BLURRED BOUNDARIES

BLURRED BOUNDARIES

Questions of Meaning in Contemporary Culture

BILL NICHOLS

INDIANA UNIVERSITY PRESS
Bloomington and Indianapolis

The paper used in this publication meets the minimum requirements of American National Standard for Information Sciences—Permanence of Paper for Printed Library Materials, ANSI Z39.48-1984.

∞™

Manufactured in the United States of America

Library of Congress Cataloging-in-Publication Data

Nichols, Bill.
Blurred boundaries : questions of meaning in contemporary culture / Bill Nichols.
p. cm.
Includes bibliographical references and index.
ISBN 0-253-34064-0 (alk. paper). — ISBN 0-253-20900-5 (paper : alk. paper)
1. Documentary films—History and criticism. 2. Historical films—History and criticism. 3. Motion pictures in ethnology. 4. Documentary television programs—United States. 5. Television broadcasting of news—United States. I. Title.
PN1995.9.D6N538 1994
070.1'8—dc20 94-2205

1 2 3 4 5 00 99 98 97 96 95 94

For Cathy and Genya,
who make all things possible

CONTENTS

PREFACE

A variety of evidence ranging from reality TV to how-to publishing points to a pervasive hunger for information about the historical world surrounding us. But our hunger is less for information in the raw than for stories fashioned from it. The global reach and structural complexity of late twentieth-century reality calls for story telling that can appear to encompass it. We hunger for news from the world around us but desire it in the form of narratives, stories that make meaning, however tenuous, dramatic, compelling, or paranoid they might be. What kind of world do we inhabit, with what risks and what prospects? Tales we label fiction offer imaginative answers; those we label nonfiction suggest possibly authentic ones.

Inevitably, the distinction between fact and fiction blurs when claims about reality get cast as narratives. We enter a zone where the world put before us lies between one not our own and one that very well might be, between a world we may recognize as a fragment of our own and one that may seem fabricated from such fragments, between indexical (authentic) signs of reality and cinematic (invented) interpretations of this reality. (I use *indexical* to refer to signs that bear a physical trace of what they refer to, such as the fingerprint, X ray, or photograph.) Stories offer structure; they organize and order the flux of events; they confer meaning and value. But stories are not a phenomenon occurring naturally. They are themselves a product of history and culture. When stories set out to represent the world around us, they enter into the realm of those blurred genres like historiography and documentary that use imaginative techniques to tell the tale of actual occurrences. The occurrence does not announce its own beginning or end, its predecessors or consequences, its implications or significance. Only those who look back upon it can provide such things, and, inevitably, more than one tale can be told for any one occurrence.

What position do we occupy when we encounter tales about the historical world? Do such tales not distinguish themselves partly by the fact that they offer an escape from the neo-Kantian realm of nonpractical, so-called purely aesthetic experience? Do such tales not blur the boundary between aesthetics and action? Are they not meant to serve a cautionary or galvanizing role? Do they not also become yet another form of commodity consumption at the same time as they urge us, directly or indirectly, to do more than simply consume them? And do such tales not perpetuate the institutional power and status of those who make, or criticize, them, even as such activity allows for contestation, subversion, and transformation?

For reasons such as these the definition of nonfiction, documentary, or even historiography remains highly elusive, and strongly debated. Claims of authenticity butt up against evidence of story telling; claims of objectivity confront signs of dramatic intensification; claims that what we see belongs to the historical world of actual occurrences come up against indications that the act of representation shaped and determined the event in fundamental ways. These blurred and often paradoxical categories are less in need of resolution than of recognition as the defining qualities of claims about the real and our relation to them. To debate such issues is not necessarily to resolve them. It does, however, locate us within a particular interpretative arena, with a definite history and a familiar array of issues and arguments, such as (1) narrative, rhetoric, and meaning, (2) style and effect, (3) content and validity, (4) ethics, ideology, and politics, and (5) institutions, disciplines, and their consequences.

One of the most blurred of recent boundaries lies precisely between fiction and nonfiction. When a single idea about the nature of reality, a common set of shared values and collective purpose, does not prevail, a considerable blurring of previously more sharply maintained boundaries is in the offing. These blurrings of what used to be effective distinctions may be not simply logical confusions but the arena within which major political, or ideological, contestation occurs. Which styles confirm a preexisting reality and which confound it? What counts as evidence? What interpretative strategies gain acceptance? Which explanatory schemes convince? What types of narrative prevail?

Deliberate border violations serve to announce a contestation of forms and purposes. What truths, drawing from what ethics, politics, or ideology, legitimizing what actions, do different forms convey? What forms, drawing from which aesthetic and political traditions, do different stories require? In what ways does the videotape of the beating of Rodney King by officers of the Los Angeles Police Department adopt a form that appears to guarantee a truth? And does it? How do the people and events represented in Randy Shilts's *And the Band Played On* enter into sharply different representational patterns in book and film; why, and to what effect? In what ways do the complex, collage-like structures of Eisenstein's *Strike* or Renée Tajima and Chris Choy's *Who Killed Vincent Chin?* address conceptual truths as well as empirical ones? Do they provoke a sense of historical consciousness? Do they document the visible world or that active process by which we make of the visible something of value? What is the content of the form, in Hayden White's memorable phrase, and what blurred boundaries are up for grabs when we approach questions of truth, history, meaning, and value in this arena of visual documentation and textual interpretation?

Such questions motivate the essays that follow. Each one takes up a different piece of the puzzle of contemporary culture and examines the ways in which earlier modes of thought and representation become blurred or altered. Examined are: documentary epistemology (the relation of knowledge to nonfiction form, particularly the boundary between embodied and disembodied knowledge); the legal status and rhetorical use of videotape as evidence in court trials such as the two that followed the Rodney King beating; the strange simulation of historical reality achieved by reality TV shows; the currently precarious status of a once secure ethnographic film tradition; the innovative nature of recent nonfiction film and video that confounds fact and fiction, documentary and the avant-garde ("performative documentary"); the history or genealogy of the documentary tradition as a form of received wisdom now in need of considerable revision; and the efficacy of recent attempts in documentary and fiction to sustain a sense of historical consciousness in the face of a postmodern tendency to forget the past.

At issue in these explorations are realism and its successors. What do the blurred boundaries of recent practice identify as a referent? Is there any "there" there, beyond the frame? To what do they refer, how do they do so, and with what end in mind? Does the adoption of a referential gesture amount to falsification? Or does the long arm of linguistic-based attacks on the referent fail to account for the inseparable link between the photographic image and what it refers to? The referent (that which came before the camera and microphone) participates in the forging of a cinematic or videographic world in ways quite distinct from written texts of every kind (even those that cite original documents and primary sources). How can we account for this distinction? How do film and video makers, and viewers, make meaning from indexical signs that continue to display traces of what they refer to while remaining clearly distinct from this referential realm?

Nonfiction film, documentary in particular, has always posed the question of the referent that poststructural linguistics has done so much to eliminate. Clearly, signification resides within the selection and arrangement of indexical representations, not in indexicality per se any more than in things themselves. When variations in selection and arrangement are minimal, closely governed by prescribed protocols, the representation falls into the class of what anthropologists call "mere film" and prize highly, for much the same reasons that dentists prize X rays, doctors value magnetic resonance images or CAT scans, police value fingerprints, meteorologists and military strategists treasure satellite photographs, and science generally cherishes "facts" or "data."

Once selection and arrangement occur in less carefully regulated ways, all the issues of truth, objectivity, authenticity, power, knowledge, and control that make the interpretive arena so vital and contentious arise. What then remains of the referent? We may often sidestep this question by thinking in terms of the simple semiotic model in which "cat" is an arbitrary sign that stands for actual cats but is itself only a signifier, a sound or set of graphic marks, capable of standing for whatever we choose. We must then attach our own image of a cat as a conceptual signified as evidence of our own knowledge of the code containing cats. The referent escapes the resulting chain of material signifiers and conceptual signifieds. But what about those other "cats" out there that are not entities and not representable by substantives? What about the "cats" which are actions and events, relationships and processes involving both others and ourselves that, if representable at all, require predicatives? These cats are the subjects not of mere film but films, cinematic texts. Perhaps our emphasis on people, places, and things, on facts and figures, has obscured our understanding of the degree to which the indexical film image, as utilized by nonfiction, has as its referent a temporal dimension. And is this temporal dimension not the domain of lived experience rather than strict chronology? Is it not, in other words, history?

Taking this notion one step further, nonfiction might arguably have a series of modes of representation (expository, observational, interactive, reflexive, performative, and so on) but also two principle forms of referent. Historiographic films (which might readily blur the boundary between fiction and nonfiction) address as their referent our relation to the historical past. Ethnographic films (which readily blur the boundaries between subjectivity and objectivity, observer and observed) address as their referent our relation to the historical present, usually the moment of filming. In this regard, reality TV, the Rodney King beating, ethnographic film, and performative documentary all share common ethnographic terrain while Eisenstein's *Strike* and the films treated in the final chapter (particularly *JFK* and *Who Killed Vincent Chin?*) address questions of history and historical consciousness more forcefully. Both, however, entail the other. These two referential domains are primarily heuristic and nonexclusive. They do not necessarily correspond to actual ethnographic or historical films. Some ethnographies will have a historical referent, and some histories will include an ethnographic referent as well.

In viewing the scene in *Silverlake Life* when Tom Joslin lies dead and Mark Massi mourns his passing, the tremendous impact of such a moment lies, I believe, in the remains of an ethnographic referent that is not in the image, not in the visible evidence of death, not in the authentic location footage or in the historical moment now marked by it, but in the relation between all these aspects and the experiential moment of encounter itself when this event unfolds again, not only as it was experienced at the time of filming by Mark Massi, and hence ethnographically, but also as it unfolds for the first time, for us. We experience the extraordinary indexical bond of history and the future we construct from it as they intertwine in the referential force field shaped in the present moment of historical consciousness.

Blurred Boundaries pursues issues across the border zones between film and television, television and video with considerable frequency and with a premeditated disregard for their relative autonomy. Neither technology nor artistic medium provide secure partitions against the blurring forces examined here. These essays adopt a different boundary, between the historical and ethnographic, which, though blurred, allows for useful distinctions.

The book, organized in collage fashion, grants each essay relative autonomy from its companions; but each essay sets out to contribute to a larger design. Each was written or rewritten specifically for this volume. Slippage and excess are necessary to invoke a whole that cannot be made to fit a Procrustean bed of linear causality or logical explanation but has system, structure, and reasons of its own. The interrelationship among chapters is not intended to provide a single, clear snapshot of our present moment or a linear, causal narrative of our past. The collage effect, if I might call it that, strives to interfere with these traditional goals of realist representation in criticism as much as in art. Each essay contributes a separate and distinct perspective on a larger whole such that both the parts from which the whole is made and the whole that only exists as an act of interpretive summation remain inextricably related. The chapters are not subordinated to an overarching theme or logic but go their own way, adopting different styles and argumentative strategies suitable to their specific subjects.

Some have asserted that there is no such thing as documentary, most notably Trinh T. Minh-ha in her essay "Documentary Is/Not a Name" (*October,* no. 52, Spring 1990). *Blurred Boundaries* makes a different assertion: not that boundaries and categories do not exist or that they are the work of taxonomic conquistadors (some are, but with no categories at all culture itself would disappear), but that the categories and boundaries surrounding documentary and reality, fact and fiction, defy hard and fast definition. This is a very different thing. Concepts such as love, reality, and play have clearly prompted more attempts at definition than kisses, clocks, or checkers, but such concepts are no less a part of our lives for doing so. Their elusiveness, the degree to which conventional understandings can be defended, adapted, subverted, or rejected, figures into their qualitative nature. This is no less true of the domains examined here. Documentary, nonfiction, reality television, ethnographic film, argument and evidence in court trials, performative documentary, historical nonfiction, and the genealogy of documentary itself defy simple definition and resist static identity. They change, and they change as part of a larger historical whole that also changes in ways we may not be able to control but which we must try to understand and shape.

Chapter 1, "Embodied Knowledge and the Politics of Location," completely rewritten from its appearance in *CineAction* (1991) for inclusion here, examines the differences between embodied and disembodied knowledge, particularly as these differences take form in the writing and film/video work of women and people of color. Later, the notion of embodied knowledge is contrasted with the far more delimiting notion of localized knowledge that figured heavily in crucial parts of the first trial of the LAPD officers accused of beating Rodney King.

Chapter 2, "The Trials and Tribulations of Rodney King," considers the way in which the George Holliday videotape served as evidence. Evidence of what? Evidence of a specific event or confirmation of an interpretive frame? This question is central to the chapter. Additionally, addressing the question of why the first trial resulted in verdicts of "not guilty" (with the exception of one unresolved charge) takes us into issues of rhetoric and the law more generally. The profound sense of injustice prompted by the videotape itself and then by the first not guilty verdict raise important issues about the self-evident truths of raw footage and the presence of crucial factors other than the widely presumed insularity and incipient racism of the first jury (presumptions that were never fully verified).

Chapter 3, "At the Limits of Reality (TV)," turns to the upsurge of reality TV shows such as *Cops, Code 911,* and *America's Most Wanted.* Despite their proximity to the documentary tradition, these shows, as part of a televisual realm of talk as distraction and news as nonhistory, swallow up the reality they refer to. The shows are a peculiar ethnographic fusion of fiction and nonfiction serving a distinct set of purposes from works considered in other, later chapters.

Chapter 4, "The Ethnographer's Tale," is the only previously published chapter that has not undergone major revision. First presented as a paper at the Nordic Anthropological Film Conference in 1991, and then published in *Visual Anthropology Review* (1991), the essay examines the various ways in which the ethnographic film tradition is in trouble. Among these "troubles," the work of the very people who have served as the subjects of traditional ethnography is foremost, supported by an increasingly critical and innovative reconceptualization of the basic nature and mission of the anthropological enterprise itself.

Chapter 5, "Performing Documentary," details ways in which recent, innovative work in film and video both continues and undercuts aspects of the documentary film tradition. Most notably, these works draw emphasis away from the historical referent and toward elements of expressivity without, however, constructing works that would normally be considered fictions. The blurred boundaries that result are of considerable significance.

Chapter 6, "Eisenstein's *Strike* (1925) and the Genealogy of Documentary," argues that *Strike* deserves to be treated as a milestone in the development of the documentary tradition. Dziga Vertov's *The Man with a Movie Camera* (1929) has held this position in relation to the contribution of silent Soviet cinema to documentary, and this place is clearly well deserved; but Eisenstein continues to be regarded as more peripheral despite the ways in which he himself blurred boundaries between history and reenactment, fact and fiction, objective representation and subjective treatment. Every introductory film history book still speaks of Eisenstein in terms of how his concept of montage contributed to film history, and then either explicitly or tacitly treats this history as the history of fiction film. Almost every introductory history then bemoans how his contribution became ignored or coopted in subsequent mainstream practice. None of these books consider the obvious: that Eisenstein's greatest contribution (like Luis Buñuel's for *Land without Bread* [1932]) lies in what he contributed to a blurred border zone of fiction and nonfiction joined together for the purposes of historical representation. Ever since Dziga Vertov attacked Eisenstein for relying on the narrative traditions of other arts, claiming the representation of reality and the discovery of a truly cinematic form for himself, a doxa has persisted that relegates Eisenstein to a category that does not suit him. Far more wide-reaching reevaluations of "the documentary tradition" are in order; this chapter attempts to inaugurate a process of revision.

Chapter 7, "Please, All You Good and Honest People: Film Form and Historical Consciousness," works through four texts (using *Land without Bread* as a genealogical precursor) to reflect on how historical consciousness might be engendered by works of film or video. *JFK* moves toward nonfiction from the fiction side of the border and toward political history from the paranoid side of interpretation; *Who Killed Vincent Chin?* works similar terrain but within a more fully documentary vein and without a paranoid dimension. These two works, which may engender a sense of historical consciousness by dint of the form they adopt, are contrasted with *Dear America: Letters Home from Vietnam* and the multiple programs and shows that make up domestic network coverage of the Gulf War against the Iraqi government of Saddam Hussein where historical consciousness became severely displaced by other alternatives. This chapter returns us to the questions we began with: how knowledge becomes embodied and how embodied knowledge is necessarily historical, situational, and goal-directed. This content to a changing form identifies the transformative potential of documentary representation: to speak of the real, to interpret its meaning, implicates us in the continuing construction of the very reality we discover over against us. Such is the goal of many of the texts discussed here, including this book itself.

ACKNOWLEDGMENTS

The material contained in *Blurred Boundaries* represents a set of sustained forays into questions of boundaries, border zones, and limits, written more or less at one time, in the spring and summer of 1992. Two chapters have been previously published: "Embodied Knowledge and the Politics of Location" appeared in radically different form in *CineAction* 23 (Winter 1990–91): 14–21, and, in slightly revised form, in Michael Renov, ed., *Theorizing Documentary* (New York: Routledge, 1993), 174–91. Originally based on ideas that became part of the final chapter, "Representing the Body: Questions of Meaning and Magnitude," of my *Representing Reality* (Bloomington: Indiana University Press, 1991), the essay has been completely revised and rewritten here. A second essay appeared elsewhere in a form only slightly different from its present one: "The Ethnographer's Tale" first appeared in *Visual Anthropology Review* 7, no. 2 (1991): 31–47. It also appears in Peter I. Crawford and Jan K. Simonsen, eds., *Ethnographic Film Aesthetics and Narrative Traditions* (Aarhus, Denmark: Intervention Press, 1992), 43–74, and in Lucien Taylor, ed., *Visualizing Theory* (New York: Routledge, 1994). "The Ethnographer's Tale" was first given as a paper at the Nordic Anthropological Film Conference, Oslo, Norway, May 21–24, 1991.

A portion of "Please, All You Good and Honest People," entitled "Historical Consciousness and the Viewer: *Who Killed Vincent Chin?*" has been reprinted in Vivian Sobchack, ed., *The Moving Image, Modernism and the Representation of History* (New York: Routledge, 1994).

Special thanks are due to Elizabeth Block, Ian Crawford, Jane Gaines, Catharine Greenblatt, David MacDougall, Michael Renov, and Lucien Taylor for comments and suggestions they made on various chapters. I owe an extra debt of gratitude to Catherine Soussloff, who made many valuable suggestions and helped provide an environment in which love and work could flourish equally.

BLURRED BOUNDARIES

1

EMBODIED KNOWLEDGE AND THE POLITICS OF LOCATION
AN EVOCATION

Overture

> [The post-Enlightenment] self as it is visible in poetry and autobiography, as well as other forms of expressivity . . . is a coherent, unified, self-aware agency, constructed both by the Christian discourses on the disembodied nature of the spirit and by the Cartesian ego which knows itself by its own act of thought.
>
> —Leslie Devereaux, "Cultures, Disciplines, Cinemas"[1]

* * *

Traditionally, the word *documentary* has suggested fullness and completion, knowledge and fact, explanations of the social world and its motivating mechanisms. More recently, though, documentary has come to suggest incompleteness and uncertainty, recollection and impression, images of personal worlds and their subjective construction. A shift of epistemological proportions has occurred. What counts as knowledge is not what it used to be. The coherent, controlling self that could make the world and others its objects of scrutiny is now fully one itself. Multiple (constituted of diverse subjectivities), split (conscious/unconscious), sedimented (bearing the trace of past selves and previous experience), what such a self knows and what we know of such a self evades ready determination. History and memory intertwine; meaning and action, past and present, hinge on one another distinctively. Documentary and fiction, social actor and social other, knowledge and doubt, concept and experience share boundaries that inescapably blur.

* * *

We are entering a realm of specificity and corporeality, of embodied knowledge and existentially situated action. Embodied knowledge differs sharply from the localized knowledge and algebra of probability at work in the two trials of the police officers who beat Rodney King. Localized knowledge constrains inquiry to a carefully delimited frame. Embodied knowledge exceeds such frames. Its inclusiveness (self plus other, body plus mind, system plus environment) makes such knowledge a strong approximation of wisdom. Embodied knowledge accords with Pascal's dictum, "*Le coeur a ses raisons que la raison ne connaît point.*" Social actors no longer serve, here, as witnesses or experts, examples or illustrations, not even as voices of authenticating testimony regarding lost or repressed histories. Pleas of charity and cries of outrage recede; different voices, less exhortatory than personal, more exploratory than conclusive, speak.

* * *

Historical reality is under siege. Imperfect utopias and diverse affinities propose themselves as alternatives to the ordered lives constructed by the master narratives of Platonic reason, Christian salvation, capitalist progress, and Marxist revolution. How do we tell what happened in the past if we do not have the familiar framework of the logic of problem solving, the theology of damnation and redemption, the economics of progress, or the politics of revolution to guide us? How do we represent—meaning to depict, to speak for, and to argue about—what is no longer present under these conditions? And, as a corollary, how do we represent individuals who speak, now, in hopes of recovering a time past?

The act of representation no longer seems as clear cut as it once did. The issues of specificity and corporeality bring to a focus tensions within the domain of representation. They sharpen questions of magnitude posed by the felt tension between representation and represented. Photographic images are always of concrete, material things recorded at specific moments in time, but are often made to point toward more general truths or issues. The indexical bond of point-for-point correspondence between photograph and source anchors an iconic sense of typicality (the image is of a house but it also, by resemblance, stands for all houses of that type) and a symbolic layer of connotation and ideology (the image of a house may signify warmth and shelter, danger and foreboding, affluence or poverty). To what extent can the particular serve as illustration for the general? To what extent is the general a misunderstanding of the concrete, the everyday and what this means for historically located individuals? The body is a particularly acute reminder of specificity and the body of the filmmaker even more so. Where do filmmakers stand and how do they represent this stance? Do they represent their own knowledge as situated or omniscient? What consequences follow?

History and Memory

> I don't know where this came from, but I just have this fragment, this picture that's always been in my mind. My mother, she's standing at a faucet, and it's really hot outside and she's filling this canteen, and the water's really cold, and it feels really good, and outside the sun is just so hot it's just beating down, and there's this dust that gets in everywhere and they're always sweeping the floors.
>
> —Opening voice-over commentary by Rea Tajiri on the image she has of her mother in a Japanese American relocation camp, *History and Memory* (1991)

> Because of the laws that existed at that time, a Japanese couldn't own any property, and so it was impossible for my mother to buy a house or buy any property and so she bought the house in my name. While I was in the army at Camp Shelby, I got word that the house, which I owned, was condemned because the United States government took it over for the navy. . . . I asked for permission to visit and was denied permission. What happened eventually was that the house all of a sudden disappeared. What happened . . . we'll never know, because all of a sudden the house wasn't there any more.
>
> —Rea Tajiri's father, describing an event during World War II, *History and Memory*

* * *

[Narrative] is a mean of symbolizing events without which their historicality cannot be indicated . . . because historicality itself is both a reality and a mystery. All narratives display this mystery and at the same time foreclose any inclination to despair over the failure to solve it by revealing what might be called its form in "plot" and its content in the meaning with which the plot endows what would otherwise be mere event. Insofar as events and their aspects can be "explained" by the methods of the sciences, they are, it would seem, thereby shown to be neither mysterious nor particularly histori-cal. What can be explained about historical events is precisely what consti-

> tutes their non- or ahistorical aspect. What remains after events have been explained is both historical and meaningful insofar as it can be understood. And this remainder is understandable insofar as it can be "grasped" in a symbolization, that is, shown to have the kind of meaning with which plots endow stories.
>
> —Hayden White, *The Content of the Form*[2]

* * *

What plots shall we choose? What tangible, concrete forms shall we give to this reality and mystery called history? Can documentary, for example, plot its way to history with reenactment? Reenactments came to be denounced as fabrications in the days of observational cinema; then, more recently, filmmakers resurrected them as a legitimate way to address what is not available for representation in the here and now. But unlike the written account, the reenactment lies anchored, indexically, to a present distinct from the past it re-presents. The very authenticity of the image testifies to the use of source material from the present moment, not the past. This presents the threat of disembodiment; the camera records those we see on screen with indexical fidelity, but these figures are also ghosts or simulacra of others who have already acted out their parts.

Spoken testimony came to be seen as an antidote for the "body too many" problem of reenactment (the bodies of those in the reenactments were "extras," never matching the historical bodies they represented). Social actors, witnesses, could speak now about what they know of historical events. The indexical image authenticates testimony now about what happened then. With historical footage from the time recounted appended to it, indexicality may guarantee an apparent congruity between what happened then and what is said now. (The historic footage enjoys the legitimating power of indexicality while the spoken testimony determines its meaning.) Like reenactment, this technique diminishes the mystery of presence/absence, then/now, history itself that may persist when we can see in what witnesses say now the continuation of the past in the present, its corporeal incarnation through speech and action.

* * *

The motivation in the present for using reenactments or historical footage—as a willing backward to conjure the past present memory requires—calls for address. Spoken testimony's indexical anchorage in the present moment of recounting is also where motivation and purpose for a particular story of "what happened" takes root. With skill and effort, the pressure of the past on the present moment of recounting (a historical latency) can become as much a subject of the story told as the history ostensibly recounted. The web of implication between past and present thickens due to the choice of plot itself. The implantation of the past (as memory, multiple subjectivities, and the unconscious) within bodies that are otherwise but convenient vehicles for true stories requires figuration as fully as some crystallized sense of the past itself. Some, like Errol Morris and Claude Lanzman, cultivate this web impressively.

* * *

> They [Morris and Lanzman] show how lies function as partial truths to both the agents and witnesses of history's trauma. . . . It is the repetition in the present of the crime of the past that is key to the documentary process of Lanzman's film. . . . The truth of the Holocaust thus does not exist in any totalizing narrative, but only . . . as a collection of fragments.[3]

> Claude Lanzman's film *Shoah* is an exception [to the impossibility of representing what "must remain unrepresentable"], maybe the only one. Not only because it rejects representation in images and music but because it scarcely offers a testimony where the unrepresentable of the Holocaust is not indicated, be it but for a moment, by the alteration in the tone of a voice, a knotted throat, sobbing, tears, a witness fleeing off-camera, a disturbance in the tone of the narrative, an uncontrolled gesture. So that one knows that the impassible witnesses, whoever they might be, are certainly lying, "play-acting," hiding something.[4]

* * *

How much more powerful might this web of implication be when realized less at the level of thematics, of testimony as confession, and more at the level of textual form, and plot, itself? Confession, with its inadvertent revelation of truths (the past's structuring but invisible presence) by social actors who think they are giving testimony about the past rather than betraying how the past persists in them, in their very act of speaking, grants us the power to extract and manage (secret) knowledge—what the body knows but cannot openly say.

Retrospection, as a viewing process requiring us to draw together fragments independent of what social actors inadvertently betray, operates through a collage-like principle to *embody* the repetition of the past in the present regardless of the filmmaker's ability to coax confessional, self-revealing testimony from his or her subjects. (This proposition forms the theme of chapter 7, and uses *Who Killed Vincent Chin?* and *JFK* as its central examples.) Crucial, though, to both efforts—to coax confessions from witnesses and to find forms (plots and structures) that reveal the force of the past on the present and future—is the way in which what is no longer present finds material embodiment in what is. History acts; it retains agency in a time when the loss of history and forgetting of the past is a commonplace of postmodern criticism.

A Body in Question

We cannot discuss embodiment, specificity, and the particular for long without addressing the peculiarity of the often absent filmmaker who urges us to draw larger lessons from the specific ones he or she learned and filmed. This is an old convention in documentary. It feels "natural" for events to refer to larger issues. They fall into place along the plot lines of our master narratives.

* * *

> The invention of needs always goes hand in hand with the compulsion to help the needy, a noble and self-gratifying task that also renders the helper's service indispensable.[5]

* * *

The politics of location, questions of magnitude, issues of embodiment all address the filmmaker as well as those filmed. These politics, questions, issues stress the local over the global, the specific over the general, the concrete over the abstract. The experience of place and subjectivity is tactile, everyday, corporeal. Films like *History and Memory, Extremely Personal Eros, Silverlake Life: The View from Here,* and *Unfinished Diary* are not exercises in the expansion of self by the construction of an Other which then displays the welcoming features of an old, familiar friend. They are more basically and vividly reconstructions of the self (as remembering, desiring, displaced, or even dying) and of the filmmaker as self most centrally of all.

* * *

> I watched the muscles of her back, her figure, her legs, and the beauty of the body so hidden to us, whites, fascinated me. . . . At moments I was sorry I was not a savage and could not possess this pretty girl.
>
> —Bronislaw Malinowski, *A Diary in the Strict Sense of the Term,* 255–56

> Between himself and the bodies of the Trobrianders, between himself and the nirvana of merging with the landscape, Malinowski interposes his ethnographic writing and its prerequisites—photographs and theorizing. All are the means of objectifying his feelings, of converting feelings into magisterial observation guided by pure, untainted theory. The Malinowski of the published ethnographies surveys the world with cool authority; it is his home, his oyster, cradling pearls of wisdom. The Malinowski of the *Diary* under-

> stands fully the universe of transcendental homelessness—and the furious desire for the primitive it helps to produce.[6]
>
> —Marianna Torgovnick

* * *

Mobility and travel no longer serve as a symbol for the expansion of one's moral framework, the discovery of cultural relativity, the heroics of salvage anthropology, the indulgence of secret desires in strange places, the rituals of self-improvement, or as training in the civic responsibilities of empire. Movement and travel no longer legitimate, ironically, the subject's right to *disembodied speech, disembodied* but *master* narratives and mythologies in which the corporeal "I" who speaks dissolves itself in a disembodied, depersonalized, institutional speech of power and knowledge. Instead, movement and travel become an experience of displacement and dislocation, of social and cultural estrangement, of retrieval, survival, and self-preservation.

* * *

> The true picture of the past flits by. The past can be seized only as an image which flashes up at the instant when it can be recognized and is never seen again. . . . For every image of the past that is not recognized by the present as one of its own concerns threatens to disappear irretrievably.[7]
>
> —Walter Benjamin

* * *

> I began searching for a history, because I knew all along that the stories I had heard were not true, and parts had been left out. I remember having this feeling growing up, that I was haunted by something, that I was living in a family full of ghosts. There was this place that they knew about. I had never been there, yet I had a memory for it. I could remember a time of great sadness before I was born. . . . I had no idea where these memories came from, yet I knew the place.
>
> —Voice-over commentary by Rea Tajiri, *History and Memory*

For Rea Tajiri, the image which flits by is that of her mother filling a canteen against the desert backdrop of Camp Poston, wartime home to several thousand Japanese Americans. The image does not disappear but grows, with incremental, *bricoleur*-like accretions, into *History and Memory.*

(The film plots its story in the form of a collage of written text, disparate voice-overs, old home movies, reenactments, clips from feature films and wartime documentaries, photographs, and synchronous, interactive footage in the present.) Her father's story of their stolen house becomes her own as she moves her own voice and memory into the past that came before her: "Much later in camp, we heard that our house was stolen, literally uprooted and moved to another location. To this day we have no trace of it."

Things and places from the past (Camp Poston, the family's missing house) return as photographs and stories. Tajiri herself ventures to the site of the past, to the relocation camp, staging the ritual (physically, corporeally) of seeking the touch of authenticity: to put oneself in physical contact with this (altered) geographical referent, to receive its imprint, to let the past reverberate through what it has become, and what we make of it.

* * *

For Rea Tajiri movement and travel become the experience of dislocation and displacement, of loss and alienation, of exile and resistance. Tajiri explores and enacts strategies of remembrance and resistance practiced through an *embodied*, corporeal discourse of self-representation.

* * *

The politics of location points to the importance of testimonial literature and first-person filmmaking.[8] Testimonials are first-person, oral more than literary, personal more than theoretical. Such work explores the personal as political at the level of textual self-representation as well as at the level of lived experience. It contrasts with the traditional essay where the authorial "I" speaks to and on behalf of a presumed collectivity. The "I" of testimonials embodies social affinities but is also acutely aware of social difference, marginality, and its own place among the so-called Others of hegemonic discourse.

* * *

Hara Kazuo possesses a massive affinity for positions of (contested) marginality. His remarkable film *Extremely Personal Eros: Love Song (1974)* (1974) carries an explosive charge in its relentless exploration of marginalized lives similar to Robert Frank and Alfred Leslie's *Pull My Daisy* (1959), John Cassavetes's *Shadows* (1959), Jean Rouch's *Les maîtres fous* (1954), or Shirley Clarke's *Portrait of Jason* (1967). And, although largely unseen and unaccorded the praise these other films have earned, it exceeds them, presenting a degree of personal risk and self-exposure unheard of at the time of its own making.

Hara uses an observational camera style in a patently interactive context, fashioning a film (with his personal partner, Kobayashi Sachicko) on the day-to-day life of his past partner, Miyuki Takeda. Hara does not observe, nor does he interact as filmmaker to subject (via the charged form of the interview, for example). He suspends himself in the presence of the other; he makes the filmed space of bodily presence precarious, fraught with peril for himself (his sense of self) and the two women equally complicit in this personal but public display of eros.

Miyuki, like Hara's own mother, becomes a barmaid, working in Okinawa, living with Paul, an African American in the U.S. Navy. Hara and his companion, Kobayashi, who records the sound, follow her there, but Miyuki is not a compliant subject. She berates Hara on camera, in front of Kobayashi, for his cowardice and passivity. She taunts him with the demand to have the birth of her son (the one she wants to have with Paul) filmed by Hara, and the threat to make him "a really wild boy." Hara does later film the birth of Miyuki's mixed-race daughter, on camera, in her apartment, atop a shower curtain and newspapers, with only Hara and Kobayashi present, filming and recording.

* * *

This is no portrait of Japanese outsiders, of bohemians and misfits, rebels and feminists, presented from a typically observational or even interactive position. No disembodied forms of knowledge are privileged over those phenomenologically embodied and manifest in Hara and his subjects/collaborators.

* * *

After Miyuki gives birth, she calls her mother on the telephone. We only hear Miyuki's side of the conversation.

> It can't be helped.
> I did everything myself. Rei [her other child] watched.
> It's almost white.
> I can't kill her now. Of course, I'll raise her.

* * *

Just as Okuzaki, the protagonist of Hara's later, much more widely circulated film *The Emperor's Naked Army Marches On* (1987), obsessively returns to the past to discover the fate of his fellow soldiers (they died in World War II as a result of cannibalism by his own officers, it turns out), Hara also returns, obsessively to the past, his own past. He embodies this encounter in the present moment, in palpable tensions (in bodies and across space) as he films his own subjection to the dialectic of memory and history constituting a present that would not otherwise be:[9]

> You have to become empty and receive of the other. When you make a film about a strong character, you become confused within yourself. In that

state of confusion the world starts to look different. Documentary filmmaking could be such if you make a film in that state of mind, you can show your audience something special. . . . As a documentarist I want to become involved with a character and see how I myself become changed in the course of the relationship.[10]

* * *

Domestic space as the locus of emotional intensities, travel as a receding fantasy, the past as images that flit by, eluding the grasp of those who made them: these centripetal forces gather themselves around the two men whose lives, and deaths, constitute *Silverlake Life: The View from Here* (Tom Joslin and Peter Friedman, 1992). Initiated by Tom Joslin to document the final days of his lover, Mark Massi, and himself (completed by their friend, Peter Friedman), the film defies all conventions of the home movie even though it is one. It addresses pain, anger, and death. It testifies to Joslin's and Massi's way of being in the world in the specificities of camera style, in the seemingly clinical but entirely humane gaze at the K.S. (Kaposi's sarcoma) lesions on Mark's body, in the casual long takes of Mark displaying his body with pleasure and defiance at a friend's retreat (out of sight of host and friends who may not know how to respond), and, after an unexpected reversal in which it is the initially healthier Joslin who dies first, in Mark's own extraordinarily humane gaze on the emaciated, inert body of the man he loved:

> This is the first of July, and Tommy's just died. At home he died. And I sang to him. I sang to him. "You are my sunshine, my only sunshine. You make me happy when skies are gray. You'll never know, dear, how much I love you. Please don't take my sunshine away."
>
> Isn't he beautiful? He's so beautiful. This is for you, Tommy, all of us, all of your friends will finish the tape for you, OK? We promise. We promise. Bye, bye, Tom.
>
> —Mark Massi in *Silverlake Life: The View from Here*

* * *

Mark Massi holds the shaking camera, aimed at the dead body of his lover in the bed they have shared for years. Knowledge, in its traditional association with a coherence and control, demands expansion to encompass tremulous, immediate experience itself, for such moments must be called a form of knowing. Not only form (diaristic home movie) but style (the shaky camera view, the quiver in Massi's voice, the palpable sense of space between the quick and the dead as Massi's camera tenaciously holds to its view of Joslin's naked, inert body) attest to a knowledge embedded in the heart and suffused with wisdom (knowledge of that larger system of which we are a part).[11] The reality and mystery of historicality announce themselves as death whose meaning emanates from that "plot" in which love and memory mark the present with an image from the past.

Body Politics

> Erotic possession. Penetration. Knowing the other. Intellectual and carnal knowledge. This universe of eroticism is suffused with power: taking possession, doing something to someone else. The (male) European subjectivity in search of the boundaries of itself.
>
> My own experience of eroticism is closer to Eros. It is replete with difference, full of Yes. In touching I am touched, suffused by touch, and in the mutual movement toward each other I come to a place of *no* boundaries. I experience my self as the other; *there is no possession in it.*
>
> In the movement of desire, in knowing, can there be the mutual experience of no boundaries? What can we know? What is the pursuit of knowing for? To know the other without knowing the self, without opening the self to being known, is truly an act of taking possession.[12]
>
> —Leslie Devereaux

* * *

A politics of location inevitably poses questions about the body.[13] We may think of the body as the most local and most tangible aspect of ourselves. How do we reach the experience of "no boundaries" (Devereaux) when to blur the self and other is to confound the epistemology of Western thought, and to jeopardize the social division of the sexes? *Our Marilyn* (Brenda Longfellow, Canada, 1988), for example, asks how to represent, in cinematic form, the female body—not as idealized nude, or object of desire, not as temptress or provider, but as a body-*in*-action.

Locus of action and source of agency, the body of "Marilyn" (signifying, here, "their Marilyn," Marilyn Monroe, and "our Marilyn," long-distance swimmer Marilyn Bell, and the body of the voice-over narrator who seeks her own identity in the terrain between these choices) eludes categorization and the stasis of fixed identity. The desired Marilyn represents a state of being-in-action, not a frozen icon or image, not a character in someone else's narrative, but a *vehicle* for the presentation of self.

* * *

> I have proposed the term "experience" and used it to designate an ongoing process by which subjectivity is constructed semiotically and historically. Borrowing Peirce's notion of "habit" . . . , I have then sought to define experience more accurately as a complex of habits . . . , the continuous engagement of a self or subject in social reality.
>
> The point of my return to Peirce . . . was to restore the body of the interpreter, the subject of semiosis. The subject, I have argued, is the place in which, the body in whom, the significate effect of the sign takes hold and is real-ized [*sic*]. . . . The notion of habit as "energetic" attitude, a somatic disposition at once abstract and concrete, the crystallized form of past muscular/mental effort, is powerfully suggestive of a subject touched by the practice of signs, a subject physically implicated or bodily engaged in the production of meaning, representation and self-representation.
>
> —Teresa de Lauretis, "Semiotics and Experience"[14]

* * *

To act is to affirm or construct an identity, and to identify with such a process is to forge an identity bound up in this very act, a sense of self as being-in-action. Habit, as somatic memory, crystallizes past effort and experience; it hinges present on past in a manner yet still open to change, to transformative action. The act of viewing, like the act of representation and self-representation, can be precisely such a form of being-in-action.

* * *

The Body Beautiful (Ngozi Onwurah, Great Britain, 1991) renegotiates the bond between mother and daughter. Without the formally reflexive turns of *Daughter Rite* (Michel Citron, 1978), with more performative than metacommunicative effort, with more emphasis on expressive and poetic aspects of its plot and form than referential ones, *The Body Beautiful* offers a compelling portrait of a Nigerian British daughter's affirmation of love for her white British mother's arthritic, deformed body (scarred by radical mastectomy).

"In touching I am touched, suffused by touch"; this could be Ngozi Onwurah's credo. She, the daughter, turns her homage to action. After she comes to see her mother as others see her (when other naked women in a steam bath recoil from the sight of a body that is no longer "mother" but an alien and disturbing presence), Onwurah stages a "touching" ceremony in which there is no possession. She has a naked young African British man carry the unclothed body of her mother to a bed surrounded by diaphanous curtains. In this clearly theatrical space a ritual unfolds, of loving, caressing, and tenderness. Ngozi (played by an actress while her mother plays herself) looks on, from an apparently separate space (the world of fashion modeling that is hers, the place of *metteur-en-scène* in a most extraordinary sense). These are the signs of love, and this is the body of her mother on which such signs take hold and are realized. Madge Onwurah is "touched by the signs of emotion," by this remarkable representation of love. This is *testimonio* of an exceptional kind, embodied knowledge of profound degree.

* * *

> I have been forty years a slave and forty years free and would be here forty years more to have equal rights for all.
>
> —Sojourner Truth

> In Sojourner Truth's words you hear the coming together, the marriage of the public discourse and the private experience, making a power, a beautiful thing, the true discourse of reason. This is a wedding and welding back together of the alienated consciousness that I've been calling the father tongue and the undifferentiated engagement that I've been calling the mother tongue.[15]
>
> —Ursula K. LeGuin

* * *

We hear the sound of such an undifferentiated engagement in Ngozi Onwurah's commentary:

> I wanted to tell her that I loved her. That I was sorry, but the words wouldn't come. And the truth was, that if she hadn't been my mother and if I hadn't loved her or known her incredible strength, if I hadn't come from inside that body that everyone wanted hidden away, then I, too, would have turned away.
>
> [As Ngozi Onwurah curls against the naked, sleeping form of her mother, she utters the film's concluding words.]
>
> A child is made in its parents' image, but to a world that only sees in black and white, I was only made in the image of my father, yet, she has molded

me, created the curves and contours of my life, colored the innermost details of my being. She has fought for me, protected me, with every painful, crooked bone in her body. She lives inside me and cannot be separated. I may not be reflected in her image, but my mother is mirrored in my soul. I am my mother's daughter for the rest of my life.

—Ngozi Onwurah's voice-over, *The Body Beautiful*

* * *

The essential gesture of the father tongue is not reasoning but distancing—making a gap, a space, between the subject or self and the object or other.

In our Constitution and the works of law, philosophy, social thought, and science, in its everyday uses in the service of justice and clarity, what I call the father tongue is immensely noble and indispensably useful. When it claims a privileged relationship to reality, it becomes dangerous and potentially destructive.

Using the father tongue, I can speak of the mother tongue only, inevitably, to distance it—to exclude it. . . . It is primitive: inaccurate, unclear, coarse, limited, trivial, banal. The mother tongue, spoken or written, expects an answer. It is conversation, a word the root of which means "turning together." The mother tongue is language not as mere communication but as relation, relationship. It connects. . . . It is written, but not by scribes or secretaries for posterity; it flies from the mouth on the breath that is our life. . . .[16]

—Ursula K. LeGuin

* * *

Another mother and daughter. The maternal relation in diaspora (*Measures of Distance,* Mona Hatoum, Lebanon/Canada, 1988). The mother, there, in Beirut, the daughter, here, in Vancouver, reading the letters her mother has written; the tape recordings of their conversations, in Arabic, without subtitles, playing under; Arabic script written in black across the surface of the image, its points and curls resembling the barbwire that scars the Lebanese cities and countryside; vague, diffuse patterns of shape and texture underneath the Arabic, patterns that gradually come into focus as photographs of Mona Hatoum's mother, naked, veiled only by diffusion and the overlay of script:

You asked if you could use my pictures in your work. Go ahead and use them, and don't mention a thing about it to your father.

—Mona Hatoum's mother's letter, *Measures of Distance*

When you asked me questions about my sexuality, your father said, "What's all this nonsense you're occupying your mind with?" I suppose he wonders why you're not communicating with him in the same way.

> I suppose he still can't forgive you for taking those photographs in the shower. It's as if you had trespassed on his property and now he feels that there's some exchange going on between us from which he is excluded. He calls it "women's nonsense."
>
> —Mona Hatoum's mother, *Measures of Distance*

* * *

Testimonial rooted in experience; conversation witnessing the personal; knowledge drawn from the intimacy of bodies. The mother tongue has its reasons that reason may not understand when it privileges its own (peculiar) relationship to reality:

> I have not been able to send you any letters for the last few months, because the local post office was completely destroyed by that car bomb back in April and there is no sign of them fixing it. . . .
>
> I personally felt as though I had been stripped naked of my very soul. And I'm not just talking about the land and property we left behind but that our identity and sense of pride in who we are went out of the window.
>
> —Mona Hatoum's mother's letter, *Measures of Distance*

* * *

The politics of experience, and location, yield, not surprisingly, the most forceful stories among those who have tasted exile or diaspora, those who are female, gay, or lesbian, and members of those groups known in the predominantly white, overdeveloped regions of the world as "people of color" (presupposing a colorless ground against which rainbow-hued figures stand out). These works constitute a vital dimension to that type of documentary described in chapter 5 as performative.

* * *

> From the retention of preoedipal attachments to their mother, growing girls come to define and experience themselves as continuous with others; their experience of self contains more flexible or permeable ego boundaries. . . . Boys come to define themselves as more separate and distinct, with a greater sense of rigid ego boundaries and differentiation. The basic feminine sense of self is connected to the world, the basic masculine sense of self is separate.[17]
>
> —Nancy Chodorow

Films like *Measures of Distance* or *The Body Beautiful* do not need to be analyzed so much as experienced and, through that experience, understood. Differences circulate within the realm of social experience, suspended, in the free play of semiosis. Yet, social difference always risks hardening into oppositions and aligning itself along the fault lines of the social imaginary—them/us, either/or, masculine/feminine, Arab/Jew, black/white.

These films leave differences "at sea," circulating around questions of crucial importance. They refuse to generalize or conclude, to make abstracting the general from the particular a more privileged form of knowledge than the wisdom of what we experience, and understand, directly. The personal "mother tongue" commentary in *Our Marilyn, Unfinished Diary, The Body Beautiful,* and *Measures of Distance* (and still other films like *History and Memory* or *Tongues Untied*) struggles to be heard in a different key, where blurred boundaries between self and other testify to a subject "touched by the practice of signs, a subject physically implicated or bodily engaged in the production of meaning, representation, and self-representation."[18]

These films bring the force of history, memory, and knowledge down to the level of immediate experience and individual subjectivity. How does a text restore that order of magnitude which characterizes lived experience when it can only make representations of what lies beyond its bounds? One set of answers involves the power of those contingent subjectivities affiliated with a self that makes meaning in the company of others.

2

THE TRIALS AND TRIBULATIONS OF RODNEY KING

Voodoo Semiotics

> The revolution has come.
> Off the pig!
> It's time to pick up the gun.
> Off the pig!
>
> —Black Panther chant

> I'm 'bout to dust some cops off . . .
> Die, die, die, pig, die!
>
> —Ice-T, "Cop Killer"

> Bad boys, bad boys; whatcha gonna do; whatcha gonna do when they come for you?
>
> —Theme song, *Cops*

> I just want to say, you know, can we, can we all get along? Can we get along? Can we stop making it horrible for the older people and the kids? We got enough smog here in Los Angeles, let alone setting these fires. It's just not right. It's not right.
>
> —Rodney King

> "The Rodney King story was pitched from day one," Ruth Slauson, senior vice president for movies at NBC, said. "One agency called and simply said they were offering the L.A. riots. I said, "'What exactly are you representing?'"[1]

Just beyond the borderland of reality TV, and in rebuttal to it, looms the March 3, 1991, beating of Rodney King by officers of the Los Angeles Police Department, their subsequent trial, the California state jury's verdict of not guilty on all but one count, the aftermath of large-scale violence, and the subsequent verdict of guilty against two of the four officers in the federal, civil rights trial.

"Rodney King," as signifier for this larger array of events that so massively exceeded his own body and his own experience, bursts beyond the frame of spectacle, of sensation and banality, and viewer response run to ground. Frames collide. Excess (history itself) spills out. Response to this tape did not pour into the gutter of grounded sensation and compensatory consumption. Collective outrage demanded redress—not charity or penance. Violent response, symbolic action at its most indignant, burst beyond the frame of representation.

The trials and tribulations of Rodney King place us squarely within a social arena where a struggle for interpretive hegemony unfolds. ("The Rodney King trial," of course, is a misnomer: Mr. King was never on trial, four members of the LAPD were.) A few moments on a spring night when what was, by all appearances, an extraordinary application of brute force by the LAPD to the crawling, cringing body of Rodney King call into question the public policies of the last thirty years, the endemic racism within public institutions, the politics of visual analysis, and the often suppressed relation of class to racial discrimination, if not outright apartheidization. These few moments, replayed and debated over and over partly because they can never answer the very questions we ask of them, haunt us with the specter that, since 1896, when in *Plessey v. Ferguson* the United States Supreme Court declared the doctrine of "separate but equal" unconstitutional, social practice has not adapted to this apparently all too radical legal standard.

Reality TV always flirts with disaster, both in the sense that danger, contingency, the randomness of violence, and the precariousness of life are its staples and in the sense that what it represents may prompt or demand response that exceeds its frame. The struggle for interpretive dominance is, in part, a struggle to address questions of magnitude. Many natural catastrophes seem to fit perfectly within the tele-frame: sympathy and charity are the best we can do, we may as well let them be tele-mediated. But those among the ruins have other needs, pose other demands, raise other questions—if their voices can elude or exceed the tele-frame. Rodney King's body has become a focal point for such voices.

This raw, crude footage in which a man is being beaten carries an indexical whammy. (I mean indexical in terms of the trichotomy proposed by Charles Sanders Peirce. Iconic signs resemble their source [drawings, for example]; indexical signs bear a "point-for-point correspondence" with their source [X rays, photographs, fingerprints, for example], and symbols bear an arbitrary relation [words, Morse code, national flags].)[2] This footage of King is the raw to reality TV's cooked. It is rebuke, not companion, to the simulacrum. The relation of signifier to referent cannot be displaced by endless chains of signifiers and the signifieds we forge to accompany them. We wince, we gasp; we experience this brutal event with moral outrage. Representations of violence often have this effect. They cry out for response; they retain the power to produce visceral effect. This is even more true when what we see, the imagistic signifiers, bear an indexical relation to an event that occurred before the camera that we take to be a historical event, not a staged, scripted, or reenacted one.

What the insulated world of tele-vision could not contain was Rodney King's metonymic linkage to a far greater community. What was done to him had been done to others like him. Tele-atonement and grounded sensation would not contain the excess this metonymy invoked.

In speaking of the effects of a text, including the Rodney King tape, we cannot dismiss questions of magnitude as a misguided belief in the referent, a delusional belief in some antecedent realm to which the recorded image refers.

This effort amounts to voodoo semiotics.

Reminding ourselves that images of a man being beaten are only signifiers, floating in the ether of an autonomous signifying practice, may be formally correct but also strangely alienated. Critics like Jean Baudrillard, who refutes the "reference principle" by which an image might refer to a real world or anything anterior to itself, opts to celebrate how alienated we have all become.[3] He wants us to enjoy a decathected free-fall through the shadow play of simulacra. Perhaps the best we can do is what Baudrillard suggests. But along comes a moment such as the beating of Rodney King and the historical referent once again cuts through the inoculating power of signifying systems to turn our response to that excess beyond the frame.

Interpretive Frames as Morality Tales

The very outrage that the Rodney King footage provokes can prove hazardous. Outrage can be the spark of revolution, the driving force that propels people to demand an end of one regime and to inaugurate another. But outrage risks diverting political praxis to the form of a morality play when it settles for immediate outlet and surface redress. The legal system reinforces this risk when it narrows its focus to the singular event and a positivist frame.

What goal do we have as we formulate a response to outrageous acts? Is our goal revenge? Justice? Revolution? (a word that has become very close to unspeakable in the time of a global economy and cyborg identities). Is it the pleasure of discharging moral outrage itself? Has the shape of public response, including our own outrage, followed the contours that transformative social praxis requires, or does it spill into the Manichean, localized, and dramatic channel marked out for it by the mainstream media?

These are important questions, for they shape the organization of our response and the nature of our interpretive frame.

Such questions confront us at a moment when any sense of a progressive, let alone revolutionary, movement falters. Recent conflicts such as the Gulf War against Saddam Hussein or the invasion of Panama have produced little more than ad hoc resistance that dissolved as soon as the most intense fighting died down. The bloody civil war and genocide in Bosnia-Herzegovina has not produced a Left position of any prominence, and the lively debates on health care in 1993 went on without any significant contribution from a militant, organized, or even coherent Left.

The Left's political strategy has paralleled the repetition and forgetting that characterize media news. We hurdle from one indignity to another, from one crisis to the next, less intent on discharging outrage in radically transformative action than on keeping conscience and witness barely alive.

Now, with Rodney King—another symptomatic eruption of the violence that marks the maintenance of social order—comes the risk of forgetting once again. Response risks being limited to another localized discharge. Public response rises and falls in relation to the pulsations and rhythms of media coverage itself. Alternative ways of seeing that cast broader questions become forgotten. (Can justice be considered complete while racism and exploitation corrode the body politic from within?)

Cooked and channeled, emotional investment rises and falls along the dramatic curve provided by the news system. Like a team sport there are preparations and plans followed by one side (the prosecution) making its case as best it can, then turning the ball over to the opposing defense. Summations bring the issues to a point. Speculation on what the jury will decide offers a crescendo. Speculation on public response and police preparedness pitch the tension higher. The verdict serves as climax, from which momentum shifts to a follow-up story of violent protest or a new story entirely, leaving only a denouement provided by profiles of the jurors and perhaps the progress of legal appeals by the convicted officers.[4]

Games and sporting contests provide a functional analogy: like history, the outcome of a particular game cannot be predicted but the clearly defined nature of any one sport encourages a wide range of informed analysis. Once the game has occurred, the factors that led to a specific outcome can be identified with some precision. Action and interpretation reach resolution inside a predefined frame. Paradigms governing the interpretive debate itself remain excluded. These governing protocols and assumptions escape the scrutiny of the positivist frame.

Media news mutates into a simulacrum, a copy of a world that only exists within its own frame. The indexical whammy of the beating of Rodney King gets reinscribed, as facts get fitted to a frame, within the dramatic curve it initially exceeded. Excess, drained of its potential to rupture all frames, flows into the channels of moral containment. Class division and racial apartheid, symptomatically inscribed on the body of Rodney King, go unrecognized. The obviousness of the raw evidence testifies to specific acts of brutal assault, not sweeping allegations. To what class do these actions belong? Of what class are they members? Such questions do not fit the prevailing judicial frame. They have a marginal role in the media coverage. Instead, media news, and all of us who move to its rhythm, assume that images will speak for themselves, that aberrations will be corrected, rogue cops punished, Rodney King vindicated. Finding the officers guilty from the outset, the news media waits for the judicial system to catch up with it, using its own confidence in the system as the basis on which to castigate the twelve Simi Valley jurors in the first trial and to spin cautionary tales against violence and mayhem in anticipation of the outcome of the second.

The case of these four LAPD officers reverses the standard pattern of reality TV and TV police programs like *Dragnet, Starsky and Hutch, Hill Street Blues,* or *Hunter.* Here, the police pursue suspects who are always and already criminals. (In this domain, we can tautologically define criminals as anyone pursued by the police.) Police force is always provoked by criminal acts, police suspicion, and fear always justified by criminal treachery. The media coverage of the Rodney King incident, though, suggests that the narrative positions can be reversed, yielding rogue cops and innocent victims, without necessarily changing the localized, game-like focus. The surrounding context in which interpretive struggle takes place—from what constitutes appropriate use of force to how crime and poverty can be eradicated—remains untouched. Away from the television sets, in large segments of Los Angeles, outrage explodes at the most immediate and visible targets (motorists of the wrong color, Korean shops, or the police themselves). This, too, will provide fuel for the media fires.

We may swing from targeting the police officers to scapegoating the jurors; we can call the cops and jurors racists, decry the anesthetizing tactics of the defense in showing the footage over and over; but these responses are evasions. Their class basis in bourgeois morality tales is patent. Such tales dwell on the emotional intensities and individualized dilemmas that beset the class in the middle, afraid of falling and eager to rise. As members of the middle class, or its professional, managerial elite, we can identify with the melodramatics of villainy and vindication, brutality and punishment. In doing so, we play right into the game the media news has perfected.

The Rush to Judgment

Why the prosecution lost the first trial remains inadequately explained within the interpretive frame the media established. Both the media and the Left blamed the not guilty verdict on the jury's racism. This was assumed, not proven. Like the dismissal of slow-motion and freeze-frame analysis of the videotape, presumed racism invokes a mythic (highly ideological) interpretive frame in which the jury's verdict serves as confirmation rather than puzzle. Confirmation of what? Of racism in Simi Valley. Of the insidious nature of slow-motion analysis. Of the failure of inhabitants in a suburban sanctuary to do justice for the inner city. Inevitably, such explanations beg important questions. The most crucial might be, If the jury was right, and these officers were innocent, in the specific context of the first trial, how can this be explained; and, once explained, what remains unaccounted for beyond this (localized) interpretive frame?

Why was the Simi Valley trial of *California v. Powell, Koon, Wind and Briseno* lost? This is not a question of ultimate truth, but of how a specific outcome occurs in a particular interpretive arena, through specific strategies and rhetorical moves, with distinct forms of appeal to fact, and authority, and with inevitable but veiled ideological assumptions.[5] Basic assumptions and controlling frames require address, but such address must occur within a specific context. Were arguments made that could convince not only the "racist" jurors of Simi Valley but *us* as well? What political counter-interpretation could channel moral outrage into effective action, *even if* these four officers were all found innocent—in the second trial as well as the first? The successful conviction of two of the four officers in the federal trial alleviates the need to answer such questions (as it simultaneously relieves the Rodney King incident of its power to galvanize), but this alleviation is more a problem than a solution if we do not step aside from media jubilation to draw more lasting lessons.

The first trial resulted in a verdict of innocent because (1) the prosecution failed to make a compelling case and (2) the defense lawyers, particularly Darryl Mounger, representing Sgt. Stacey Koon, made a brilliant defense.

The prosecution rushed to trial under Proposition 115 which permits the elimination of preliminary hearings, with the cross-examination of witnesses, in order to seek a grand jury indictment directly, with a guarantee of a trial date within sixty days of the indictment. The rush, fueled by political pressure, hinged heavily on the positivist fallacy: the videotape offered the proverbial smoking gun. The prosecution could treat its images as raw evidence, as incontrovertible answer to a carefully formulated and often debated question: When are the police out of control? Answer: when they beat an errant motorist with metal clubs more than fifty times.[6] The prosecution neglected to consider the image as symptom in need of diagnosis. The prosecution chose to treat the tape as evidence, exposing itself to compelling counter-arguments that it was no such thing (in and of itself).

The argumentative naïveté of the prosecution fed into the defense lawyers' strength. The defense lawyers systematically set out to construct an interpretive frame in which the videotape itself would serve as confirmation. Confirmation of what? Of the rough and brutal nature of police work. Of the risk and uncertainty that confront officers in the street. Of the dire necessity of controlled force to safeguard the men in blue and preserve the lives of suspects who might otherwise be killed. (One *New York Times* headline read, "Blows Saved Rodney King's Life, Officer Testifies" [March 23, 1993].) The overall defense strategy, reconstructed here from a variety of sources, presents a cogent, coherent, convincing interpretation.[7] Although not immediately compatible with many people's imagined relationship to justice, it proved quite plausible to the Simi Valley jury, very possibly for reasons other than their own preassigned racism.

Placing the videotape evidence within a larger context was crucial to the defense lawyers' interpretive strategy. Rather than a constant irritant, this embarrassing piece of grit grew into a pearl. The lawyers argued that the officers did not just start beating Mr. King out of the blue as the videotape implies. Important, mitigating events occurred before the tape began. These events could be interpreted to portray Mr. King as a dangerous suspect who required felony arrest (which, in turn, mandated the "proned out" position flat on the ground that Rodney King failed to assume).[8] The video then demonstrates the determined, casebook efforts by well-schooled cops to arrest a potentially violent man without resorting to deadly force (choke holds and the gun).

Rodney King not only sped on the L.A. freeways and city streets but ignored stop signs, red traffic lights, and the pursuing California Highway Patrol (CHP) officers. (Whether these violations were known to the LAPD officers at the time of the arrest remains unclear.) Once he stopped, Rodney King was ordered out of his car by the CHP officers. (A police helicopter overhead may have rendered these orders unintelligible.) When King did eventually get out of the car, he "danced around. He waved at the helicopter. Worse, he reached into his pockets, an exceptionally dangerous action since he hadn't been cuffed and searched and the officers on the scene had no idea whether he was armed."[9]

Although in his book Koon describes these as events that occurred before his arrival (which, therefore, may not have been known to him until later), Koon also uses them to conclude that this is a dangerous suspect. Sgt. Koon uses these events to construct an interpretive frame for King's actions, a frame that treats all King's subsequent behavior as confirmation: King was a serious threat who "knew all the tricks to take out a police officer."[10] Koon's own direct observations confirm the interpretation he retrofitted to the scene. King seemed under the influence of alcohol or stronger drugs, he was sweaty and "buffed-out" (heavily muscled), "a physical condition often associated with ex-cons."[11] He spoke gibberish and ignored repeated commands to lie on the ground, face down, hands behind his back. He was probably "dusted" (under the influence of PCP).

Koon goes to get his TASER (an electrical stun gun) and returns to find King responding to an order from CHP officer Melanie Singer by turning his back, grabbing his butt and gyrating "his hips in a sexually suggestive fashion" (33). As she advances on Mr. King, with her gun drawn, Sgt. Stacey Koon assumes command of the situation. He orders her to back away.

Sgt. Koon, striving to avoid a deadly confrontation, orders four LAPD officers to swarm Mr. King and handcuff him. (When forced to the ground, face first, King probably broke his cheekbone, according to Koon.) But before the officers can cuff him, Rodney King throws them off. Koon: "I think to myself, 'Oh, shit! He's turned into the Hulk!' . . . My officers are in immediate danger" (37).

Convinced by this demonstration of superhuman strength that King is on PCP, Koon orders his men to back away as he gives additional commands verbally for King to lie down with his hands behind his back. Instead Mr. King "cocks" his legs once again, "it looks like he's getting up to come after me or one of the other officers. . . . And so I TASED him" (38).

Mr. King makes "a bear-like moan . . ." and is then "groaning like a wounded animal. . . . So I TASE him again" (38). He continues to groan and lies on the ground, perhaps ready to comply with their commands.

It is only now that the George Holliday videotape begins. Everything up to this point is crucial to the interpretation the defense will make of the tape. Justification and motivation for what follows resides in this prior set of events for which no video record exists.

From this point on, the testimony of witnesses must correspond to, or at least not contradict, what the videotape shows.[12] As Sgt. Koon describes what happens next, Rodney King rises again and rushes Officer Powell. Because he could have moved in other directions (assuming he had his wits sufficiently about him to do so after two tasings and an inebriated condition),[13] Koon describes this action as volitional on King's part ("He chose to collide into Officer Powell") and defensive on the part of Powell ("He defended himself with his metal PR 24 baton, unleashing a furious series of power strokes. The first one hit King's collarbone. King was knocked to the ground, doing a one-point landing, face first, into the asphalt" (40). Striking the ground a second time may also have broken King's cheekbone.

The next minute and a half are the portion of the event millions witnessed on TV. Whether King was struck in the head cannot be determined. (If he were hit in the head by a baton it would constitute "assault with a deadly weapon" since head blows can kill and are not allowed unless deadly force is itself allowed.)

Hours and hours of court time centered on the videotape. Three points require examination: (1) the narrative argument made by the defense about what happened, (2) the expository style used to unfold this narrative, and (3) the exact role of the videotape in advancing the argument.

1. The defense lawyers developed the argument, with considerable success, that Rodney King, not the police officers, was in control of the entire

event. The officers consistently responded to King's actions. They were always on the defensive; they feared for their lives.[14]

Based on the pattern of conduct presumably established by events prior to the start of the tape, every subsequent action by Mr. King becomes aggressive, not evasive. Even after receiving numerous blows, at 4.28.18 (4 minutes, 28 seconds, 18 frames) on the videotape, just as Officer Briseno stomps on the back of King's neck, with two other officers in close proximity, Koon continues to see a serious threat:

> Lawyer Mounger: "Do you believe he was trying to get up?"
> Koon: "Yes, I do."
> Mounger: "And what did you think he was trying to get up to do?"
> Koon: "He was gonna get up and arm himself and possibly attack Officer Wind here in the background, Officer Powell, Officer Briseno."[15]

Another prime example occurs at an earlier moment when, after being struck a series of baton blows, Mr. King rolls away from the officer striking him. Although this particular moment is not covered in either videotape of the trial, this is how Sgt. Koon describes Mr. King's action in his book, *Presumed Guilty*:

> King began rolling toward Officer Wind [away from Officer Powell]. Wind backed quickly away. He knew what was happening.
>
> Rodney King was doing the "Folsom Roll." To the casual viewer of the videotape, it appeared as though King were rolling away from the officers in an effort to avoid getting hit. But he wasn't being hit at the time. [Two seconds earlier, King had just received five seconds of continuous blows from Powell and Wind; he could have no way of knowing when they would resume or for how long.]
>
> King wasn't avoiding blows. He was rolling *toward* Officer Wind—he was doing the "Folsom Roll": Any LAPD cop who's dealt with ex-cons is familiar with the "Folsom Roll." . . . It's a technique for disarming an officer while proned out on the ground. The idea is to roll into an officer and tangle up his legs, then reach up and grab a gun belt and holster while the officer is off-balance. Then the officer is down and the suspect has the weapon. You can see where that leads. (42–43)

The hypothesis that the suspect might be an ex-con because he was "buffed-out" is now treated as a fact, and a movement that "the casual viewer" would regard as defensive reflex becomes converted by street-wise cops into an offensive threat.

This conclusion results from shifting the placement of interpretive punctuation marks in the flow of a continuous action. If we punctuate the events in a series of actions involving two parties, A and B, such that A causes B's response which then causes further behavior from A and so on, we would have the causal chain, A / B / A′ / B′ / A″ / B″. But if we shift our punctuation marks, or framing, one space to the right, or left, suddenly B becomes the causal agent and A the respondent: B / A′ / B′ / A″ / B″ / A‴. This shift in framing is tantamount to the difference between saying "The officers struck King with their batons (A) which caused King to roll on the ground to escape the blows (B) which led an officer to strike King again (A′)" versus an account based on shifting the causal bracket: "King executed a Folsom Roll (B) which caused an officer to step back (A′) but King continued to roll (B′) which forced the officers to strike him again (A″)."[16]

Both causal series are supported by the same raw data. In cases such as this, involving intersubjectivity and multiple motivations that may not be conscious, the interpretive frame, not visual evidence, determines the causal bracketing.

The prosecution might have countered this argument with a metacommentary on the technique of punctuation itself, or it might have adopted the concept of social gest proposed by Bertolt Brecht (adapted, of course, to a court of law). What Brecht suggested was that certain individual actions convey within them a complex set of social power relations: they are signs, not motor responses. In this case, King's "Folsom Roll" could be a sign of self-protection as he uses bodily movement to avoid physical harm. Here is an apt example provided by Roland Barthes regarding Brecht's idea of social gest:

> What then is a social gest? It is a gesture or set of gestures (but never a gesticulation) in which a whole social situation can be read. Not every gest is social: there is nothing social in the movements a man makes in order to brush off a fly; but if this same man, poorly dressed, is struggling against guard-dogs, the gest becomes social.[17]

2. The style adopted by the defense team, and Sgt. Koon in particular, exemplifies a distinctly administrative or bureaucratic use of language. This style of speech epitomizes the one-dimensional thinking that Marcuse criticized so aptly in 1964.[18] The social exists on a flat plane of action and effect; no space for critical consciousness or dialectical thought persists. The description of volitional actions eliminates any sense of human agency, of a conscience or consciousness capable of alternatives. People do what their institutional or operational frame requires them to do. Individuals become cyborgs (cybernetic organisms, a living form of artificial intelligence) trained to execute policies and procedures. To the extent that they do so, no questions of personal motivation, intention, bias, or desire call for attention.

Police officers, for example, do not hit or kick people vindictively; they do not act from anger or hatred. (They may have to contend with fear but their training gives means of doing so.) Police officers embody the procedures and protocols for which a value-free operationalism trains them. No opportunity for the infiltration of personal bias or social prejudices like racism presents itself (only feelings of fear and self-preservation). Tactics, procedures, command and control structures possess the false concreteness and objective giveness of facts of nature. The template they offer transcends divisive issues of race, class, or gender to guarantee technocratic equality for one and all.

This stylistic operation pervades Stacey Koon's written account of the Rodney King incident, *Presumed Guilty,* but is even more rampant in the court testimony itself.[19]

To pulsate back: In describing a pause by Officer Powell in his beating of Rodney King, Koon, on the witness stand, says, "He got to a point where he's flat again, and Officer Powell kind of pulsated back to evaluate. And Mr. King started to rise again."[20]

The fatigue factor: Regarding a later point in the tape when the officers again seem to have paused, Koon comments, "My officers are going through a fatigue factor here."

The compliance mode: And still later, at 3.52.20, Koon's lawyer asks him for his thoughts: "I'm getting a concern, scared. I'm getting a little frightened here now because this gentleman has just been subjected to a multitude of blows with the metal PR 24 and there's no evidence he's going to go into compliance mode."

The stomping motion: When Officer Briseno forces King flat to the ground by striking him in the back of his neck with his boot, Koon states, "Officer Briseno applied a stomping motion that struck Mr. King in the neck, back area here and then Mr. King again was on the rise." When asked if he saw any "kicks" during the beating, Koon replied, "I wouldn't consider them 'kicks,' but I saw a stomping motion by Officer Wind, yeah." He is asked again if there were no kicks: "Not what I consider kicks, no." Was there a pushing motion? "Pushing, yes. I saw pushing, stomping motion."[21]

Tasing: Koon, describing Rodney King's response to the effect of 50,000 volts of electricity from the TASER gun: "He continued to rise to his feet and I TASED him a second time."

Koon's lawyer, Darryl Mounger: "And what did he do after you TASED him a second time?"

Koon: "He repeated this groan, similar to like a wounded animal, and then he, I could see the, I could see the vibrations on him. He seemed to be overcoming it."[22]

Officer Laurence Powell continued this same style of testimony, adding a personal element when it conveyed fear rather than anger. Michael Stone, Powell's lawyer, asks him, "Did you strike Mr. King for the purpose of punishing him?" Powell answers, "No."

"Did you strike Mr. King for the purpose of hurting him?" "N . . . no, not for the purpose of hurting him."

"Did you strike Mr. King in anger?"

"No."

"Describe your mental state at the time you were striking him."[23]

Powell: "I was completely in fear of my life, scared to death that if this guy got back up, he was gonna take my gun away from me or there was gonna be a shooting and I was doing everything I could to keep him down on the ground."

Charles Duke, an expert witness for the defense, also adopts a language in which physical forces act without conscious agency. Prosecutor Terry White asks Duke, who stands before a monitor on which the videotape has been frozen at 4.03.02, with King on the ground, one leg drawn up toward his torso, "What action have you seen at this time?"

Duke: "He had his knee in a cocked position and the baton's blow struck and it straightened it out."

Prosecutor White: "The baton blow straightened out his leg?"

Duke: "It caused it, him to move his leg in a straight position."

White: "Did it cause him to move his leg from pain?"

Duke: "I don't know."[24]

This line of defense could have been more forcefully countered by the prosecution. (Other experts could have described how people typically protect themselves from violent blows, but the prosecution called no such experts.)[25] The prosecution might have also attempted to introduce contextual evidence about typical or likely police conduct when minority suspects prove recalcitrant or less than deferential. The popular press presented such information. It clearly contradicted the image of beleaguered, well-trained, highly disciplined cops struggling to survive the mean streets of the inner city. Suzanne Espinoza's article in the *San Francisco Chronicle,* for example, describes the informal, everyday attitudes and beliefs of L.A. cops on the beat:

> In dozens of interviews, police officers said a badge and uniform no longer win them automatic respect and cooperation. Too many times, they say, officers are driven to using fists, batons and harsh language to counter hostility and disrespect. . . . "Every L.A. cop who saw that tape knew exactly what happened," said one officer who did not want to be named.
>
> Because of such hellish experiences, officers said they are likely to "fight" or beat a person who crosses the line between cooperation and resistance, regardless of race or ethnicity.[26]

The defense lawyers established a false concreteness. They created an interpretive arena in which physical force is applied or delivered by procedural mandate, with no personal inflection. This use of force has at its base institutional policy (to follow correct procedure for a felony arrest) and personal fear (by a large cohort of armed police, with a police helicopter overhead) but not anger, prejudice, or vindictiveness.[27]

3. The exact role of the videotape emerges in relation to the previous

two points. The defense goal is to build an interpretive frame, via points 1 and 2—Rodney King's control of the situation and the officer's operational obedience to policy and procedure—that will produce meaning for which the Holliday videotape appears to be raw evidence (the return of the historical referent, what really happened). In fact, however, the videotape serves as confirmation. The meaning of the tape (as opposed to its indexical correspondence to a prior event, the actual beating), however, is the signified of the interpretive frame's signifiers, not an external referent. As a signified, meaning is what we, audience or jury, attach to a signifier, to render it intelligible. Without a signified a signifier is noise even if it has a referent: a blurry, underdeveloped photograph may be *of something*, but a viewer may call it undecipherable. The viewer has no signified, such as "prize fight," to attach to make it meaningful.

In this case, we attach the meanings posited by the defense lawyers but believe that these signifieds derive not from the interpretive frame as signifier—the form of the discourse—but from the referent of this signifier, the historical event of which the videotape is raw evidence. The work of signification within the tape, and within the act of interpretation, becomes erased in favor of transparency. This completes the work of confirming underlying assumptions (an interpretive frame) in the guise of presenting hard evidence.[28]

The punctuation of the causal chain by Sgt. Stacey Koon such that King's actions constantly prompt police responses, putting King in control of the situation, is one example of this process. An interpretation that frames King's action as aggression, as a "Folsom Roll," generates as its signified the "fact" of King's control. The act of interpretation clearly constructs this specific meaning; it does not inhere in the external referent (those events whose indexical trace stands before us).

The performative or rhetorical dimension of the argument, though, is to prompt belief that this meaning comes directly from this discourse's referent, the historical event, and *not* from the form of the argument. The tape confirms this claim, but does so in the guise of raw evidence of a fact, King's "Folsom Roll," and meaning, his control of the situation, that has been produced in the manner of ventriloquism: as confirmation in the guise of brute evidence. (It is not I who speak but the "evidence," the historical world, itself.)

What makes this interpretation stick, if it does, is the rhetorical force of its claims. Ethical credibility—astute lawyers and honest police officers; convincing argument; tacit, or streetwise, knowledge; visual evidence; the appearance of logic if not logic itself; and compelling effect—tapping preexisting emotions about "buffed out" black males, urban danger, and the police as the thin blue line between chaos and civilization: these classic modes of rhetorical proof provide the raw material of courtroom argument.[29]

The sticking power of such proofs, certainly in this case, hinges heavily on the degree to which its claims correspond to the social imaginary within which the listener, or jury, already lives. The social imaginary consists of those social relations members of one group imagine they have to their actual relation to another group. As a realm of the imaginary (rather than the symbolic where differences prevail over oppositions), these relations are image-based, not make-believe. They move toward either/or, them/us polarizations.

Once applied to groups, the social imaginary becomes a map (or interpretive frame) defining the territorial claims and boundaries that divide us according to race, class, gender, age, nation, language, religion, ethnicity, and so on. When the construction of an interpretive frame that draws on evidence which in fact confirms the meaning the frame itself produces works (achieves believability), it matches up with the social imaginary its subjects already occupy.

Moving beyond this map to address the great social divides themselves requires moving beyond the production of meanings as though they were inherent in the historical world or documentary representations of that world; it requires a social symbolic in which the act of framing, contextualizing, and interpreting is as central as putative claims to fact made by means of a rhetorically induced subjectivity that only confirms what already exists in the social imaginary.

Visible Evidence

The defense argument appeared to fly in the face of common sense. But it took the *form* of a positivist, scientific interpretation. It did what any good examination of evidence should do: it scrutinized it with care and drew from it (apparent) substantiation for an interpretation that best accounted for what really happened. That the form of interpretation used by the defense fit such a classic mode—especially the revelation of a "true" reality beneath the deceptive certainty of surface appearances by means of special techniques like slow motion and freeze framing—may be a major reason for its success in the first trial. (It was not until the second, federal trial that the prosecution adopted an equally impressive form for the interpretation of the evidence.) The success of the defense was also the major reason why the tactics, if not the form, they adopted was so constantly attacked, even by experts who might well have known better.

What we have heard so far from "experts" on the use of videotape evidence often amounts to denial of the very tenets of interpretive investigation. The experts' eagerness to claim that slow motion and freeze framing "distort" reality seems based on the fear that, if these tactics worked for the defense and against Mr. King, they must be bad techniques. These attacks do not examine the more specific strategies that blur the boundary between confirmation and evidence. Instead they throw out the tools of close analysis as well as the result of an apparent injustice. In an "Op-Ed" article in the *New York Times,* Patricia Greenfield and Paul Kibbey argue that analytic techniques like slow motion and freeze framing distort meaning. They also assume that some conclusions "are more accurately taken from real-time video or witnesses."[30]

The polarity they set up echoes the assumptions of the prosecution, media-orchestrated sentiment heard after the first trial, and the indignation that fueled the subsequent violence: the Holliday tape, seen in real time, speaks for itself. Violence has been done; justice must be had. Scrutinizing the tape the way one would scrutinize the slow-motion replay of a sports event deceived a jury already prone to deception thanks to its lack of technological sophistication and its incipient racism.

What such arguments fear most is that the analytic techniques themselves were not at fault, that the jury was not anesthetized, and that the case was won and lost for other reasons.

George Holliday's videotape was not an edited film. It was raw footage. To slow it down for examination harkens back to Muybridge's use (in 1875) of multiple cameras to prove that a running horse's hoofs are all momentarily off the ground at the same time. It is what researchers routinely do to understand rapidly occurring processes in greater detail.

When what we watch is actual violence, slow motion and freeze framing identify the application and effect of that violence graphically. This can be profoundly disturbing, not soothing. The violence is not staged or rehearsed. Nor is it choreographed, nor edited to hide the staging. We are not left with *only* slow-motion renditions of staged violence, as we are in fiction films, but with a detailed dissection of actual events. The tape remains constantly available for real-time viewing. The purpose of viewing a different, slower or frozen version of the same thing is not entertainment or aesthetic pleasure. The spectator, or juror, uses these devices for other ends. In this context close analysis hardly creates an "aesthetic" of the sort associated with Hollywood fiction.

By framing denunciations of close analysis in terms of the use of special effects in fiction films, these attacks demean the jury and hamstring the prosecution. They must only repeat, over and over, "Believe your eyes; watch the tape." No interpretive frame is necessary. Every attempt at analysis will "distort" the truth. Unmasking the production of meaning—not by slow-motion viewing, but by the rhetorical treatment of the videotape as evidence for what it in fact only confirms—becomes impossible.

Had slow-motion analysis revealed that blows were struck to Mr. King's head, groin, or spine (the zones of "deadly force"), the same experts would no doubt be praising the virtues of the techniques they so quickly disparage when it does not produce the results they (morally or politically) desire. Of course, slow motion is a "distortion." So is the raw footage. (It puts three-dimensional events onto a two-dimensional surface, produces foreshortening, and introduces problems of graininess, focus, and sound.) *Any* post facto account, be it from an eyewitness, participant, prosecutor, or historian, distorts. History, which is what we must reconstruct here, is always a matter of story telling: our reconstruction of events must impose meaning and order on them, assign motivations, assess causes, and propose moral judgments (in this case, guilt or innocence).

This is where the prosecution failed. It didn't make a convincing case with the evidence at hand. The prosecution's narrative of "what really happened" was flimsy. It simply and contentedly said, "Believe your eyes." But the defense said, "Look again; this isn't what it seems." For this jury, at least, reasonable doubt was sufficiently established. (It is important to note one crucial exception: the jury could not decide on Officer Powell's possible use of excess force ["assault under color of authority with great bodily enhancement"], the most damning charge of all.)

The desire to discover facts others have not seen, the urge to interpret, the wish to make raw footage speak the truth of an event rather than confirm the interpretation applied to it, possesses a power similar to that of the confessional. It is a power hard to resist, although that is what the prosecution in the first trial asked the jury to do. In the second, federal trial, one juror spoke with considerable pride about the jury's own decision to look again, to see what they, too, might discover beneath the surface detail:

> "What we decided is to chuck all [the expert witnesses'] opinions," the goldsmith said. "We said we're going to interpret it ourselves. That's our job. . . ."
>
> In the case of Officer Powell, jurors found guilt even though some gave little weight to hours of testimony by a Government witness called to prove that Mr. King was repeatedly hit in the head by Officer Powell. The clincher instead was a baton blow to Mr. King's chest as he seemed to be motionless on his back near the end of the beating. In trial that blow was referred to in passing by a Government witness and it was not stressed in the closing arguments.
>
> "There was no doubt," the welder said. "It was so clear a violation of any human right I can imagine. It was like chopping wood, and King was just lying there on his back."[31]

In a similar spirit a hypothetical line of prosecutorial argument might run like this: On close examination of the tape, is it so clear that Laurence Powell strikes the first blow in self-defense with a checked swing as Rodney King rises from the ground and moves toward him? (This is the first blow we see, within two seconds of the tape beginning.) One might argue that Powell anticipates Mr. King's move (how? was Mr. King goaded into rising?), steps back, "cocks" his wrists, and unleashes a tremendously brutal blow to King's shoulder and possibly his neck or head. Slowing the action makes Mr. Powell look like a baseball batter whose swing is only "checked" by the forward momentum of Mr. King's body as he topples toward Mr. Powell and plummets to the pavement face first.

Did this devastating blow so terrify Mr. King that all his subsequent actions were an attempt to avoid more blows? To "prone out" is to render oneself totally vulnerable. Who would do so if the very people demanding it also appear determined to beat you, possibly to kill you? Is this story plausible? Could it not be told with slow motion and freeze frames in convincing detail? Would the difference in the interpretations then reside not in the abuses of close analysis but in the plausibility produced by the form of the interpretive frame and by rhetoric effect? By trying to put the prosecution on ontologically superior ground—the evidence is in the tape, the indexical image guarantees its own meaning—such arguments abandon the arena of interpretive struggle for a moral high ground secured by blind belief.

Rolling in the Dirt

The videotape debate has been a major obfuscation so far. No image can *show* intent or motivation. Images, whether in real time, slow motion, or freeze frame, can, however, help corroborate a narrative account of what happened. This corroboration is best supported by close scrutiny and careful analysis. Mr. Holliday's videotape is raw footage, the latent pearl in the oyster. It does not speak for itself.

The defense played to the order/anarchy model of reality TV. They adopted the *Grand Canyon* point of view, with its vertiginous moments of the sublime as both awesome and terrifying sight.[32] They concluded on just the right note of valiant public service by those who constitute the thin blue line. This summation tapped into the image of police patrols valiantly enforcing the geopolitics of a globalized apartheid that keeps some of us safe behind our closed doors and walled communities, under virtual house arrest in the constructed spaces of reality TV, airports, freeways, and shopping malls, on this side of the metal detectors and security systems standing between them and us.[33]

The defense lawyers readily admitted violence had been done, that what we saw was brutal. But the defense also posed a question for which the prosecution had no clear answer: What do you expect, what else could they do? (How such a question constructs a "you," a social subjectivity that beckons to a great many of us but within a highly loaded, ideological [classist and racist] frame, might well have been a subject for the prosecution's own closing statement.)[34]

"*What do you expect?*" The video confirmed what the defense set out to argue: Here was a dangerous, hulking suspect in control of a potentially deadly situation; here were operationally proficient, professionally neutral police officers fearful for their lives but determined to do their job. As Officer Laurence Powell's attorney, Michael Stone, put it:

> There were many opportunities, I suppose, for Officer Powell to avoid the risk, and the threat, to his own personal safety that was occasioned by the incident that these officers confronted that night. But he determined to stand his ground; he determined to take the necessary steps to do his duty. As a result of those choices he made that night of March 3rd, 1991, early in the morning, he's sitting here as a defendant before this jury. It's not Rodney Glen King who's sitting here, but Officer Laurence Powell, Sgt. Stacey Koon, Officer Ted Briseno, and Officer Tim Wind.
>
> What do we, ladies and gentlemen, as members of the community, expect from our police? What is it we want them to do? These officers, these defendants, do not get paid to lose street fights. They don't get paid to roll around in the dirt with the likes of Rodney Glen King.
>
> These are not robo-cops, ladies and gentlemen. They hurt, they feel pain, they bleed, and they die, just like everyone else. And we leave it to them to take care of the mean streets so that we can safely enjoy our lives.
>
> I decline the challenge to play the video again. You can play the video all you want, backwards, forwards, slow motion. It will be available to you as a piece of evidence. I've seen it enough and I think you have, too.[35]

This summation is exceptionally persuasive (within the frame that has constructed "you" as one of those with much to lose from "the likes of Rodney Glen King"). It taps into the preexisting fears that those outside the urban bantustans might have of them. It is a moment in the defense's finest hour, and it was not successfully rebutted.[36]

What do we expect our police to do? (And which "we" are we when we ponder this question?) Roger Parloff wrote in *The American Lawyer* that as presented in court the evidence for reasonable doubt was compelling. He runs through a point-by-point account of events prior to the tape and events in the tape, and concludes that, from the legal perspective of evidentiary argument, the defense made a solid case. Outrage at policies that allowed such an event to occur were misplaced if they cause the cops who must follow them to be convicted. (The policies, even if racist or inappropriate, were not on trial in this particular case. Instead of being subject to legal scrutiny, as they might be in a class-action suit, or in a legislative investigation, they served as a key element in the officer's alibi of operational professionalism and adherence to established procedure.) Parloff editorializes:

> LA police officers are trained to force suspects into the prone position, because that is the procedure that is supposed to best guarantee their own safety. If that procedure and training ought to be reexamined, the time and

> place to reform it is not a criminal prosecution of 4 officers who were required to follow it.
>
> I should add that if you are unwilling to put yourself in the officer's shoes—because you cannot imagine yourself or anyone you love choosing to become a police officer and having to subdue a resisting suspect—then you are not a fit juror for this case. You may also be a class bigot.[37]

The judge adhered to previous legal precedent that required the determination of guilt to be made from the point of view of a "reasonable police officer," not a civilian witness. This ruling together with the emphasis on the very compelling question of "what do you expect?" supported an interpretive frame that localized this event at the expense of larger patterns of police policy or conduct and their perceived impact within specific communities. Since police policy was not on trial, it could not be debated, and the media's commitment to factual reporting served as a convenient alibi: unless some other agency reassessed policy, press reports could justifiably remain focused on this one incident. Whether alternative tactics such as the use of velcro blankets, nets, or other similar restraints might achieve the desired result less violently never entered the public debate.

A Loss of Class

The ability to solve problems by means of an algebra of probability provides one definition for "street smarts." Using such an algebra requires an ability to develop and follow tacit conventions describing the boundaries of a discrete situation or event, character types, their usual behavior, the motivations and intentions governing specific encounters, and their likely result. (More formalized and explicit descriptions arise in institutional settings where generalization rather than participatory involvement in specific situations is the primary goal.)

An algebra of probability submits specific facts to formulaic calculation. Behavior, and criminality in particular, becomes measured by probabilities governing similar people, doing similar things, in similar situations, with similar motives, goals, and results. Such an algebra replaces personal knowledge of specific individuals—their family history, past behavior, typical traits, and established goals. It is the algebra of the city and of the management of populations. Embodied knowledge yields a potential and a wisdom: a being-in-action conducive to historical consciousness that contrasts sharply with the reductive and objectifying algebra of probability. (This algebra is clearly akin to the algebra of need William Burroughs used to describe drug addiction in *Naked Lunch.*) In later discussions of *Strike, Who Killed Vincent Chin?*, and many performative documentaries I implicitly contrast embodied knowledge, which yokes together the particular and the general, amplifying both, with this algebra of probability, which subsumes the particular (and the body) into the general, reducing particularity to raw material for operational procedures.

Class antagonism and racism draw on an algebra of probability, a virulent Malthusianism, to describe black males as prone to commit violent crimes; poor neighborhoods as hotbeds of drugs, gambling, and prostitution; people of color as more likely to break the law. Instead of treating specific cases symptomatically, tracing them back to controlling structures, an algebra of probability uses each specific case to confirm the already answered question of class and racial superiority. Yoked to power, and instruments of force, such an algebra becomes a major tool in the maintenance of those class, racial, and ethnic divides that constitute the social imaginary.

Once we leave the street for the courtroom, American jurisprudence moderates the application of this algebra of probability in the determination of guilt or innocence. The extent to which individuals can be assumed to behave in a certain way based on evidence of past conduct, for example, is carefully controlled. (The regulation of assumptions regarding behavior has formed a central part of the debate in cases of alleged rape where past sexual conduct has often been used to discredit a charge of rape. The issue is also central to the idea of product "recalls" and class-action suits when the probability of hazards or the breadth of injury reaches a certain limit.) Neither Rodney King's previous convictions, nor previous accusations against Officer Powell for excessive force, nor Officer Briseno's sixty-six-day suspension for excessive force (kicking a handcuffed prisoner) and reports of his abusive behavior in a prior marriage were ruled admissible.[38] The events of March 3, 1991, were isolated from such factors that may have made these events symptomatic in significant ways.

Such an effort to regulate the use of an algebra of probability stems from the positivist aspect of American law. It puts the onus on the prosecution not to prove guilt by dint of a pattern of conduct likely to place the suspect in the present situation or shape what he or she does but by dint of specific evidence pertaining to the immediate situation itself. For someone who has habitually broken the law, and for members of groups characterized as frequent lawbreakers (young black males, for example), this control of past information has clear benefit since guilt cannot be proven simply by association. (To the extent that skin color cannot be hidden, such control may be only partial, expressly forbidding what may nonetheless be tacitly assumed. Attorney Stone's reference to "the likes of Rodney Glen King" clearly works to trigger an implicit, racist assumption rather than point to any specific instance of past conduct.)

For someone who belongs to a group characterized as law-abiding, this control can work the other way: tacitly allowing assumptions that cannot be expressively undercut to persist. "Altruistic police protect us from those who would cause us harm," for example, is the type of assumption an astute defense lawyer can readily exploit when "we" belong to the propertied classes. Scouring the thirty-page survey used to select the first jury, for instance, the defense lawyers and the four officers pointedly sought out fifty-something candidates who "had a stable life and an investment in the community."[39] (They also accepted a Filipino and a Hispanic juror, along with three jurors with experience in the military or as security guards, one brother of a retired LAPD sergeant, and three National Rifle Association members.[40] The prosecution's rush to trial, and overconfidence, allowed the defense to empanel jurors whom an algebra of probability indicated would be disposed toward the police side of the story.)

Probability and positivism sometimes confirm one another—by producing mathematical formulas for social pattern, and sometimes conflict—where probability erases those distinguishing marks of singularity that define the historical. Legal doctrine allows the algebra of probability to operate within limits (themselves subject to contestation) regarding character, past behavior, or jury selection, but it also demands specific charges pertaining to a specific event. This positivist frame works to maintain a boundary that might otherwise blur between the specific case at hand and the social issues that underlie it.

Among these larger issues is the use of legitimate force in civil (nontotalitarian) society. "What do we expect" from our police? When "we" is the state itself, the answer is the maintenance of law and order. The police stand as the key form of coercive domestic force. They constitute one of the state's principal RSAs (Repressive State Apparatuses in the terminology of Louis Althusser).[41] In a civil society, however, the state's right to use force is not itself secured by force but by ISAs (Ideological State Apparatuses like the educational system, the mass media, electoral politics, and the judicial system) where arguments legitimating the use of force take persuasive, rather than coercive, form. The Rodney King incident was one example of this process.

This amounts to the legitimation of force or violence by ideological means within an arena of interpretive struggle. In doing so, the raw fact, the brute reality of violence, often recedes beneath the arguments made on behalf of its use ("law and order," "public safety"). (State approved violence is a gritty piece of raw data best transubstantiated into the precious stuff of ideological mystification.) We (white, middle-class citizens in reasonably secure communities) have little direct contact with the border zone—the streets and public spaces, the ghettos and communities—where police violence is an everyday occurrence and less a form of protection racket (sold to us with budgets and ballots) than harshly imposed repression governed by an algebra of probability.

The raw use of force can hardly be denounced if it is a brutal but necessary part of the social order. ("What do you expect?"—if exploitation and racism are not themselves addressed.) To ask *whose* order begins to move us away from a Malthusian algebra of social control and toward the arena of interpretive struggle. To read the Rodney King incident not as a confirmation of or departure from preexisting probabilities (and stereotypes) but as the symptomatic display of class and racial contradiction requires a broader frame than juridical positivism allows. The prosecution's challenge was to push the interpretive frame in this direction, by implication and suggestion if necessary, just as Attorney Stone's "the likes of Rodney Glen King" remark did from the other direction.

Demonstrating the intrusion of racial and class antagonism into the operational proceduralism of Sgt. Koon and his men is where the first prosecuting team failed and the second succeeded. The federal attorneys developed a far more systematic set of arguments, including, quite crucially, testimony from Rodney King himself, that generated the vivid impression of a hapless motorist whose brutal beating was de facto punishment for unspecified and untried crimes (crimes, the prosecutors suggested, that amounted to angering the police by appearing to defy their authority). In this interpretation, police conduct yielded symptomatic evidence of anger, frustration, and a desire to punish a less than obsequious black male rather than demonstrating conformity with classic police procedure for subduing dangerous, defiant suspects.

The videotape served to confirm this alternative view, presenting apparent evidence of excessive, unwarranted force whose purpose could be best explained symptomatically rather than probabilistically: What we saw was not what police typically do (although it may be that); it was what these specific police did in this specific situation from which personal motive and individual feeling are no longer evacuated. Abiding by the requirements of the positivist frame governing the trial, the federal attorneys chose not to introduce symptoms of class or racial conflict as primary factors but to disclose the symptomatology of personal vindictiveness, the pleasure of power, and the desire to punish that gave both a more complex and recognizably human face to the four officers on trial.

This form of symptomatic reading turns the singularity of the case to limited advantage. The case becomes, at least potentially, the "royal road" to the political unconscious and social structure. It removes the particular from the web of surface detail enclosing it, of "what everyone can see." It spares the prosecution from pitting a pious recitation of self-evident truths against an intriguing tale of hidden truth. Rather than transporting the incident from the realm of (bourgeois) human nature to that of a cybernetic operationalism in the face of a monstrous (subhuman) threat, the federal attorneys dwelled on the irruption of human nature (King's fear and terror; the officers' impulse to punish) and the familiar story of an all-too-human capacity to turn, in the heat of the moment, the best-laid plans, policies, and procedures awry.

Narrative and rhetoric pitched at this level reflects a shrewd pragmatism aimed at winning this case within predefined legal limits. This interpretive frame, however, reverses terms (reassigning power to the police, converting King's dangerous threats to fear and panic) but does not alter the controlling, humanist frame of individual behavior and responsibility. It does not travel far enough down the "royal road" that leads to other factors and forces than individual responsibility as social basis and legal cornerstone.

Class and Magnitude

What is to be done? As a start, break with the identificatory frame that binds us, as spectators, to a crime in terms of moral outrage rather than social change. Break with the narrative strategy of media reporting that develops suspense, anxiety, and catharsis rather than investigation, contextualization, and transformation. Break with the dramatic curve that constantly runs outrage to ground, short-circuiting efforts to move beyond the frame of immediacy to those structures and patterns responsible for the production of immediacy, sensation, and closure.

We return to questions of magnitude, of what carries us beyond the apparent evidence of the videotape per se, and beyond the specific drama of these two trials of four LAPD officers. A felt tension between representation and represented (the question of magnitude) involves the recognition of visual evidence as symptomatic evidence, not of psychic disorder necessarily, but of historical struggle most certainly. The production of such tension was the goal of Bertolt Brecht and those who have followed his example if not his specific strategies. At its best, such perceptible tension reminds us that moral outrage demands resolution outside the representational frame ideology provides for it (imaginary relationships [mis]recognized as our actual relationship to our social situation, relationships that appear capable of presenting pearls without a shell, truth without a frame).

Questions of magnitude diminish when the incident provides prima facie evidence of the appropriateness of existing policies, such as Sgt. Stacey Koon apparently believed. In his book he describes (after the fact) his first reactions to learning that the Rodney King incident had been videotaped:

> "BITCHIN" I thought. "This is great! They got it on tape! Now we'll have a live, in-the-field film to show police recruits. It can be a real-life example of how to use escalating force properly. Take it up and take it down. Watch what the suspect does. If he moves, control him. If he doesn't, cuff him. The guys are going to love this one. It's true stuff. Bitchin."
>
> Maybe it was naive, but it never occurred to me that the videotape, which I hadn't seen at the time, could be interpreted otherwise.[42]

The Rodney King case epitomizes exceptional violence by officers of the law much more for those outside the ghetto than for those contained within. In places like South Central Los Angeles, the incident may not pose questions of magnitude so readily. Instead of generating a felt tension, the incident can deflect issues of the social gest and symptomatic reading back toward those of an algebra of probability, stereotyping, and scapegoating (involving police conduct, whites, and local shopkeepers). It can diminish a sense of the possible, of alternative visions, and articulations, of what might be.

A sense of prima facie evidence prevailed in South Central L.A., but less in terms of a model of exemplary conduct than typical terrorism:

> But on the grass-roots level, especially among gang youth, Rodney King may not have quite the same profound resonance. As one of the Inglewood Bloods told me: "Rodney King? Shit, my homies be beat like dogs by the police every day. This riot is 'bout all the homeboys murdered by the police, about the little sister [Latasha Harlins] killed by the Koreans, about twenty-seven years of oppression. Rodney King just the trigger."[43]

If "ordinary fascism" requires the routine, day-in, day-out containment of anger within the urban bantustans—accepting drugs and violence as endemic to this border zone between civilization and its discontents, and acting more to prevent the infection of the greater body politic—the L.A. police motto, "To Serve and Protect," is better interpreted as "To Discipline and Punish." Without the patina of noble fatalism provided ex-cop Deckert by the movie *Blade Runner,* the police become contemporary bladerunners for a new world order whose greatest fear is not the destruction of its own environment but its overthrow by those parts of itself, these people, defined as expendable, as wholly other. "Off the Pig" and "Power to the People" are slogans that retain their resonance when issues of probability and stereotypes, racism and exploitation, opportunity and abandonment, let alone due process or affirmative action, go unresolved.

Who Killed Vincent Chin? answers its own title's question with a complex indictment not only of the one individual responsible, Ronald Ebens, but with a powerful critique of the racism, sexism, and class bigotry that made Ebens's act a case of social gest. The corresponding question here is, Who Beat Rodney King?

The answer I suggest includes, at the very least, an understanding of how and why King's experience follows the racial and class fault lines of a global economy that has decimated the working-class populations of Los Angeles and rendered them and their reserve pool of unskilled labor redundant. Mike Davis puts it this way in his pamphlet on the L.A. riots of 1992:

> A core grievance fueling the Watts rebellion and the subsequent urban insurrections of 1967–68 was rising black unemployment in the midst of a

> boom economy. What contemporary journalists fearfully described as the beginning of the "Second Civil War" was as much a protest against black America's exclusion from the military-Keynesian expansion of the 1960s as it was an uprising against police racism and de facto segregation in schools and housing. The 1992 riot and its possible progenies must likewise by understood as insurrections against an intolerable political-economic order. As even the *Los Angeles Times,* main cheerleader for "World City, L.A.", now editorially acknowledges, the "globalization of Los Angeles," has produced "devastating poverty for those weak in skills and resources."[44]

Police work, in this reconfigured context, pursues a far more overtly repressive function than televisual simulacra would allow, and relies on brute force far more routinely as a "bitchin'" instrument of control. A global economy's need to isolate and contain, not communism, but those made superfluous to its constituency of consumers and producers; a bureaucratic apparatus's tendency toward the operational control of unlawful conduct based on an algebra of probability; and a masculinist mentality's tendency to assert physical dominance when ridiculed or challenged are what we find symptomatically inscribed on the body of Rodney King.

The risk, though, remains of seeing trees instead of forest. Middlemen, culturally and often ethnically distinct police or local entrepreneurs, become the visible and outward sign of an invisible and pervasive system that robs local communities of social integrity and economic autonomy. "In the case of Los Angeles, it was tragically the neighborhood Korean liquor store, not the skyscraper corporate fortress downtown, that became the symbol of a despised new world order."[45] Scapegoating is a symptom of the *absence* of class analysis, historical consciousness, and political praxis.

How can priority be shifted from four police officers, on the one hand, and neighborhood merchants, on the other, to a system that is everywhere and nowhere, a system for which "fortress downtown" is but a more visible and more imperious sign of that for which it stands? The answer surely does not run in the direction of reading out the evidence of a postmodern aesthetic within this fortress design as Fredric Jameson's extraordinary but disassociated and undersynthesized reading of the Los Angeles Bonaventure Hotel does.[46] This is not a question of aesthetics but of an economic system that adopts a postmodern aesthetic of surface, reflection, self-sufficiency, and imperviousness as its own.

Spatial apartheid, the physical separation of races and classes, must surely be overcome as much or more than any mystifying incomprehensibility to the global economy. What everybody 'n the hood already knows is that the locus of the most dehumanizing looting and pillage of all is not the work of violent indignation but of urban planning, economic strangulation, and educational stultification within racial bantustans and the routine sale of "police protection" to those outside these zones. When the beating of Rodney King is understood as the symptomatic gest of an entire social system, justice for Rodney King cannot be satisfied within the melodramatic frame of the trial of Stacey King, Laurence Powell, Ted Briseno, and Timothy Wind. Transformative social praxis exceeds that frame.

3

AT THE LIMITS OF REALITY (TV)

A riot is the language of the unheard.

—Martin Luther King

The world watched in horror as over 200 bodies were pulled from the rubble.

—Host, *Code 3,* describing the aftermath of a gas explosion in Guadalajara, Mexico

Mondo Video: Non-Friction's Finest Hour[1]

Story telling is television's forte. In addition to drama with its obviously fictional form, news, talk shows, game shows, quiz shows, nature shows, sportscasts, and the recent phenomenon of "reality TV" all erect narrative frames around the situations and events they relay to us. Any firm sense of boundary which such shows attempt to uphold between fact and fiction, narrative and exposition, story telling and reporting inevitably blurs. Everyone and everything can be ripped from its historical ground and contained within this televisual scaffolding.

The ubiquitous and instantaneous quality of television consumes vast quantities of evidence. The sense of aura described by Walter Benjamin vanishes—"[a work of art's] presence in time and space, its unique existence at the place where it happens to be."[2] Everything is up for grabs in a gigantic reshuffling of the stuff of everyday life. Everything, that is, is subject to interpretation by television as a story-telling machine. (It also remains subject to reinterpretation by viewers themselves.) The struggle for interpretive hegemony that ensues (who can make their story stick?) relocates social experience within highly charged webs of significance that only remain as stable as the persuasive power supporting them.

Here is one story from the tele-tale vidi-machine, "The Story of Sadistic Women":

> A white male in his thirties stands by his car in a short-sleeve shirt at night in Miami. The police have stopped him for using a megaphone as he

drives. He speaks into the night as bystanders fill the background and four or five officers mill around, more bemused than concerned: "I was informed they put micro-stimulators into the uteruses of women, they artificially stimulate them sexually which is how they create sadistic women, and they put the sound of pleasure into the inner mind with implants, like implanted teeth, or the tonsils are removed, or stitches in front of the left ear (his hand motions toward his head, throat, and ear), and then they maneuver women into intimidating men and they maneuver the men into responding rather than out the door at the woman.

"And my wife was being used in a sadistic fashion against me."

The man's narrative ends on an upbeat, conclusive note. He seems satisfied with his tale. Case closed. The police talk among themselves during this monologue, inaudibly, until one declares there is "no crime" here to concern them. The man belongs in a different institutional frame, perhaps (they do not say) the therapeutic one.

He is about to be erased from reality TV.

An officer approaches him and says, "Just do me a favor, when you leave here, put the megaphone away and go home." The man goes to his car. The other police watch and begin to disperse, nonchalantly. One cracks a smile. The officer: "Good night. Good luck." They shake hands.

Fade to black as the end-of-show logo for *Cops* appears.

The same police officer speaks, his voice emanating from the ensuing blackness, "Put the seat belt on there and have a safe night."

—*Cops*[3]

What story does reality television tell most generally? "The Story of Sadistic Women," as I have coined this one sequence from the reality TV show *Cops,* may seem atypical. The police are not in danger; they do not effect an arrest; violence does not erupt; they have encountered, in some basic sense, "the wrong man." But this sequence, mixed in with other scenes of patrol-car footage, drug-dealer arrests, and potential shoot-outs, is of a piece with them. The threat of civic disruption is in the air (we do not know in the first few moments if this man really does pose a physical threat to others or himself); the need to patrol the boundaries of normalcy remains controlling. The man, clearly disturbed, falls outside the realm of criminality and can be treated lightheartedly (with no indication of effort to find him the help he apparently needs). The harmless discharge of tension does not signal a failure of the system. Quite the contrary: the border patrols operate; threats are assessed, measures taken.

Most important, we are there, on the street, with the cops. We share their point of view and subjectivity. We are invited to nod and wink with them. They, together with us, their tele-partners in reality, can move on to other situations, other risks and potential disruptions to the social order. Once again, we learn "the system works."

To account for the prevalence of such stories on television calls for us to scrutinize the mechanisms of televisual narrative, the premises of reality

TV, and to ask how this form has totally eviscerated an already suspect documentary tradition dedicated to guiding and directing civic-minded action.

Reality TV includes all those shows that present dangerous events, unusual situations, or actual police cases, often reenacting aspects of them and sometimes enlisting our assistance in apprehending criminals still at large. Such programs include: *Cops, Top Cops, Code 3, America's Most Wanted, The F.B.I.: Untold Stories, American Detective, Manhunt International, Rescue 911, I Witness Video.* At the boundaries of these phenomena lie standard TV news and the tabloid journalism of *A Current Affair, Hard Copy,* or *Inside Edition.*

Remarkably, these shows tend to emphasize a compelling mixture of what Lévi-Strauss called, to distinguish the external facticity of nature from the social significances of culture, the raw and the cooked. Reality TV lurches between actual situations and events of startling horror, intense danger, morbid conduct, desperate need, or bizarre coincidence (the raw) and cover stories that reduce such evidence to truism or platitudes (the cooked). (We might term this "the ideological reduction" of reality TV.) The startling or bizarre, desperate or intense, is given an offhand and commonsensical ring: "Isn't it incredible; life's like that (and you are there)." The strategies and effects are different from fiction, and different from the often no less bizarre and unsettling work of the avant-garde.[4] Reality TV aspires to *non-friction*. It reduces potential subversion and excess to a comestible glaze.

Affronts to the Body

> "You still got hair coming out your mouth where you been biting on your girlfriend, don't ya?"
>
> The suspect is thoroughly drunk. The camera zooms in to an extreme close up of his mouth, revealing several long, blonde hairs, and holds on this shot. The concluding logo, *Cops,* appears and, offscreen, the voice of the same officer speaks, "The way his mouth looked, looks like he liked the taste of blood."
>
> End of show.
>
> —*Cops*

The combination of the raw and the cooked, evidence and story, produces a spectacular oscillation between the sensational and the banal. Without the sensational contents, the stories might well dissipate into repetition and boredom. Without the reassurance of the narrative frame, the sensational might only prompt disgust and revulsion. Some ethnographic films which present typical behavior from other cultures which flies in the face of our (Eurocentric) sense of the normal and natural, such as female circumcision, extensive scarification of the body, the extraction and consumption of cow's blood as a dietary staple, or the skinning of animals for their meat and fur, can produce a vivid sense of nausea in viewers.[5] These forms of behavior, like the beating of Rodney King, dwell, graphically, on apparent insults to the body, invasions of its physical integrity, or affronts to its status as outward manifestation of an internal self or soul.

Our culture tends to place abattoirs, tattoo or body piercing parlors, and death beds off limits visually, and aurally. (Despite the markedly more vivid depiction of graphic violence to the body in fiction films where such violence is a "special effect," the detailed, clinical reporting of such actions remains heavily taboo-laden. A documentary representation of the type of autopsy performed in *The Silence of the Lambs* on a severely decomposed body remains close to unthinkable. The closest approximation is Stan Brakhage's *The Act of Seeing with one's own eyes,* which films several autopsies in a Pittsburgh morgue; many find viewing it utterly unbearable.)

A physical screening off of the most horrifying affronts to the body serves the same function as a narrative frame: to eliminate threat and discomfort, to reassure, to reclaim for culture those very practices that seem beyond its pale. "Affronts" to the body politic and cultural order produce endless fascination. Reality TV continuously peeks behind the screen, flirting with the taboo and forbidden, with the frontier beyond the law. The frontier is what marks the boundaries of culture and society. Patrolling them, peering over the shoulder of the police, confirms the order law produces. The raw, the savage, the taboo and untamed require recuperation. We flirt with disgust, abhorrence, nausea, and excess seeking homeopathic cures for these very states. Reality TV provides a curative for disease through the (repetitive, tiresome) tale it tells. This meta-story, the ideological reduction, makes the strange banal. (As such, it is diametrically opposed to the goal Russian formalism set for art: *ostranenie,* to defamiliarize or, as Brecht would have it, alienate, by making the familiar strange.)

Reality TV and the Death of Documentary

Documentary film, as conceived by figures like John Grierson, Dziga Vertov, Paul Rotha, Robert Flaherty, or Pare Lorentz, served a social purpose. This form arose in response to the sensationalized, oversimplified representation of reality offered by the average fiction film. Documentary might treat reality creatively in Grierson's words (i.e., with narrative and dramatic techniques), but the intent was to mobilize viewers to act in the world, with a greater sense of knowledge or even a more fully elaborated conception of social structure and historical process.

The call to action—or at least the call to be predisposed to look favorably at certain patterns of problem solving by the benevolent intervention of government in the conflicts occasioned by industrial progress, for example—placed documentary in much closer alliance with rhetoric than aesthetics. A disinterested eye that engaged a work of art without regard to practical effect or immediate consequences had little value. A committed eye that engaged the world with a renewed sense of purpose and responsibility held greater sway.

Traditional modes of documentary representation strive to address viewers in ways that would fulfill this sense of purpose and responsibility.[6] Among the characteristics which serve to distinguish these modes of documentary representation from fiction are:

1. Adherence to the principles of rhetoric that govern the discourses of sobriety. These discourses include economics, medicine, law, geography, military strategy, history, anthropology, psychoanalysis, journalism, documentary, and science generally. Such discourses attempt to represent the state of affairs in the historical or natural world itself rather than offer openly imaginative representations of it. Their sobriety allows such discourses to count narrative technique among their rhetorical strategies but with little stress on *complex* narrative form or on the construction of imaginary worlds. Documentary, for example, adopts narrative structure (a beginning, middle, and end) and narrative techniques (such as realism, subjective points of view, expressive performances, and so on) but in ways distinct from fiction.

2. An emphasis on making arguments through the use of visible or audible evidence. Visible evidence includes images that constitute, illustrate, or counterpoint the argument. In one way or another they work to authenticate the film's claims to represent some aspect of the historical world. Verbal evidence includes testimony by witnesses or experts and by narrating authorities who speak on behalf of the film or its producing agency. The argument may be made through the direct commentary of authorities, such as news anchors or TV show hosts, or indirectly through the film's perspective as it is conveyed by such means as composition, lighting, music, or, most notably, editing.

3. Questions of style are experienced, at times, as questions of ethics. The proximity of the camera to its subject or the relentlessness of its gaze may provoke discomfort when it obtains evidence without regard for tact, or perhaps even decency. The paparazzi of Rome have been a notorious emblem of this issue, but it readily extends beyond this craven disregard for privacy to other situations where the camera records that from which we may wish to turn away or that in which we may feel compelled to

intervene. Filmmakers enter the historical arena to engage with their subjects. How they acquit themselves remains evident in the resulting style. It provides, in part, an indexical trace of lived encounter.

4. The representation of people (social actors) confronts us with the body of the historical person, heir to all the vicissitudes of life, and subject to the finality of death. The representation of death itself, such as we see in the Zapruder footage of President Kennedy's assassination or in an episode of *I Witness Video* when a police officer's patrol car camcorder records his own death by gunfire from suspected drug dealers, affects us differently from fictional representations, no matter how realistic imaginative simulations may be. "Thus, while death is generally experienced in fiction films as representable and often excessively visible, in documentary films it is experienced as confounding representation, as exceeding visibility," according to Vivian Sobchack.[7] Here, at death's door, we find documentary endlessly, and anxiously, waiting. It hovers, fascinated by a border zone it cannot ever fully represent.

Actual violence or death always betrays physical affronts to the body itself. The irreversibility of historical time prevails. We and the text share a sense of historical being, and nothingness. An indexical record of the ultimate bodily insult, death, carries an impact no staged performance can duplicate. A text alone, however, cannot guarantee that what we see is death itself or actual violence. The authenticity of the representation will often depend on the assumptions we bring to it and the expectations we form of it.

5. The tradition of documentary film opens up questions of magnitude. Fiction directs our attention to the historical world in various ways, but documentary opens up a felt gap for the viewer between the representation and its historical referent for the viewer. (The sense of a gap implies an awareness of the representation, the referent, and the difference between them all at once.) We have the impression that any sense of completion, any resolution to the conflicts and issues posed by the text, requires action in the historical world itself. The gap is both spatial (the image, present, re-presenting that which is now absent) and temporal (we, here, witnessing what calls for response elsewhere). This felt gap yokes us as viewers to the historical world that exceeds representation; its reminds us that, as viewers, we, like the documentary filmmaker, remain *in* history.[8]

None of these characteristics exist in reality TV.

The Documentary Tradition, Network News, and Reality TV

Television network news is the linchpin between the documentary tradition just described and the very different world of reality TV. (Network news now includes CNN as a national and, even more than NBC, CBS, or ABC, international news organization.) Network news oscillates vividly between sobriety and spectacle. It upholds the tradition of informed citizenship in its structure of credible news anchors and diligent reporters, objective reporting styles, canons of validation for evidence, and priority for issues pertaining to the nation-state (its economy, foreign affairs, domestic politics, and so on).[9]

Network news makes heavy use of melodramatic codings in its representation of reality. It recounts events as a tale between forces of good and evil, between "our" family and "theirs," in foreign news, and as a tale of conflict, rivalry, sacrifice, or betrayal among members of our own family, in domestic news.[10] Through the (dramatic but historiographically simple) story structure used to encase specific events, the news as data for decision making can readily slide into news for entertainment.

The boundary between news and reality TV blurs as the news stresses audience participation in the ritual of news production itself rather than in the world outside the frame. Network news may well be said to present the news of the day as attractions offered by anchor/showpeople, but the news does not invite our assessment of its rhetorical operations or of the events it reports. (This is where its perversion originates.) The news makes vicarious participation in the news *show* a higher priority than decision making and responsible action. Reality TV raises vicarious participation to an art, using the newsworthiness of its events as little more than a blatantly cooked-up alibi. Reality TV elicits a pleasure built on participatory involvement in the "show" and the game of "show and tell" it performs for us.

The precarious position of network news between the principles of inculcating civic responsibility and of fulfilling an expectation of spectacle sometimes crystallizes in a single story. One example of such a story was Dan Rather's "live" report from Kuwait City shortly after its liberation during the Gulf War of 1991. The report began with Dan Rather, in khaki field clothes, speaking directly to his replacement in the studio, Charles Kuralt.

Mr. Rather then indicated that he wanted to show us something just off camera. He began to move away and as he did so the report cut to another shot of Mr. Rather entering a building converted into a bunker. The viewer could quickly determine from the sizable spatial leaps between shots and the smooth flow of Rather's speech over them that this segment had been previously recorded and significantly edited.

Nonetheless, caught up in the throes of immediacy, Dan Rather audibly puffs as he climbs a ladder to the rooftop. He warns the cameraman, "Watch out, Chris, booby traps," as though imminent danger still surrounded them. He opens packing crates feigning no idea what is inside only to "discover" rocket launchers. All this is accomplished in accord with the pretext that the viewing audience might believe that CBS and the U.S. military allowed a civilian reporter earning millions of dollars a year to wander among booby traps, lethal weapons, and live ammunition in a bunker not already secured.

What such episodes betray is the proximity of news to circus. Such episodes betray what becomes the fundamental *raison d'être* of tele-reporting, tele-talk, tele-discourse in all its forms: self-preservation against the electronic oblivion of "zapping." Maintain the viewer's involvement. Tell stories that, though simple in structure, are rich in gripping power. The grip, however, may exceed the grasp.

A special NBC news report on urban violence was a show whose grasp of what it sought to represent faltered even as it strove to maintain its grip on viewers precisely through a virtual confession of incommensurability. This episode of *The Brokaw Report,* according to Tom Brokaw, star, host, and nightly NBC news anchor, would address the question of "what begets violence in American society."

Planned before the uprising that followed the verdict in the trial of the four policemen accused of beating Rodney King, the show, on June 5, 1992, focused on Oakland, California, as its research site. Brokaw's intrepid foray into this world beyond the newsroom takes on the burden of a moral sensitivity usually lacking in crimestopper shows. He wants to know how life can be so unfulfilling that "the idea of killing somebody or the risk of being killed is so routine that it's terrifying."

What is even more terrifying is how far apart Brokaw's world and the world he examines remain. Brokaw seems aware of this. His moral concern is more lament than exhortation, more dismay than troubleshooting, more despondency than optimism. Those who report on the world in the belief that such reports contribute to the future shape of the world confront a land that time forgot, where the future has collapsed into repetitive deprivation, where violence is the only extra-televisual sensation, and where dying is the price of staying alive. In short, this is the world of reality TV brought to life, a simulation of a simulation too shockingly real and incomprehensible for its kinship to be acknowledged.

An extraordinary sense of precariousness in the face of values and attitudes beyond all comprehension pervades the show. Try as he will, Brokaw cannot bend his subject to fit the cheery summation offered by *TV Guide:*

> In addition, the show considers the impact of the media, including the depiction of violence in television, films and music, incidents of violence among youths (reflected in the need for metal detectors in some inner-city schools); and methods of dealing with the problem.
>
> —*TV Guide*

> Two years ago, in order to meet this and other problems, New York City's Office of School Safety started buying handcuffs . . . an average of two pairs of handcuffs for each school.
>
> —Jonathan Kozol, *Savage Inequalities*

This eternal seesaw of problem/solution is precisely what Brokaw cannot master. What solution can there be when there is no future? What benevolent, liberal, consoling problem-solving devices can there be when time collapses into an interminable "now" where living or dying is secondary to the *act* of being? Brokaw, not only despite his best efforts but also because of them, cannot reach the very people he encounters as anything other than failed consumers, the bad children of a TV nightmare in which the market share is zero and sponsorship nil. This would be the network equivalent to inner-city despondency, and it is, for now, unimaginable to those who make the news.

Reality TV and Social Perversion

> Isn't it time you felt that way again?
>
> —Saturn car ad
>
> It protects you like a man, treats you like a woman.
>
> —Lady Speed Stick ad
>
> Kill the germs. Keep the kids.
>
> —Liquid Dial ad

Reality TV is to the documentary tradition as sexual "perversion" was to "normal" sexuality for Freud. The biological purpose of sexuality—reproduction—is no longer served by perversions that have purposes of their own. Similarly, representations whose purpose is to absorb and neutralize all questions of magnitude no longer serve the ostensible purpose of news: to facilitate collective action based on fresh information. (Perverse purposes need not necessarily be condemned; perversity's willingness to disregard social and moral codes lends it great potential for subversions of all kinds. Each case requires separate assessment. Sexual perversities can have great value for what they reveal, and refuse, of our culture's prohibitions and constraints; the value of the perversity of reality TV may lie in the gleeful abandon with which it mocks, or rejects, civic-mindedness and the positivist social engineering behind it.)

Reality TV extends into the zones that threaten to erupt within network news itself but normally remained repressed. Reality TV anneals the felt gap opened by historical consciousness between representation and referent. Dan Rather's strangely hallucinatory tour of an Iraqi bunker reveals the symptomatic return of this repressed. Believing himself surrounded by booby traps, in constant bodily peril, Rather acts out a tableau of vicarious concern for American lives that might have been lost. News becomes dramatic spectacle, a simulacrum of eventfulness for which there is no original (this *is* the moment of discovery, and danger, such as it is, for Rather).[11]

It's sorta like havin' a seat in the front row of life.

—Patrol car officer, speaking of his job, *Top Cops*

While most of the outrageous events the realities and tabs are concerned with actually happen, they fortunately happen somewhere else, to someone else. And that allows us to be discrete voyeurs, occupying front-row seats for these displays of human folly.

—Van Gordon Sauter, "Rating the Reality Shows," *TV Guide*

Reality TV's perverse kinship with traditional documentary film, network newscasting, and ethnographic film lies in its ability to absorb the referent. The digestive enzymes of reality TV (its distracting quality and spectacle, its dramatic story lines and self-perpetuation) break the referent down into palatable confections that do not represent an absent referent so much as cannibalize and assimilate it into a different type of substance. The historical world becomes reduced to a set of simulations and idle talk (Heidegger's *gerede*). The webs of signification we build and in which we act pass into fields of simulation that absorb us but exclude our action. Referentiality dissolves in the nonbeing and nothingness of TV.

What characterizes reality TV most broadly is the production of a feeling tone in the viewer similar to that produced by an exceptional acrobatic feat, superb magic tricks, or the sudden appearance of a full-scale helicopter thirty feet above the stage in *Miss Saigon:* "Isn't that amazing!"

Now, how are they going to get the wife over here, because she can't swim.

—Elderly husband of a woman still trapped in her car by a torrential flood in the Arizona desert, *Code 3*

A reality TV special, *Miracles and Other Wonders* (June 5, 1992), reported the story of Barney, a black truck driver, who played good samaritan by deviating from his route to answer a distress call from a driver suffering a heart attack. Voice-over comments by the host accompany a reconstruction of the events, like the traditional *benshi* presenter of Japanese silent films. Barney finds the man and radios for paramedics who are able to stabilize the man and get him to a hospital where he recovers. The oddest part of the story, though, is that when they examine the man's car, they see no trace of the CB radio he would have needed in order to contact truck driver Barney.

This apparent act of telepathy would have been amazing enough, but

> several years later Barney succumbs to a heart attack of his own while trekking through remote country on a fishing trip. Friends manage to get him to a nearby Indian village but despair that the nurse who only visits once a month will not be there. Miraculously, she is. Even more miraculously, she is not alone. Her father, a cardiologist, happens to accompany her. The man steps into the room where Barney rests and, lo and behold, it is the very man Barney saved all those years before! His quick action spares Barney from certain death.
>
> Isn't that amazing!

When we return a woman needs your
help to find her long-lost twin brother.

—*Unsolved Mysteries*

This ebb and flow of detached consumption, distracted viewing, and episodic amazement exists in a time and space outside history, outside the realm in which physical, bodily engagement marks our existential commitment to a project and its realization. "Project" refers to Sartre's idea of an engaged, committed life in the world, and in the body, where every "experience" remains charged with importance in this larger context—exactly what reality TV denies or perverts. Here we have disembodied but visceral experience, a freewheeling zone in which the same set of emotional responses recycle with gradually diminishing force until the next raise of the ante in the production of spectacle.

These responses are keyed to a conventional story format. It is something like a perversely exhibitionistic version of the melodramatic imagination: provide a "hook" by underlining an important aspect of the case—its scale, severity, uniqueness, or consequences; offer a dab of location realism; sketch in characters quickly; dramatize sensational aspects of the case—usually aspects of intense threat to human life and bodily integrity; move swiftly to an emotional climax; and urge a specific response—grief, alarm, fear, consolation, shock. Conclude the episode with a resonant moment and perhaps a pause for affective response to the marvelous and terrifying, the challenging and remarkable, the extraordinary and corrupt.

In a phrase, "Isn't that amazing!"[12]

A chronicle of contingent, futureless moments strung together in a protracted morality play produces an entire telescape that does not so much screen us off from reality, or refer us back to it, as beam us aboard a tele-visual simulation. Our subjectivity streams toward the videoscreen that welcomes us to its cyborg circuits of information, noise, feedback, and homeostatic redundancy. Instead of a charge up San Juan Hill (filmed by Vitagraph employees J. Stuart Blackton and Albert E. Smith in 1898), we see a charge into a suspected amphetamine lab (on *Cops* in 1992). The first charge was represented as news, as a report on the finality of the already done (with clear awareness of how public opinion might be shaped by such reports).[13] The second charge, even if news in some sense that is not examined, hangs in suspended animation: every moment, every action, takes shape around the sensation of contingency. We *are* at the moment of filming: "Nothing has been changed, except, You are there." Desperate criminals or terrified children may pop into the frame. Shots may be fired or profuse apologies offered. Suspects may submit immediately, in resigned silence or sullen anger, or they may resist, shouting, twisting, flailing at their captors. The stress on a sense that "You never know what might happen next," and the parallel admonition to "Do your part to help bring criminals to justice," makes this richly constructed sense of contingency a vital element in the pervasive "now" of tele-reality. Social responsibility dissolves into tele-participation.

Our subjectivity is less that of citizens, social actors or "people," than of cyborg collaborators in the construction of a screen-world whose survival hinges on a support system designed to jack us into the surrounding commodity stream, around which an entire aesthetic of simulated pleasure exists. We cannot read these shows as built upon a prefigurative ground that would entail a particular moral or political stance toward the surrounding world.[14] Documentary film had a vested interest in our behavior and disposition beyond the theater. Reality TV has a vested interest in subsuming everything beyond itself into its own support system of circulating exchange values. This circulatory system incorporates the only behavior that really matters: consuming. Careful explication of episodes or shows serves little point at all, at least in the conventional terms of textual analysis and narrative structure. Their meaning comes from elsewhere, from the tele-world to which they belong and in which "we" are constituted as messages-in-the-circuit of contingency, participation, consumption.

Reality TV, then, plays a complex game. It keeps reality at bay. It succeeds in activating a sense of the historical referent beyond its bounds but also works, constantly, to absorb this referent within a tele-scape of its own devising. Reference to the real no longer has the ring of sobriety that separates it from fiction. Such reference now *is* a fiction. Participation is fully absorptive. The gap is sealed, the referent assimilated. We enter the twilight border zone of virtual reality.

The Tele-Sacramental

An odd characteristic of this ebb and flow of sensation and banality is its simulation of a spiritual dimension, well beyond the televangelism that exhorts us to participate by phoning in our donations as the crime shows urge us to call in our tips. Reality TV offers a continuous confessional for the sins of the world. It promises the absolution of sins when we participate in the redemption of everyday life. (Phone in, stay tuned, consume.)

Reality TV tenders charity for "those poor people" it parades before us as victims of violence and disaster. It urges faith—in the ceaseless baptism in the tele-real for those wishing never to be bored again. It offers hope for a future constantly collapsing into an ever-expanding present.

> Now, when her daughter's killer escaped the death sentence, police say she showed up with a loaded gun. More in a moment.
>
> —*Hard Copy*

Reality TV may not be "intimately bound up with women's work," as Tania Modleski argued on behalf of daytime soap operas, but it is bound up with everyday experience.[15] Reality TV shares many of the characteristics Modleski assigns to fictional soap operas such as a participatory quality (connection to versus separation from); a sense that characters or social actors are "like me"—unlike stars who are of decidedly different status; an emphasis on knowledge of what others might do or think (troubled characters, potential dates, criminals at large) rather than strictly factual "know how";[16] acceptance and acknowledgment that viewers are subject to "interruption, distraction, and spasmodic toil";[17] multiple plot lines; and casts of characters who may not know each other. As Modleski argues, soaps have a special meaningfulness for their target audience; they are more than filler, audiovisual wallpaper or escape. So is reality TV.

> All suspects are innocent until proven guilty in a court of law.
>
> —Voice-over introduction, *Cops*

> We asked for your help last week and you provided some good leads. If you see Peter Fisher, call 1–800-CRIME-92.
>
> If you see James Ashley, call us right now.
>
> If you think you know who kidnapped little Terry Molini, call our hot line tonight. . . . Please have the courage to call.
>
> —John Walsh, host, *America's Most Wanted*

"Shrift": the confession of one's sins, especially to a priest in the sacrament of penance (*Websters*).

"Short shrift" originally meant the abbreviated sacrament offered to criminals condemned to die and thence took on the meaning of summary treatment. The tele-confessional offers only short shrift. Now, see this. Act now. Tomorrow is too late.

> If you know anything that can help solve this case, call us at 1–800–876–5353.
>
> —Robert Stack, *Unsolved Mysteries*
>
> Thanks for a nation of finks.
>
> —William S. Burroughs

Reality TV patrols borders and affirms the law. It also offers a therapeutic ritual for encounter with what lies beyond the law. Reality TV substitutes the confessional dynamics of viewers who phone in their response for the confession that cannot be: the criminal's penance. Neither we nor the tele-confessional itself can grant forgiveness for those whose guilt is not the point. But we can obtain it for ourselves. What Foucault says of confession as a strategy for the regulation of sexuality seems to apply vividly, but not to the suspects whom we encounter as much as to our own vicariously participatory dynamic:

> [The confession] is a ritual that unfolds within a power relationship, for one does not confess without the presence (*or virtual presence*) of a partner who is not simply the interlocutor but the authority who requires the confession, prescribes and appreciates it and intervenes in order to judge, punish, forgive, console, and reconcile; . . . and finally, *a ritual in which the expression alone, independently of its external consequences,* produces intrinsic modifications in the person who articulates it: it exonerates, redeems, and purifies him; it unburdens him of his wrongs, liberates him, and promises him salvation.[18] (italics mine)

But the redemptive virtue of our calling, as it were, is not stressed as much as the purgation of fear through the sensation/pleasure of vicariously participating—a simulation of the form of the confessional without its content. Our engagement is less in terms of a civic duty than in terms of the perpetuation of a moment, here and now, when confessional engagement is always possible. We have the pleasure of situating ourselves within a cybernetic feedback loop, absolved, over and over, of all necessity to step beyond it.

The spiritual quality of this appeal permeates a dimensionless surface of sensation. The phatic bond—the open channel, the phone operators "standing by," the pleas of "Don't go away," the possibility that you may have something to contribute at any moment—offer the sensation of connectedness, of tele-communion. Here is a connectedness that affirms the work patterns and social hierarchies from which we allegedly escape. Vicarious participation as (virtual) confession constructs spirals of power and pleasure:

> The power that lets itself be invaded by the pleasure it is pursuing; and opposite it, power asserting itself in the pleasure of showing off, scandalizing, or resisting. . . . These attractions, these evasions, these circular incitements have traced around bodies and sexes, not boundaries not to be crossed, but *perpetual spirals of power and pleasure.*[19]

Reality TV offers communion drawn from atomized, dissociated figures who remain so; a sense of engagement, empathy, charity, and hope built on a disengaged, detached simulation of face-to-face encounter; and a sense of coherence and continuity, if not suspended animation, at a time when ideas and values *feel* worn, ineffective, abused, and bandied about. Here is another form of televisual perversion: the (virtual) conversion of spiritual ritual to social, institutional, hierarchical purposes of its own.

Spectacle: Grounded Sensation

Tele-spectacle treats sensations the way an electrical circuit treats shorts: it runs them to ground. The very intensity of feeling, emotion, sensation, and involvement that reality TV produces is also discharged harmlessly within its dramatic envelope of banality. The historical referent, the magnitudes that exceed the text, the narratives that speak of conduct in the world of face-to-face encounter, bodily risk, and ethical engagement ground themselves harmlessly in circuits devoted to an endless flux of the very sensations they run to ground, a perfect balancing act of homeostatic regulation.

Transitions from one attraction to the next are moments of risk. Alternatives to "Isn't it amazing" threaten to intrude. "Stay tuned," "Don't go away," "More in a minute." These endless pleas to maintain the phatic connection between show and viewer while our hosts mysteriously "go away" underscore the urgency of self-promotion. The pleas implore us to grant these denizens in a box the right to persist, as though it were in our power to annihilate them. And perhaps for a fleeting moment we believe they are at our mercy as we decide whether or not to grant them a continuing presence in the telescape they hope to share with us.

An orchestrated sense of distraction saves the day.

> After an extensive profile of ex-baseball pitcher Denny McLain which touched on his jail term for drug use, his rehabilitation as a radio talk-show host, and the death of his daughter at the hands of a drunk driver, the male co-host intones, speaking to the camera (us), "No family should endure that much tragedy."
>
> His female co-host looks toward her partner, pauses, then, looking back toward the camera, responds, "Now, if you need to try pulling a few rabbits out of the boudoir, try the *magic* of making love."

A set of ads follow, then a story on Dr. Miriam Stoppard's new book, *The Magic of Sex.* At its conclusion the co-host says, "Now, when her daughter's killer escaped the death sentence, police say she showed up with a loaded gun. More in a moment" (another set of ads follow).

—*Hard Copy*

The melodramatic novel arose at a time when contending classes, the aristocracy and bourgeoisie, could see their own precarious class situation played out in fiction (for example, the sentimental novels and romantic dramas of the eighteenth century that surround the French revolution, such as *Clarissa* and *Nouvelle Héloïse, Emilia Galiotti* and *Kabale und Liebe*).[20] Reality TV offers another version of this effort to represent anxieties of social stability and mobility at a time when economic solvency, let alone prosperity, hangs in doubt. The fate of middle-class "in-betweeners" is uncertain, split as it is between a richer and more insulated upper class and a despondent and more isolated "underclass." White-collar, mid-level managers in Ohio may suddenly find their work delegated to a monitoring system and computer network based in Osaka in these days of transnational globalization. Paranoia may be one form of response to a system without a center; in this case, responsibility diffuses into an amorphous, unrepresentable "they."[21]

Reality TV, though, stems anxiety less with paranoia than with a schizoid-like detachment from and reconstruction of the "reality" it re-presents. Beset by dreams of rising and nightmares of falling, plagued by the terror of pillage, plunder, and rape, the "target" audience for reality TV (white, middle-class consumers with "disposable" income) attends to a precarious world of random violence and moment-to-moment contingency (as inexplicable to viewers as it was to Tom Brokaw).

The decimation of the men within the population is quite nearly total. Four of five births in East St. Louis are to single mothers. Where do the men go? Some to prison. Some to the military. Many to an early death. Dozens of men are living in the streets or sleeping in small, isolated camps behind the burnt-out buildings. There are several of these camps out in the muddy stretch there to the left.

—Safir Ahmed, *St. Louis Post-Dispatch* reporter, quoted in Jonathan Kozol, *Savage Inequalities*

In 1991, 21,859 white students earned Ph.D. degrees. In the same year, 933 black students earned Ph.D.s, the first year the percentage of black students earning doctorates had increased in thirteen years.

—*S.F. Chronicle,* May 4, 1992

The aesthetics of immediacy, conjured in a timeless, spaceless telescape of mediated reality, drowns out the descriptions, like Ahmed's, that urge us to further action beyond exclamation or dismay. An aesthetics of sensation underlies reality TV: Its claims of authenticity, its construction of an endless "now," its preference for the chronicle, the random and the unforeseen over the order and cohesion of historiography and the problem-solving discourses of a technocratic order all come at a time when master narratives are a target of disparagement.

Under what conditions does the need to represent contingency and to reject order prevail? One answer is: Contingency looms when an elite, or ruling class, can no longer convince others or itself of its rightful primacy (when hegemony fails). Unpredictability, uncertainty, contingency: they loom as symptoms of incomprehension masquerading behind an aesthetics of sensation when those for whom hegemony has failed demand alternative visions and different futures. These demands cannot be understood in the form they are spoken. "A riot is the language of the unheard," asserted Martin Luther King, Jr. Instead these demands register as noise, confusion, chaos. Their negation of what is and their transformative call for what ought to be cannot be contained. They lie beyond the law. Those who speak no longer convince us that they can speak for others; a dumb silence haunts the endless talk. "We" may be "the people," but "we" are also many, and among that many are diverse cultures and subcultures, affinity groupings and collectivities that lie beyond the pale of reality TV.

An insistence on *differences that make a difference* confounds a sense of hierarchy, undermines standard reference points, and questions received notions of quality or excellence. This diffusion of power and control may seem closely akin to the form of reality TV. But there is a major difference that makes a difference. Reality TV may be as sensational as it wishes, it may be as seemingly decentered, ahistorical, and futureless as it chooses, but, in its present manifestations, it is never critical of the hierarchy perpetuated by its own form or of the power rooted in its dynamic of vicarious (or virtual) participation. Reality TV can be as heterogenous, dispersive, self-conscious, and reflexive as all get out, but it never calls our own position as virtual participant and actual consumer into question. It can tolerate our talking back and mocking its own self-mocking forms but not our refusal to listen to its (empty) talk at all.[22]

We presume immunity from this perversion or dis-ease at some peril, however. There is a risk that the *form* of political struggle may take on qualities akin to those of reality TV. The simple dramatic envelopes placed around localized events that rapidly play themselves out, passing our attention on to their successor, are a dangerous model for political struggle. Such dramatic protest rituals allow for sharply focused moral outrage but often channel it into partial or token victories that leave basic structural conditions unchanged. Celebrating the conviction of two LAPD officers for beating Rodney King "ends" the story, on the episodic level, but does nothing to address the social conditions that underpin it structurally.

The danger exists that actual struggles will take their cue from the rhythms of reality TV: specific issues and events will become a target of concern or outrage; emotions will wax and wane in keeping with the dramatic curve of televised coverage (Three Mile Island, the Gulf War, Anita Hill and Clarence Thomas, the Panama invasion, "ethnic cleansing," Rodney King). Coalitions, support groups, ad hoc committees and rallies will spring up. Collective identities take shape and a common agenda will emerge. But the specific event will eventually reach a point of resolution. The forces once mobilized with fervor and outrage will disperse, potentially available for the next contingency. Such a pattern constructs a reactive politics that may mirror, in disturbing ways, the very forms of absorption and distraction that should be among its primary targets.

Reality TV seeks to reimagine as broad a collectivity or target audience for its sponsors as possible. Hence the tendency to represent experience as spectacle framed only by the banalities of a crude morality play. This form of orchestrated spectacle stands in an antithetical relationship to the project of an existential phenomenology.

Reality TV and Political Consciousness

What reality TV (a phrase that shows no embarrassment at its oxymoronic ring) eliminates is any coming to historical consciousness. By historical consciousness I mean something akin to consciousness raising: an awareness of the present in relation to a past active within it and a future constantly being made in the thick of the present, together with a heightened consciousness of one's relation to others in the common project of the social construction of reality. Such a consciousness holds production and consumption, past and future, in a dialectical relationship. It is what films like *Who Killed Vincent Chin?* and *JFK,* discussed in chapter 7, may bring into being, and what reality TV perverts. We can turn off the tube to go shopping with no alteration in the distracted state of consciousness a perpetual "now" encourages.

The founding principle of surrealism—the juxtaposition of incommensurate realities as a jarring act that forces the beholder to see things anew, casting off old habits and assumptions, seeing the strange quality of the familiar in ways that propose alternative values and action—this collage principle becomes absorbed by a telescape from which it cannot escape. There is no "Aha!" on reality TV. A subsuming "logic" absorbs all incommensurate juxtapositions. It denies contradiction by refusing to propose any frame from which more local gaps, disturbances, or incompatibilities could be rearranged coherently. Reality TV is one significant piece of a postmodern aesthetic in which what was once incompatible, incommensurate, and contradictory—experiences that compelled us to search for resolution, if not revolution—coexist inside a boundless envelope of presence that banishes historical consciousness from its bounds.

Coda: Tele-Vision in the Days after the L.A. Uprising of 1992 (The Rodney King "Riots")

> Thomas Mitchell [an armed, black male bank robber] could be anywhere, but if he's in *your* neighborhood, call us at 1-800-CRIME-91.
>
> —John Walsh, host, *America's Most Wanted* (italics mine)

> "Financially at least, it's going to be a long, hot summer," Perot told the group. "Now I don't have to tell *you* who gets hurt first when this sort of thing happens, do I?"
>
> "*You* people do, *your* people do. I know that, *you* know that."
>
> —Ross Perot, speaking to the NAACP (italics mine)

> Our relation to television can be summarized as one in which a medium structured to prevent dialogue with the other in our society has developed a fictional form of dialogue; television cannot satisfy our desire for subjectivity, but it can displace it. It caters to both our desire for mastery and pleasure in identification as well as our wish to share in subjectivity through recognizing and being recognized by others as a "you."
>
> —Margaret Morse, "Talk, Talk, Talk"[23]

When a sweet grandmotherly sort has to tell *you* how black people once were chained in iron masks in the canebrake, to keep them from eating the cane while they harvested it, and that these masks were like

> little ovens that cooked the skin off their faces—when *you* hear that grandmotherly voice and realize she once was a girl who might have been *your* girl, and someone caused this pain on her lips and nobody did anything about it but keep living—this gives *you* a tendency to shout, especially when confronted by an opportunity to speak to a smarmy talk-show host or a snarling highway patrolman.
>
> —Robert Wiley, *Why Black People Tend to Shout* (italics mine)

In the wake of the first trial of four LAPD officers for the beating of Rodney King, those who stepped outside this tele-logue and took to the streets to enact a form of symbolic action can say, "I'm not the *you* you think I am." Instead of talking back to the box in a game complicit with the simulation of the impression of direct address to *you* (a generic plural always disguised as a discrete singular, divide and conquer at its finest), those who decided to shout in the street began to forge an alternative dialogue.

"An exchange of views" between tele-talk and *you,* which demands of *you* nothing but your willingness to consume—time, spectacle, the sponsor's commodities, rioting, and war—finds itself run to ground. Viewers reclaim their identity as social actors, taking back the ground that makes us one (one people whose face-to-face encounter affirms diversity). Violent retaliation, often aimed at the very objects we have been urged to joyfully consume, becomes an active form of speech, symbolic action that, instead of *talking back* to television, *takes back* the historical world.

In its own unique form of incomprehension and revenge, tele-vision represents such re-appropriations as mayhem, as self-destructive chaos, as sensation and catastrophe of the highest order. The thin blue line, and its Echo, that thin blue glow cast across the land, waver between the voices of repression and charity. *You* must do something for "those people": "We know" and "*you* know" that this must not happen again. "We" must ensure the social order, forcefully, or increase the downward trickle so that "they" may regain the hope "we" have taken from them, or, in an equivocation *you* will understand, both.

Though broken, the prevailing frame has yet to shatter. Tele-vision sweeps on, ready for the next crisis or contingency. The panoptic camera adjusts its rhetoric and makes "color adjustments" as necessary.[24]

Meanwhile, the interpretative arena remains alive with voices, and actions, which, even when pitched to a defiant shout, remain unheard in the telescape around them.

4

THE ETHNOGRAPHER'S TALE

Preamble

Ethnographic film is in trouble. Not entirely due to what ethnographic filmmakers have done, or failed to do, but also because of the nature of the institutional discourse that continues to surround this mode of documentary representation. And not entirely due to either of these factors, but also because of the ground-breaking, convention-altering forms of self-representation by those who have traditionally been objects (and blind spots) of anthropological study: women/natives/others. For over ten years a significant body of work has been accumulating that comes from elsewhere, telling stories and representing experiences in different voices and different styles.

Ethnographic film has represented a valuable, concerted effort by those who share anthropology's principles and objectives regarding the representation of other cultures to members of our own. Ten years or more ago, exploring other cultures on film meant one of three things: analyzing the fictional works of celebrated filmmakers like Satyajit Ray, Yasujiro Ozu, or Glauber Rocha; viewing openly political documentaries of national liberation struggles, such as *79 Springtimes* (Santiago Alvarez, Cuba, 1969)[1] and *Last Grave at Dimbaza* (Nana Mahamos, South Africa, 1975); or studying films that were considered ethnographic accounts of other cultures, such as *Kenya Boran* (David MacDougall and James Blue, Kenya/United States, 1974), *Dead Birds* (Robert Gardner, New Guinea/United States, 1963), or *Jaguar* (Jean Rouch, Ghana/France, 1967). Each of these three choices had value. Each expanded our horizons and our collective sense of the possible. As we move toward the present, however, the choices are far less clear cut. New principles and objectives, not always arising from within the anthropological traditions but clearly of importance to it, call for our attention. (This "we" is not universal; ten years ago or more the collectivity it referred to was predominantly white, male, and strongly university-based with minimal inclusion of those who now represent themselves. Given the erosion but hardly supplantation of this traditional "we," I have used quotations marks around it to indicate its lack of normative authority.)

Ethnographic film no longer occupies a singular niche. Other voices call to us in forms and modes that blur the boundaries and genres that represent distinctions between fiction and documentary, politics and culture, here and there. For those situated in the larger, nonspecialist audience outside of anthropology per se, these other voices often seem more incisive, informative, and engaging. The opportunity exists to learn from and engage with the ways in which others choose to represent themselves in "autoethnographies" like *Speak Body* (Kay Armatage, Canada, 1979), *Unfinished Diary* (Mallet, Canada, 1983), *Handsworth Songs* (John Akomfrah, Great Britain, 1986), *Babakiueria* (Don Featherstone, Australia, ca. 1989), *Who Killed Vincent Chin?* (Chris Choy and Renee Tajima, 1988), and *I'm British But . . .* (Gurinder Chadha, Great Britain, 1989), and from *Surname Viet Given Name Nam* (Trinh T. Minh-ha, 1989) to *Films Are Dreams* (Sylvia Sensiper, Tibet/United States, 1989). The voice of the traditional ethnographic filmmaker has become one voice among many. Dialogue, debate, and a fundamental reconceptualization of visual anthropology in light of these transformations is, quite simply, essential.

All the Better to Vex You With, My Dear

Clifford Geertz has described as well as anyone the finely honed interpretive skills required of the anthropologist or ethnographer. His account of the subtleties, and subtle misunderstandings, arising from the conflicting worldviews of a Berber tribe, a Jewish trader, and a French colonial officer in the Morocco of 1912 captures well the "thickness" to which description might aspire—though it may be "thick" in an unintended sense as well.[2] Following Geertz, "anthropology" becomes an institutional discourse which has assigned itself the challenge of representing others. Like the truth of "indefinite approximation" championed by Sartre, Geertz prefers refinement to perfection: "What gets better is the precision with which we vex each other."[3]

Both anthropology and documentary filmmaking have caused themselves considerable vexation debating the issue of representation as a process of rendering likenesses effectively, according to criteria of realism, objectivity, accuracy, or ethnographicness. Neither discipline has vexed itself quite as much with the realization that Geertz's model creates, but does not acknowledge, representation as trouble for the Other. Who has the responsibility and legitimacy (or power and authority) to represent others, not only in the sense of rendering likenesses but also in the sense of "speaking for" and "presenting a case"? Evaluating the degree of difficulty attempted and level of sophistication attained is how "we" (objective, professional, "disciplined") vex each other more precisely at the expense of others. An unasked but crucial question is, In what way does this representation matter to those it represents?

Anthropology: Behind the Scenes

> If only he (the anthropologist) could provide us with correct, consistent accounts of himself, his gossiping organization, and the specific instances of discourse that constitute his very accounts, then there would be no need for us to carry out an ongoing critique of ethnographic ideology and its claims to represent other cultures.
>
> —Trinh T. Minh-ha, *Woman/Native/Other*[4]

Anthropological representation addresses the problems of being "on the scene" and of getting "behind the scenes" of other cultures. It has proven less adept at looking behind its own scenes, at the staging of its own representations and in debating what this activity represents as a symptom of our own cultural situation (the mythology of travel, the valorization of experimental knowledge over experiential or tacit knowledge, and the prevalence of scientism: the regulation of institutionally legitimized discourse and authority).

From this perspective, the location of anthropology's Other may reside less in another culture than in anthropology's own unconscious. Among other things, this anthropological unconscious might contain: whiteness; maleness; the body of the observer; the experiential; canonical conventions of Western narrative; narrative conventions and forms from other cultures; the full indexical particularity of the image and its emotional impact; the erotics of the gaze; textual theory and interpretation; the actual workings of the institutional procedures that determine what counts as anthropological knowledge; and the viewer or audience for ethnographic film (a group that has been largely unseen, unknown, and unexamined).

Looking at others in order to represent them may not be so easily rationalized by strictly scientific motives as some anthropologists believe. Long takes and minimal editing do not eliminate, though they may disguise, the psychodynamics that Malinowski reserved for his diary. Many different ways of seeing surround the use of a camera. As long as human agency comes into play it will do so in relation to desire and the unconscious as well as reason and science.

In film study, a considerable body of work has argued that the ways and means of cinematic representation often gain motivation from narcissistic, voyeuristic, sadistic, and fetishistic mechanisms.[5] Power, knowledge, hierarchy, and scopophilic pleasure entail one another in ways that cannot be easily avoided or denied. As Laura Mulvey argues, scopophilic identification and desire are "formative structures, mechanisms not meaning. In themselves they have no signification, they have to be attached to an idealization [like the cinema's ability to re-present reality]. Both pursue aims in indifference to perceptual reality, creating the imagised, eroticised concept of the world that forms the perception of the subject and makes a mockery of empirical objectivity."[6]

I wish to look behind the scenes of anthropology's representational mechanisms to examine its unconscious assumptions, or habits, and their implications. The purpose of this examination is to see in greater detail how the ethnographic film stages its representations, whether these representations can withstand the fundamental challenge of usefulness to Others, and then to look beyond as well as behind ethnography to other scenes of increasing interest.

The Ethnographer's Tale: Making Representations

> I have felt that my own projects vis-à-vis the Other, as representations of my own processes of self-discovery, carry with them, as the other is there as an actual person, actual other place, the questions of potential dangers that arise from the inability to do anything but misrepresent that other person.
>
> —Ken Feingold, "Notes on *India Time*"[7]

As used here, *ethnographic film* will refer to films that are extra-institutional, that address an audience larger than anthropologists per se, that may be made by individuals more trained in filmmaking than in anthropology, and that accept as a primary task the representation, or self-representation, of one culture for another. What characterizes ethnographic film as we have known it from *Nanook of the North* (Flaherty, Canada/United States, 1922) to *First Contact* (Bob Connelly and Robin Anderson, New Guinea/Australia, 1984), from *Bitter Melons* (Marshall, Kalahari Desert/United States, 1971) to *Forest of Bliss* (Gardner, India/United States, 1985), from *Grass* (Schoedsack and Cooper, Iran/United States, 1925) to *The Women's Olamal* (Melissa Llewelyn-Davies, Kenya/Great Britain, 1985), and from *Moi, un noir* (Rouch, Gold Coast/France, 1957) to *I'm British But . . .* (Chadha, Great Britain, 1989)?

Binaryism: If Veni Vidi, Can Vici Be Far Behind?

The separation of Us from Them is inscribed into the very institution of anthropology and into the structure of most ethnographic film. They occupy a time and space which "we" must recreate, stage, or represent. Once upon a time, it was easy to say, "There is no one else to do it." Under the aegis of scientific responsibility (and power), this is a sober enterprise. Ethnographic film, in fact, belongs squarely among the discourses of sobriety.[8] As systems of discourse, science, economics, politics, foreign policy, education, religion, and welfare exercise instrumental power. They operate on the assumption that they can and should alter the world itself or our place within it, that they can effect action and entail consequences. These discourses presuppose an internal (and often heavily policed) set of criteria (objectivity, canons of validation, etc.) against which specific truth claims can be gauged.

Discourses of sobriety regard their relation to the real as nonproblematic. Like Plato's Guardians their speakers return to the cave with a knowing sigh of disinterest in the shadow-play and story-telling distractions they now understand entirely and can explain to others. Through the discourses of sobriety, knowledge/power exerts itself. Through them, things are made to happen. These are vehicles of domination and conscience, power and knowledge, pleasure and reason, desire and will (although the aura of science and sobriety—acute in U.S. anthropology—has often pushed the psychodynamics of domination, power, pleasure, and desire squarely into the anthropological unconscious).

Between the "here" of anthropology and the "there" of another culture stands the border checkpoint where the passage of our bodies there and representations of them here is governed by the standards and principles of fieldwork and location filming. The separation of "here" and "there" is sharply demarcated. The predilection for "non-Western societies, particularly exotic cultures" heightens the sense of separation, of a passage to and fro, in which visible differences attest to both spatial and temporal separation.[9] The act of travel and, consequently, scenes of arrival play a central role here.[10] In film such scenes may have a literal representation, as in *The Ax Fight* (Chagnon and Asch, Venezuela/United States, 1971) and *Before We Knew Nothing* (Kitchen, Peru/United States, 1988), or they may be diffused throughout the film in an observational stance that puts distance between another culture and the person behind the camera lens. (The negotiations over representation and self-representation in *A Wife among Wives* [David and Judith MacDougall, Kenya/Australia, 1982], for example, display a reflexive turn but also continue to presuppose the separation of cultures that underpins the film's conception.)

Also central to the impression of being there, while remaining separate from the reality represented, are the indexical film image and synchronous location sound. These qualities of the realist image certify the authenticity of what is seen and heard as lifelike even though they may represent lives conducted differently from our own. Voice-over commentary is another familiar form of binary support: fabricated here, it provides an appliqué for the sights and sounds from there, embellishing them. Sometimes a voice-over from there bumps against one from here, deferentially, as in *N!ai: Story of a !Kung Woman* (Marshall, Namibia/United States, 1980). N!ai's voice-over, spoken by Letta Mbulu, is a vehicle for nostalgic reminiscence: "When [my father would] get up to go hunting . . . we'd be eating meat just like that." It is left to the anonymous male voice of anthropological authority, from here, to remind us of what Marshall's *The Hunters* (Kalahari Desert/United States, 1956) chronicled and N!ai forgets: "It took four men five days to track the wounded giraffe." (Marshall's chronicle itself bears a wishfulness similar to N!ai's for bygone times but masks it in the guise of authoritative knowledge.)[11]

Travel also underwrites the authority of ethnographic film with the powerful guarantee: "What you see is what there was (I know; I was there)." It may also guarantee that "What you see is what there would have been if I had not been there to film it (I know: I was there and can attest to the representativeness of what you see)." Being "on the scene" also allows anthropologists to identify subsequent distortions in the representations of others, in the case, for example, of footage they have shot being transformed into the dross of television documentary: "What you see is what there was, but it did not occur in this sequence, have this musical accompaniment, or bear these meanings (I know, I was there and can identify the distortions)."

Travel thereby underwrites authority by means of bodily presence although the body of the anthropologist/filmmaker usually disappears behind the optical vantage point where camera and filmmaker preside—a perspectival equivalent, but behind the scenes, of the film frame's internal vanishing point. This disappearance, once valorized as part and parcel of observational respect for one's subjects, transforms firsthand, personal experience into third-person, disembodied knowledge. Although it has been subsequently criticized as a masquerade of self-effacement that also effaces the limitations of one's own physicality in favor of omniscience and omnipotence, it remains a common trope.[12]

As accounts of the personal, physical dimension of travel recede, invocations of the transpersonal, mythical dimension, distinctive to Western culture, take on added prominence. Travel conjures associations with spiritual quests, voyages of self-discovery, and tests of prowess, with the pilgrimage and the odyssey, as well as with the expansionist dreams of empire, discovery, and conquest.[13] Movement and travel participate in the construction of an imaginary geography that maps the world required to support the sense of self for whom this world is staged.[14] Travel, which began as something spiritual or economic, takes on the aura of something scientific and representational.[15]

Going there to get the story is one important part of the overall process; returning here is equally important. The act of representation always requires distance between the staging of a representation and its maker or *metteur-en-scène,* as well as between the world represented and its viewer. Questions of authority and authenticity arise from the effect of distance. This effect can be contested, subverted, or displaced, as Brecht's theory of distanciation proposed. When left uncontested, this sense of distance—registered in the space between camera and event, in the observational stance from which it originates, in voice-over commentary, in the certifiable "ethnographicness" of sound and image, and in the construction of a factual story in accord with the canonic narrative form familiar in the West—assures the viewer of the traveler's desire for a welcome return to the fold.[16]

Talking Heads or Travel from the Waist Up

> Our primary goal is the production of knowledge. . . .
>
> —Jay Ruby, "Eye-Witnessing Humanism"[17]
>
> Only anthropology provides the cross-cultural framework that is sophisticated enough to deal with the range of variation that exists among human cultural systems.
>
> —Jack Rollwagen, "The Role of Anthropological Theory in 'Ethnographic' Filmmaking"[18]

The more crucial science and written accounts loom for anthropology, the more suspect ethnographic film becomes, especially when produced by "amateurs."[19] Science is the institutional discourse of sobriety par excellence. Ethnographic films, like studies based on fieldwork, attempt to resolve an acute contradiction between impersonal, scientific knowledge and the personal experience on which it is based: "States of serious confusion, violent feelings or acts, censorships, important failures, changes of course, and excessive pleasures are excluded from the published account."[20] Scientific knowledge travels from one mind to another, transported by bodies as cargo is by ships. Hence the disembodied quality of the voice of authority operating behind most ethnographic film. (The female voice-over commentary spoken by Mbulu in *N!ai* is clearly assigned to the physical person of N!ai as her restricted perception and opinion; the unidentified male voice-over that speaks on behalf of unrestricted ethnographic knowledge has no body; it projects itself from here to there as the voice of scientific reason, personified only by the "grain" of the individual voice used to represent it.)

Disembodied knowledge causes problems of its own. It contrasts sharply with the story-telling traditions of other cultures where experiential, embodied knowledge is more highly prized. As Trinh puts it,

> The words passed down from mouth to ear (one sexual part to another sexual part), womb to womb, body to body are the remembered ones. S/He whose belly cannot contain (also read "retain") words, says a Malinke song, will succeed at nothing. The further they move away from the belly, the more liable they are to be corrupted. (Words that come from the MIND and are passed on directly "from mind to mind" are, consequently, highly suspect . . .).[21]

The knowledge Trinh describes requires different stagings, different forms and styles of representation, from those that have characterized ethnographic film.

The ethnographic message can serve as ethnographic shroud, masking the body, and body knowledge (discussed below), from view. The shroud of the depersonalized, disembodied investigator or filmmaker also allows the race and gender of the body to be relegated to the anthropological unconscious. Like a default value in cybernetics, reference to *the* body and *the* experience of the ethnographic field-worker/filmmaker may mask the white male bodies of most anthropologists along with their distinctive ways of seeing and knowing. (Are the etic systems applied by the ethnographer as tools of the trade color and gender blind? If so, what consequences follow from such blindness?)

Feminism: The Body That Is Not One

> In my research I propose that ethnographic film and photographic images are a reflection of the gender stereotypes found in the filmmaker's (photographer's) dominant group, and thus reproduce the ethnographer's ideas and ideals about gender onto the visual representation of the cultural group being studied.
>
> —Kathleen Kuehnast, "Gender Representation in Visual Ethnography"[22]

Feminism, as the articulation of issues that are inseparably linked to the physical body and its representation, to the personal and its political ramifications, has had noticeable trouble with ethnographic practice. Clifford laments the lack of a feminist contingent in the ranks of those who apply aspects of "textual theory" to ethnographic writing, without wondering if this "lack" might not only be a deficiency but also a critique,[23] and George Marcus identifies feminism (along with poststructuralism) as one of the major forces that has prompted a reevaluation of the nineteenth-century realism supporting most ethnography only to drop it from the rest of his discussion of ethnographic writing and cinematic montage.[24]

Deborah Gordon specifies the dilemma posed by such gestures: "[Feminism] presents a face of similarity outward toward men who are its 'other.' Unlike experimental ethnography where the point is to establish a mutuality between self and other, feminism's relationship to its other is antagonistic."[25] On the other hand, films such as *Small Happiness: Women in a Chinese Village* (Carmen Hinton, China/United States, 1984), *The Women's Olamal* (Llewelyn-Davies, Kenya/Great Britain, 1985), *India Cabaret* (Mira Nair, India, 1986), and Diane Kitchen's *Before We Knew Nothing* demonstrate that the apparently subordinate position occupied by women in a culture (something perhaps more "apparent" to men than women) need not be matched by a parallel subordination in representations of that culture. The possibility of a feminist ethnographic film aesthetic, however, has received no debate at all, to my knowledge.

Feminists recognize an acute predicament of either speaking "mind to mind," even in the dialogic play of modernist distanciation, or of speaking words from the belly that are meant to be of use-value to both those who utter them and those who hear them. Feminists may therefore have trouble with both realist and modernist camps, and with "textual theory" as a politically efficacious, rather than formally sophisticated, move. They may also make trouble for all these camps by posing the simple, yet "unscientific," question of what place does realism, modernism, or textual theory lead one to occupy among the permeable, shifting, diverse subjectivities and ideological affinities operating at a specific historical moment?

The Master('s) Narrative

> We spent a hectic first day in Mina shooting as much footage of the Charriada as we could.
>
> —Jon Olson, "Filming the Fidencistas"[26]

> Actions filmed were, for the most part, spontaneous, candid, and one-time

phenomena and not the result of any deliberately planned "staging."

—George Klima, "Filming as Teleological Process"[27]

These epigraphs, taken from *Anthropological Filmmaking: Anthropological Perspectives on the Production of Film and Video for General Public Audiences,* convey one of the central themes of the book: the disavowal of aesthetic intent. If aesthetic considerations should happen to slip in, despite the rough and tumble effort to catch as catch can, safeguards must to taken. Participation in television productions based on anthropological footage generates tension largely because the anthropologist confronts a well-formulated television documentary aesthetic with only inchoate and semi-conscious aesthetic alternatives. Precepts based on content no longer carry their full weight (entertainment values and the array of televisual alternatives from which viewers might choose intrude). Precepts based on form circle back to a (discounted) anthropological content; they seldom address issues relevant to a general public audience in any detail.

What is somewhat remarkable in this context is how often ethnographic films repeat similar cinematic qualities and narrative structures, without, apparently, knowing or acknowledging it. The canonic story form in the West of an introduction to characters and setting, presentation of a disturbance or puzzle, a goal-oriented line of causally linked situations and events, followed by a resolution to the disturbance or solution to the puzzle recurs in ethnography as well as fiction. Boiled down to a schematic template by Bordwell, this story format amounts to "setting plus characters—goal—attempts—outcome—resolution."[28] It has informed films from *Nanook of the North* to *The Hunters* and from *Tourou et Bitti* (Rouch, Niger/France, 1971) to *Tong Tana* (Jan Roed et al., Malaysia/Sweden, 1990). The pervasiveness of this format in classic ethnography suggests it is not considered aesthetic at all but "natural," despite evidence to the contrary.[29]

Inherent in this preference for canonic story form is the idea of a "virtual performance," an unscripted and unrehearsed performance, which, like a scripted and rehearsed one, carries significant themes through bodily gesture, tone of voice, and facial expression. Instead of an assumed identity performatively conveyed, it is the performance of a lifetime—the condensation of a lifetime into representative moments. Filmmakers seek out those who "naturally" reveal or expose themselves, allowing their performance to engage a viewer's curiosity and empathy while masking the filmmaker's own fascination or attraction—including the erotics of the gaze—behind the naturalness of discovering familiar (Western, dramaturgical) codes of human expressivity among others. Cinematic conventions of the close-up and the long take, of the scene and the event, of continuity editing and synchronous sound reinforce virtual performances that fit the mold of classic, Western dramatic theater in ethnographies from *Nanook* to *The Women's*

Olamal (in contrast to the Brechtian alternative of epic theater and the alienation effect or the exploration of indigenous, non-Western forms).

What is most convenient about these conventions is that they not only serve to support the canonic form of narrative structure in Western society, they also literally constitute an "imaginary geography." Like the imaginary geography constituted by the traveler, explorer, and field-worker, this map to an imaginary world reciprocally and recursively constitutes the self that produces it. This reassuring coherence may be one of the reasons why ethnographic film has not more readily adopted the conventions of modernism and cinematic montage championed by Marcus.[30] Modernist conventions upset the clean separation of here and there and the coherence afforded to those who negotiate such spatial discontinuities by projecting onto other people and places systems of Western, realist representation.

When rendered subservient to scientific knowledge, to the sobriety of discourses that distinguish themselves from fiction or "just stories," these realist conventions and narrative structures rupture the phenomenal, experiential bond of passing stories from one mouth to another, of a knowledge that is fully embodied. Trinh describes well the feminist and political dimension of what is at stake when stories become an explanatory template rather than an inseparable part of a life:

> Not only has the "civilized" mind classified many of the realities it *does not understand* in the categories of the untrue and the superstitious, it has also turned the story—as total event of a community, a people—into a *fatherly* lesson for children of a certain age.
>
> This is why we keep on doing violence to words: to tame and cook the wild-raw, to adopt the vertiginously infinite. Truth does not make sense; it exceeds meaning and exceeds measure. It exceeds all regimes of truth.[31]

A fascination with that which exceeds the grasp prepares the way for fetishism. Science can serve as talismanic fetish for the production of knowledge. Other cultures, caught in the thickness of ethnographic representation, as fetishized images of a pastoral or endangered Eden, offer a reflection of the selves "we" might have been. To the extent that this process depends on another scene, separated off, distant, available for representation, others will exist within the framework of an oscillatory ambivalence. The desire to know or possess, "to tame and cook," is constantly juxtaposed to the desire for the experience of strangeness itself. The juxtaposition holds the other at the distance of fetishistic contemplation. Ethnographic realism serves this ambivalence well. The arrival scene and the distance required by the act of representation confirm the sense of otherness, strangeness. The canonic narrative format, in either fictive or expository forms, produces a sense of the familiar.

Elsewhere I have discussed this ambivalence as part of a much larger set of parallelisms between the licit knowledge produced by classic ethnographic film and the illicit knowledge produced by classic heterosexual pornography.[32] The parallels are quite extensive even though the institutional frames, discursive practices, and ostensible purposes seem sharply distinct. Parallelisms include emphasis on: (1) efforts to establish the authenticity of what "we" see via arrival tropes and scenes or via images of male ejaculation, aka "cum shots"; (2) "whole acts" defined in ritualistic, empirical terms; (3) the hierarchical effect of a voyeuristic gaze or a panoptic gaze; and (4) a fetishization of phallic power or cephalic knowledge ("talking heads"). In many ways the parallels recapitulate the mind/body split epitomized by a scientific production of knowledge. What Foucault called a *scientia sexualis* detaches itself from the body in order to understand, label, codify, and cure the body and its sexuality.[33] This detachment from that which becomes the object of study allows science, or ethnographic film, to disavow its attachment to the body. And yet, like the repressed, disavowal returns as fetish and ambivalence.

Ambivalence derives from the dependence on the other for a sense of identity which, in its imaginary coherence or autonomy, denies the centrality of the other upon whom it is dependent. In pornography this ambivalence involves a paradoxical desire for a pleasure that is not one, is not fully available. Pornography sets out to please but not to please entirely. It affords pleasure but not the pleasure that is (only) represented. The pleasure that is represented remains deferred, perhaps indefinitely, in favor of its (fetishistic) representation. The result is a gendered viewing subject caught up in a desire for this oscillatory pleasure per se. The completion of desire is deferred in favor of perpetuating a set of staged representations of desire (for more pornography).

In ethnographic film this ambivalence involves the paradoxical desire for a knowledge that is not one, that is not fully "ours" or theirs. Rather than seeking to make strangeness known, "we" seek to *know* strangeness (the mythos of travel enters here). By being beheld at a distance strangeness eludes full comprehension but supports an imaginary coherence, what Said would call Orientalism, what we might more generally call the self that constitutes itself through an imaginary geography. Ethnography affords knowledge passed from mind to mind, but not the knowledge that is (only) represented, which is *their* knowledge, embodied knowledge located *there,* in other bodies. The result is a viewing subject caught up in a desire for this oscillation between the strange and the familiar. The satisfaction of the desire to know is deferred in favor of perpetuating this set of staged representations of knowledge (by means of more ethnographies).

Break On Through to the Other Side

These parallelisms might seem to deal a fatal blow to conventions of ethnographic film that bind its representational strategies so tightly to the culture of origin that misrecognition and misrepresentation are all but inevitable. I wish to suggest that what requires concerted effort is not the redemption of ethnographic film from its apparently fallen state but heightened exploration and utilization of its material, experiential dimensions. Eliminating the perpetuation of ambivalence from the representation of experience, the body, and the other would be one important step forward. In her provocative book on hard-core film pornography, Linda Williams refuses to choose between the binary either/or of pro- and antipornography positions. She concludes by arguing that a feminist pornotopia—akin to an ethnotopia constructed by the others who have been represented as source of the knowledge produced by anthropology—is preferable:

> An ideal of bisexuality drives the quest for the knowledge of the pleasure of the other: that one sex can journey to the unknown other and return, satiated with knowledge and pleasure, to the security of the "self." . . . Of course . . . there is no such thing as a discrete sexed identity who can journey from fixed self to fixed other . . . these identities themselves are constructed in fluid relations to fictional "others" who exist only in our relation to them. . . . If the sexual other is ultimately unknowable, then all the more reason to desire this knowledge, especially now that what was once the "other" has begun to make the journey herself.[34]

Breaking through to the other side would mean making a similar journey, and helping others do so as well. The body—with its truth that exceeds all regimes of truth, its excess of physical specificity and historical situatedness—rather than being contained within (Western) story formats and ethnographic "attribute dimension grids" of the sort Heider presents in *Ethnographic Film,* might provide the focus for speculation about experience and knowledge beyond the valley where our ethnographic shepherds have built their house of science. Just as a pornotopia requires not disavowal but a more intensive exploration of the sexual imagination to represent a dispersal of pleasures no longer focused on phallocentric tales, an ethnotopia would disperse experience and knowledge far beyond the binary, realist, canonic narratives of the classic ethnographer's tale. Rather than dismissing ethnographic film for failing to fulfill (generally unspecified) criteria of anthropological validation based on a conception of anthropology as science and professional discipline, we might push forward, as Williams does, toward an ethnotopia that will not abolish experience, the body, and knowledge from the belly but affirm it.[35]

Nausea, Anomaly, Excess

> Viewers do not share the cultural context,
> and the background is not thus anchored

in familiar assumptions, but begins to float in a sea of questions. . . .

—Alison Jablonko, "New Guinea in Italy"[36]

The message goes straight to the stomach. . . .

—Tambs-Lyche and Waage, "Intimacy, Recognition and Nausea"[37]

Just because the world goes round is no reason for getting seasick.

—Italo Svevo, *The Confessions of Zeno*[38]

Sometimes bodily experience exceeds intellectual understanding. Cognitive processing and bodily experience produce contradictory responses that disorient the mind. Visceral reactions occur that are uncontained by the descriptive or explanatory grid utilized by a given film. To a large extent, such reactions are treated as anomalies. (The anthropological unconscious blocks more rigorous scrutiny.) My contention, however, is that such responses indicate a possible direction forward, toward an ethnotopia that does not arise from a discourse conveyed from mind to mind. Such an ethnotopia may provide a meeting ground for ethnographic film and those cross-cultural journeys that "others" have already begun.

Two fascinating accounts indicate just how visceral the cinematic experience of another culture can be. Tambs-Lyche and Waage report that fourteen- and fifteen-year-old Norwegian schoolchildren, shown a series of ethnographic films that included nudity, violence, and "strange scenes," were nonetheless overwhelmed by *The Nuer* (Harris and Breidenbach, Ethiopia/United States, 1970) in particular. Several students fled the classroom; "some were found vomiting, one crying." In describing their responses the students identified with the Nuer as "so much like us" but also found their actions "disgusting."[39]

Though seemingly anomalous and theorized as a hysteria-like display of emotion at behavior that could not be assimilated within a cognitive frame (partly because the film did not provide a conventional one), this report also suggests that affective, embodied response is as underexamined for spectators as it is for field-workers. Confusions and censorships, intense feelings and pleasures, failures and misunderstandings, inextricable from fieldwork but excluded from written accounts, also face exclusion from the official discourse of "lessons learned" from ethnographic films.

The Tambs-Lyche and Waage report has its echo in a study of U.S. university students' responses to a series of ethnographic films.[40] Responses, carefully monitored, varied considerably; different qualities came to the fore with different films, but *The Nuer* again scored highest of all the films shown in terms of emotional response. Typical comments were: "I didn't like the film at all. . . . I found it long and boring. . . . I was in awe when I saw it. . . . The droning of the cattle almost drove me crazy. . . . The people were dirty."[41] These emotional responses, which accompanied every ethnographic film to some degree, blocked more consciously interpretive readings of the film, leaving the student feeling boredom and disgust, or awe. This pattern recalls Mulvey's comment that patterns of identification, or scopophilia, have their own aims which create the eroticized, imagized world needed to support the subject's image of him- or herself, aims which make "a mockery of empirical objectivity."

Visceral responses present a host of questions, for viewers and ethnographers alike. Strong emotional reactions that block movement toward more generalized perspectives are not unique to *The Nuer* and its distinctively poetic, associative editing pattern. Such emotional disturbance is not limited to students: Balikci recounts how Representative Conlan of Arizona attacked *The Netsilik Eskimo Series* (Balikci, Canada, 1967–68) as unfit for American schoolchildren because it undermined morality, patriotism, and American values by means of its lack of contextualizing commentary in the face of numerous scenes of "violence and death."[42] Such disturbances are not limited to events in other cultures: Sobchack makes a compelling case for the extent to which the representation of death in any documentary is vividly different from its representation in a fiction film, a difference that prompts a qualitatively different form of response.[43] The disturbances are not limited simply to students and nonprofessionals: the extraordinarily diverse set of opinions occasioned by Robert Gardner's *Forest of Bliss* that appeared in the final issue of *SVA (Society for Visual Anthropology) Newsletter* and the first issue of *SVA Review* (1990) also give evidence of emotional reactions of such unfathomed strength that more elaborate analysis is blocked.

These responses float in a sea of questions because they lack an interpretive frame within which they can be addressed. They represent a short circuit. An aesthetic, visceral response translates into expressive excess, spillage from reactions unconnected to a self-reflective, consciousness-raising means of contextualizing and understanding them. Instead of comprehension, assimilation, and interpretation, these reactions surge past the mind in a guise that allows expression to what remains ultimately repressed within the unconscious. They are ego-defensive and boundary-protective rather than catalysts to relationality and exchange. This is not experiential or embodied knowledge as liberatory escape from Platonic hyper-rationality or sobriety. Emotion as excess represents the return of the repressed in forms that fail to lead to increased self-awareness or a heightened sense of permeable boundaries and partial subjectivities. Instead, "any scene is immediately either 'domesticated' by being naively explained as analogous to something in our culture, or it is dramatized and appears as a projection of unconscious or suppressed elements of our own culture."[44]

"Our" ability to draw body and mind together, to acknowledge fears and dread, the experiential and affective, and rescue them from a sea of repressed emotion may not be very much advanced from where it was in the apocryphal story of art critic Roger Fry and his French lover, Josette Coatmellac. Fry sent Josette an African mask from which she recoiled. What Fry's biographer casually accepted as the mask's "savage expressiveness" aroused enormous jealousy and insecurity. Fry's letters, attempting to allay her responses, failed. Marianna Torgovnick, noting that we cannot know exactly how Coatmellac interpreted this mask, draws this conclusion:

> What we can know is that others in her culture thought African masks and statues "horrors" that alluded to extreme states of sexuality, suffering, and pain, and that Josette's "intuitions" about and "misreading" of the mask were not purely personal. We know as well that she acted upon what she saw in the mask, acted upon what Fry calls her "wretched intuition," and that her action had the direst consequences most of all for herself but also for Fry. Josette committed suicide; Fry experienced gloom that he claimed overhung his life. After Josette's death, Fry considered the erotic segment of his life ended and he devoted himself thereafter to the service of "art" . . . ; he was still unaware that "art" is not necessarily a category separable from erotic life.[45]

For Torgovnick, the incident underscores the disturbing linkages of the primitive and gender. For me, it also provides suggestive evidence that the anthropological unconscious is but a minor variation on the Western, patriarchal unconscious. As long as visceral reactions of longing and desire, aversion and disgust, remain checked, to be overcome by discipline and training (including the "taming" of images by words), the crucial nexus of mind/body, gender/knowledge, experience/insight will be interpreted by a reason that cannot grasp the reasons of its own (unconscious) heart.

Shifting Paradigms and Changing Times

How can we account for our bodily response to the sight of a film? This question exceeds the bounds of debate based on a shift from a social science model to a cultural studies and textual analysis paradigm for ethnography. This shift sets up the following oppositions: (1) the transparency of representation versus the content of the form (rhetoric and style as producers more than bearers of meaning); (2) the imaginary geography of the Orientalist versus the heterogeneity of interpenetrating categories and worlds; (3) the fullness of empirical knowledge versus the partiality of experiential knowledge; (4) disembodied, impersonal reason versus a situated historical perspective; (5) a zero-degree style of institutionally regulated objectivity versus the purposeful style of intersubjective communication and exchange; (6) conventional story formats versus experimental ones; (7) self-sufficient, full narratives versus reflexive, incomplete ones; (8) realism versus montage or collage; (9) univocality versus dialogism; and (10) hierarchy versus difference.

Such a paradigm shift recapitulates the last thirty years of debate in documentary and ethnographic filmmaking that began with the introduction of lightweight, synchronous recording equipment. The same issues, posed in the 1960s around cinema verité and direct cinema, return. But the interpretive arena in which debate occurs may suffer the same flaw now as then: it is too narrowly defined, producing an oscillation between alternatives that represent the (unconscious, policed) boundaries of a system still unable to see its own (repressed) limitations. In short, how can the new paradigms of dialogism, polyvocality, heteroglossia, and reflexivity avoid the fundamental rebuke of sustaining hierarchical relations and minimizing use-value to others when the questions, technologies, and strategies are so heavily of "our" own devising?

Hardly insignificant, this paradigm shift does not yet, in and of itself, suffice to account for the nausea and excess ethnographic film may produce. What remains to be proposed, not as an alternative but an adjunct, is a reconceptualization of what visual anthropology itself might mean.

Reinterpreting the Visual

> From the first moment [of *Forest of Bliss*] then we are confronted with a central principle of Hindu thought—the juxtaposition and interpenetration of oppositions (Creation: Destruction; Life: Death).
>
> —Radikha Chopra, "Robert Gardner's *Forest of Bliss*"[46]

> I rarely can figure out what the people are doing [in *Forest of Bliss*] and when I can, the significance of the action is lost to me.
>
> —Jay Ruby, "The Emperor and His Clothes"[47]

> . . . literary practice remains the missing link in the socio-communicative or

subjective-transcendental fabric of the so-called human sciences.

—Julia Kristeva, *Desire in Language*[48]

If the status of ethnographic film within anthropology signals a tension within the field as a whole in terms of epistemological theory and modes of representation, the status of Gardner's *Forest of Bliss,* and the films of Trinh T. Minh-ha, signal a tension within visual anthropology between social science canons of evaluation and cultural theory modes of interpretation (or "literary practice" in the Kristeva epigraph). So far there has been minimal dialogue between these two camps since anthropology and cultural theory, like communication studies and film studies, occupy very distinct sites within the U.S. academy: the former located more squarely within a social science tradition geared to the interpretation of data and the latter within a humanities tradition of hermeneutic interpretation. The adoption of reflexive, text-centered strategies in many cross-cultural forms of representation has yet to be matched by a comparable adoption of cultural theory in ethnographic film criticism.

A visual anthropology devoted to the interpretation of texts might raise from the anthropological unconscious questions regarding the viewer and viewer response. Repressed questions of the body, experience, and sensory knowledge that figure forcefully into the rituals of fieldwork—even if they are largely suppressed from finished reports—might return, addressed to the viewer's bodily, affective experience of an ethnographic film. Interpreting the experience of the text and the forms of knowledge it makes possible is precisely what Chopra attempts in her close textual reading of *Forest of Bliss*.

Going further, it is not interpretation but theories of interpretation that are at stake; not one reading of a text against other readings but questions of historically conditioned and ideologically inflected modes of textual representation. Sarah Williams, in a response to a trio of commentaries on the work of Trinh T. Minh-ha, poses this more radical challenge by asking "Is it possible 'to know' difference differently?"[49] Doesn't such "knowing" require putting current practices, prevailing conventions governing the ethnographer's tale, what takes place behind the scenes of anthropological discourse into suspension? "[S]uspension is deferment, dispersion, cessation. . . . To put into suspension is to support, to hang, to postpone, to interrupt."[50]

Reviewing the scope and application of cultural theory, literary theory, hermeneutics, and interpretation is well beyond the range of this essay. Clifford and Marcus have offered a useful prolegomenon for anthropology in their *Writing Culture* and Trinh T. Minh-ha has offered a symptomatic, distanciated reading of anthropological practice designed to put its underlying assumptions into critical suspension in her *Woman/Native/Other.* There also exists a tradition already represented, though often neglected, within sociology and anthropology that offers something of a bridge from paradigms lost to paradigms regained.

A Method in the Mist

> . . . it is crucial to realize that events take place not as representatives or examples of abstract categories ("marriage payments," "dispute settlement") but as contingent phenomena [which can be] far more important than the label which is attached [by analyst or actor] to the interaction.
>
> —Marcus Banks, "Experience and Reality in Ethnographic Film"[51]

> Seeking to perforate meaning by forcing my entry or breaking it open to dissipate what is thought to be its secrets seems to me as crippled an act as verifying the sex of an unborn child by ripping open its mother's womb. It is typical of a mentality that proves incapable of touching the living thing without crushing its delicateness.
>
> —Trinh T. Minh-ha, *Woman/Native/Other*[52]

The method glimpsed in the mist shrouding current discussions of the scientific dimension of anthropology is phenomenology. The phenomenological tradition shares with ethnographic film a commitment to the appearance of things in their specificity. It takes considerable interest in the question of the body and how embodied action—performance—constitutes a sense of self in relation to others. Phenomenology addresses the issue of experience directly. It brings into focus the (largely absent) body of the filmmaker him- or herself as the organizing locus of knowledge. Phenomenology, and kindred approaches such as ethnomethodology or symbolic interactionism, offers a framework within which to displace the problematics of observation and the professional gaze with questions of interaction and participatory dynamics.[53]

Like a feminist ethnographic film aesthetic, a phenomenological aesthetic remains underdeveloped and often overlooked as a possible point of departure. (It does figure, sometimes implicitly, in the largely conversational exchange among ethnographic filmmakers attempting to articulate the problems and conflicts they experience in which bodily presence, emotional response, erotic engagement, and ethical dilemmas inextricably confront one another.) It may be no coincidence that both David MacDougall and Alison Jablonko envision an experiential or perhaps gnosiological, repetitive, poetic form of filmic organization that would foster "haptic learning, learning by bodily identification,"[54] or would replace subject-centered and linear models with ones "employing repetition, associative editing and non-narrative structures."[55]

Efforts such as these would move away from attempts to speak from mind to mind, in the discourse of scientific sobriety, and toward a politics and epistemology of experience spoken from body to body.[56] Hierarchical structures designed for the extraction of knowledge (the interview, the informant, the case study) might yield to more fully personal, participatory encounter that makes an expansion or diffusion of the personal into the social and political inevitable. Rather than "perforate" the surface of things to extract concepts and categories, falsifiable rules and generalizations, ethnographic film might, according to Stephen Tyler, respond to the call for evocation rather than representation in order "to provoke an aesthetic integration that will have a therapeutic effect. It is, in a word, poetry."[57] Its production and interpretation requires both a poetics and a phenomenology to accompany, if not displace, the "production of knowledge" and interpretation of data that prizes referential and explicit meanings—pertaining to another culture—over implicit and symptomatic meanings—pertaining to "our" own.

Beyond the Binary

> [*Appeal to Santiago*'s] sequences contain superb visual ethnography, but when finally produced, these scenes are montaged primarily for artistic effect with no respect for spatial or temporal context. . . . When the artistry becomes an end in itself, then film on human behavior can become scientifically worthless.
>
> —John Collier, "Visual Anthropology and the Future of Ethnographic Film"[58]

> [*The Nuer*] is one of the most visually beautiful films ever made. . . . But the film is almost without ethnographic integrity. By this I mean that its principles are cinema aesthetic. . . .
>
> —Karl Heider, *Ethnographic Film*[59]

> Thus, Nuer culture, or our experience of it, can be known through a formal strategy of "making strange" in order that overlooked qualities of the everyday can be rediscovered. *The Nuer* attempts to restore a sense of the poetic to the everyday world of another culture.
>
> —Bill Nichols, *Ideology and the Image*[60]

Cultural studies, phenomenology, and Tyler's particularly evocative description of a transformative ethnography conceived and practiced with social use-value foremost in mind refute the self/other opposition and its inevitable slide toward hierarchy in the service of the "production of knowledge." An interpretive method that centers on the form and texture of the text, and our experience of it, also holds the potential to bridge the divide between the practice of interpretation as the scientific derivation of data, facts, or "ethnographicness"—with code words like "cinema aesthetic" to locate the author cleanly on one side of a self-constructed art/science divide—and interpretation as a hermeneutic act that locates the interpreter, viewer, and text in the midst of both a formal and an ideological, aesthetic and social, web of significance, stylistically inflected, rhetorically charged, affect-laden.

In short, bridging the gulf between interpretation as content analysis and interpretation as discourse analysis, between seeing *through* a film to the data beyond and *seeing film* as cultural representation, may reorient visual anthropology toward questions of form and their inextricable relation to experience, affect, content, purpose, and result. The emotional distress occasioned for some by seeing *The Nuer* can compel interpretive engagement and embodied awareness. Reworking the boundaries between the anthropological "discipline" and the anthropological unconscious can challenge the domesticating/exoticizing tendencies of representation and the gaze. There is no reason why nausea should lead to protracted sickness.

To the Back of Beyond: Other Voices, Other Places

> [As anthropologist/filmmakers] we will communicate from the subjects to the audience with the minimum distortion and with the maximum effort to tell the subject's story the way they would if *they could speak* to the audience *themselves* [my italics].
>
> —Jon Olson, "Filming the Fidencistas"[61]

> To return the ethnographic gaze, both women and other non-hegemonic groups must begin to write and make visual images of the world according to their own viewpoint.
>
> —Kathleen Kuehnast, "Gender Representation in Visual Ethnographies"[62]

> Clifford's map of consciousness with its sense of history and maturation from a state of belief in total knowledge to experimentation threatens to collapse under the weight of feminism and non-Western writings which make this division unstable.
>
> —Deborah Gordon, "Writing Culture, Writing Feminism"[63]

> But feminist ethnography . . . has not produced either unconventional forms of writing or a developed reflection on ethnographic textuality as such.
>
> —James Clifford, "Introduction"[64]

New paradigms and their application risk appearing as merely fashionable—responding to the commands of late capitalism and the global economy. They risk proposing a new balance of forces on the same, old, binary checkerboard. Dialogism, heteroglossia, reflexivity, and experimentation with form can all be recuperated into new and improved ways for institutionalized ethnographers to vex each other more precisely by involving "others" more thoroughly in the process. Giving others a chance to speak (on terms not finally of their own choosing) is not a radical break with past convention. Questions of how ethnography matters to "others" remain unspecified. In what way does ethnography do more than refine a professional pursuit and project the imaginary geography peculiar to a modernist or postmodernist sensibility onto the world around it? What more can it do, if natives and women, as the traditional "others," or those not seen at all, have not participated in such debates as one among many or, more precisely, as many among one—fracturing, suspending, even dissolving that "one" into the many it too readily subsumes.[65]

New strategies for film structure and film interpretation, incorporating a poetics and phenomenology, will make a difference but perhaps not enough to know difference differently. To go beyond is to go outside. It is to discover other voices in other places that, as members of a diasporic or exiled community, frequently are neither here nor there in terms of fixed location, that bring the Third World inside the First, that have undertaken their own experimentation with form to give voice to subjectivities, perspectives, and commitments that stem from other places and other experiences rather than to improve the existing ethnographic filmmaking tradition. These are voices from which we can learn.

Pranja Parasher's *Unbidden Voices* (Parasher and Deb Ellis, India/United States, 1989) is a case in point. Structured between a biography and testimonial, between reportage and evocation, adopting an array of representational strategies similar to those of *History and Memory* such as reenactments, interviews, intertitles, quotations, superimposed images, and evocative musical passages, *Unbidden Voices* examines the life of a Third World woman living in the First World. (Manjula Joshi is an Indian woman living in Chicago, eking out a modest living.) The video's final sequence begins with an intertitle. It addresses the issue of speaking for oneself at the very moment when such speech threatens to become the words of ghosts, rendered invisible by a global economy that swallows up difference:

> When we discover that there are several cultures instead of just one and consequently at the time when we acknowledge the end of a sort of cultural monopoly, be it illusory or real, we are threatened with the destruction of our own discovery.

Unbidden Voices does more than simply define the issue. It also evokes it through the superimposition, in sequences near the beginning and the end of the tape, of a tracking shot in an Indian sector of Chicago with shots taken on the streets of India. In one passage the grainy, black-and-white Indian footage exhibits soft, earthy tones, indistinct boundaries, and numerous individuals (including a woman who pulls a veil across her face when she notices the camera). These images are then superimposed over the tracking shot in which the most distinctive feature is the sharp, bright, metallic glint of car after car parked along the street. The two images overlap but clash. No explicit commentary is required to make the point.

Marilu Mallet's *Unfinished Diary* (Canada, 1983) takes up similar concerns. Mallet speaks from and about the self, with the sense of an ever-widening web of implication that spins outward from this singular but incomplete nodal point, one among many that we see as the film unfolds. Like so many inhabitants of the great global village of political refugees, exiles, immigrants, and diasporic communities, Mallet, like Joshi, is not "one of us" in terms of the classic, conventional image of the settled native informant as key to region and culture. She lives "inside" but perceives from "outside." Her split perspective leaves her acutely aware of the emotional resonance of minor moments such as when Michael Rubbo, her husband at the time, matter-of-factly staples sheets of translucent plastic to all the windows as a heat-saving procedure. To her, the rationale is understandable but it does not eliminate the felt experience of encryptment that Rubbo's calm rationality only intensifies.

For Mallet—as for others among the dispossessed and displaced for whom "de-territorialization" is not a concept but an experience, not postmodern fact as much as postcolonial trauma—movement and travel become emblematic of dislocation, of social and cultural estrangement, of survival and self-preservation. What self is it that one preserves in the midst of dispersal and fragmentation? Mallet explores and proposes strategies of resistance, of struggle and resolution (displayed vividly in the weave of Spanish-, French-, and English-speaking voices that situates characters within their own distinct, decentered locus of communication). Location stems from an embodied, corporeal discourse, and resistance from the material practice of communication and exchange.

Mallet's placement of herself within the film as a person whose authority derives from experience more than from theories, methods, or institutional legitimacy, her displacement of the "history lesson" or "ethnographic message" from its privileged position of justification for her diaristic account, her refusal to make herself into the figure of the one-who-knows that most voice-over commentary in documentary evokes, all propose a radically distinct model of social representation.

Her scenes cannot be described as examples, models, or representative evidence in the service of an argument without betraying the very strategy she adopts. They are scenes not from *a* marriage but *her* marriage, not from *a* life but *her* life. Their significance within a wider web of implication resides in their particularity, not their typicality, their phenomenological aura, not their conceptual essence. To treat them as examples is to slide toward a Geertzian problematic where representation becomes the province of Us discussing Them in ways that no longer matter very much to Them.

Here, instead of the classic ethnographic paradigm, "We speak about Them to Us," Mallet opts for one of a series of alternatives: "I speak about myself for myself and others like me" (the form of testimonial). This opens onto yet other options such as "I speak about Us for Us"; "We speak about Ourselves to Them"; or "We speak about Them speaking about Us." This array of relations between enunciator/enunciation/audience suggests how limited dialogism and heteroglossia may be, let alone classic ethnography, when responsibility, initiative, and control reside within an interpretive frame that is not yet fully defamiliarized.

Stephen Lansing also reminds us that the model of ethnographic film discussed here, of work aimed at a larger public, is not the only pertinent model.[66] His discussion of the National Film Board of Canada Fogo Island films and other works structured for use-value for their subjects rather than for their informational or affective value to others is a salutary reminder that ethnographic film can have more than one definition or purpose.

A similar reminder runs through the videotape *Satellite Dreaming* (Ivo Burum, Australia, 1991), which surveys various efforts by Aboriginal communities to produce their own television programs and distribute them by satellite. A show produced in the town of Erenbella, "Nyiru and the Seven Sisters," details a women's dance ceremony so that other, more distant members of the group can view it. The production effort prompts one Aboriginal woman to proclaim, "They're keeping their mothers' stories really strong." Another program, from Yuendumu, *Manyu-wana,* serves as an Aboriginal version of *Sesame Street,* using Aboriginal children to teach the local Aboriginal language.

The qualities of testimonial address found in *Unfinished Diary* are suggestively taken up in other works as well. *Films Are Dreams,* for example, traces a journey to Tibet by a political refugee, Lobsang Dakpa, and the ethnographic filmmaker herself, Sylvia Sensiper. News of the journey first comes to us through a staged television news report. The device aptly introduces the theme of mediating images, memories, and discourses that the remainder of the video explores. Both Lobsang and Sensiper speak for themselves about what the journey means. In each case they envision a preexisting Tibet: the Tibet of 1959 for Lobsang, the year his exile began, and, for Sensiper, the Tibet of *Lost Horizon* (Frank Capra, 1937), the film that prefigured the world she thought she might discover. By intercutting footage shot by Dakpa and Sensiper separately, clips from Capra's *Lost Horizon,* newsreel footage of China's annexation of Tibet and the Dalai Lama's (and Lobsang Dakpa's) exile, and more formal interviews with Dakpa, the film explores the construction of the imaginary geographies that usually remains unacknowledged in ethnographic work. Characters, institutions, and nations bring their preexisting maps with them. Dissonance and conflicts arise. Contradictions reveal the premises and limitations, the dreamworld quality to imaginary geographies which, at first, seem boundless. The tension between past and present is also rendered far more palpable than a salvage anthropology of disappearing customs can accommodate. There is no direct access to that imagined realm at the other end of memory; there are only memories and dreams that make more vivid the lineaments of the present from which past and future extend.

Another film that works against the grain of the ethnographer's tale is Diane Kitchen's *Before We Knew Nothing* (Peru/United States, 1988). This film is close to a conventional ethnography in its description of living among the Ashinka Indians of the Amazon River basin, but Kitchen's stress on the physical experience of being there; her admission of being drawn to the tribe by early photographs of them as fierce warriors fending off the first waves of intruders early in the century (conveyed by cutting these photographs into the flow of present events, something like the intercut scenes from *Lost Horizon* in *Films Are Dreams*); her very limited use of synchronous sound; and her total reliance on a whispered voice-over for her own commentary construct a vivid sense of distance and the struggle to *negotiate* (rather than feign effortless) passage across it. Rather than being the space necessary for representation and fetishization of the other, personal and cultural distance provides the space for critical reflection.

The almost-whispered commentary in particular conveys a sense of intimacy and respect rather than confiding a secret or suggesting gossip. The whisper erases any sense of authoritativeness from the commentary. The grainy whisper localizes and personalizes the commentary and yet holds it apart from the visible scenes where its point of enunciation, Kitchen's body, is plainly in evidence. Now and then, like here and there, interpenetrate in the shadowy echoes of a voice that does not restore the past but identifies it as available to consciousness and the present but irreducible to these or any other essentializing formulations.

Other voices propose yet other directions. These works reconfigure strategies and assumptions that underlie the ethnographic film tradition from the outside, in relation to other concerns and priorities. *I'm British But . . .* addresses questions of identity in relation to nationality and individual subjectivity. It presents a series of interviews with young Pakistani-British individuals who begin by describing themselves as Welsh or Scottish only gradually to speak more emphatically about their position between national identities—aware of their British present, conscious of their Pakistani heritage, and unwilling to choose within an either/or binary. Like Marilu Mallet, these individuals also convey a both/and subjectivity that does not confuse transnationalism with postcolonial privilege: the residue of racism, exile, xenophobia, and repression is far too strong.

Not only *Unfinished Diary* and *I'm British But . . .* but also *Handsworth Songs* (John Akomfrah, Black Audio Collective, Great Britain, 1986), *Des grands événements et de gens ordinaires* (*Of Great Events and Ordinary People*) (Raul Ruiz, France, 1979), *Surname Viet Given Name Nam* (Trinh T. Minh-ha, 1989), and *Who Killed Vincent Chin?* (Chris Choy and Renee Tajima, 1988) offer compelling representations of the interpenetration of cultures and sensibilities in a world of guest workers, refugees, exiles, diasporic movements, and ethnic diversity.

Some, like *Who Killed Vincent Chin?*, reckon the enormous price this diversity exacts when differences serve to justify racism and conflicts turn to violence. (It follows the prolonged and desultory quest for justice in the wake of the murder of Vincent Chin by an out-of-work Detroit autoworker who mistook him for Japanese.) *Who Killed Vincent Chin?* exposes the workings of institutional and habitual racism at the level of everyday life. (Compared to the virulent ideology of racism promulgated by groups like the Ku Klux Klan, the autoworker insists he had no racial motives whatsoever. His own blindness challenges the viewer to identify and understand dynamics unrecognized or misunderstood by the murderer himself.) Like *I'm British But . . .*, *Who Killed Vincent Chin?* examines racial and cultural differences at home, not in exotic locales, and makes clear what is at stake for others when difference succumbs to objectifying stereotypes and racist phobias.

Surname Viet Given Name Nam, another film outside the ethnographic tradition but instructive to it, hinges on subverting the construction of authenticity and the representation of others as "informants" by presenting scripted and rehearsed interviews with women in Vietnam that use Vietnamese women in the United States to play the parts of the women who remained in Vietnam after they left. Trinh's film, like her earlier *Reassemblage* (Senegal/United States, 1982) and *Naked Spaces: Living Is Round* (West Africa/United States, 1985), acts as a metacommentary on documentary form and ethnographic intent. Trinh stages the other culture (postwar Vietnam) as "there," only to reveal it to be "here" in ways that demonstrate continuing difficulty for women within the sex-gender system of both cultures; Trinh subverts standard assumptions about travel, fieldwork, and ethnographic authority and she presents translation and transcription as processes that distort or betray that which they represent. Rather than allowing subtitles to give the impression of representational adequacy, Trinh sets up vivid discrepancies and counterpointing between what is said and what is written, between written speech and spoken writing. Like Godard in his fondness for building scenarios from fragmented quotations, and Sensiper in her citation of previous Tibets that circulate within an imaginary geography, Trinh constructs a reality that testifies to the overlay of discourses and imaginary sites constituting this place called Vietnam. *Surname Viet Given Name Nam* not only brings Vietnam inside the United States, it embeds the experience of cultural difference within the form of film experience itself.

Dream, Memory, History, Representation

> We need a dream-world in order to discover the features of the real world we think we inhabit.
>
> —Sylvia Sensiper, quoting Paul Feyerabend, in *Films Are Dreams*

Dreams rework everyday experience according to the distinct processes of the unconscious mind. They are a way of re-membering the past and addressing its lingering conflicts, traumas, and contradictions. Memory often plays a similar role. Adjunct or alternative to third-person historical narratives, it is another way of discovering features of the real world we think we inhabit. And in many of these films, time, memory, and the past are a recurring motif. As in Marshall's film *N!ai: The Story of a !Kung*

Woman, Before We Knew Nothing, Handsworth Songs, Unfinished Diary, I'm British But . . . , History and Memory, Passion of Remembrance (Isaac Julien, Sankofa Film Collective, Great Britain, 1986), and Aboriginal satellite programs like *Manyu-wana* or the Erenbella-based show "Nyiru and the Seven Sisters" all address the question of how the past persists in the present or of how the present includes a partiality, a lack of fullness, resulting from the undertow of the past.

No longer a repository of "our" lost horizon of idyllic bliss or savage ancestry, no longer an element held within the unconscious by an ethnographic present, the past takes on a living presence perceived and felt from the inside by those for whom it matters.[67] What has come before—often in another place, another country—confirms the self as multiple, split, and layered, built up of sedimented acts and revised memories. The hearty individuality of a Nanook shatters against such forces but is none the worse for it. What is re-membered serves to constitute a body of knowledge and experience that inflects the politics of location and subjectivity. The Pakistani British in *I'm British But . . .* , who begin by calling themselves Welsh or Scottish, conclude by remembering the massacre of Jallianwala Bagh, the kind of memory that identifies a place apart.[68]

Handsworth Songs vivifies the memory of immigrant parents and the dreams they bore with them on the boats that plied the Atlantic between England and its Caribbean islands. The film utilizes a poetic voice of reminiscence describing their aspirations in a diaristic mode that establishes a region of memory and history. Sometimes this commentary is juxtaposed with footage showing new arrivals disembarking at dockside, sometimes it accompanies the camera as it slowly tracks past poster-sized photographs of the wedding pictures of Afro-Caribbean immigrants in an otherwise dark, wall-less studio space.

These passages abut others built from journalistic, catch-as-catch-can footage covering the riots in Handsworth. There is no attempt to reconcile the two forms of representation. The memories of past hopes provide a contextualizing aura of historical consciousness for the next generation of blacks, those who made the film. It is little wonder that their imagination sees, and is compelled to help others see, ignorance, racial blind spots, and misrepresentation—in sum, incommensurate realities—where their parents saw new beginnings.

These films, a few of the many available for discussion, interpretation, and use, step beyond realist conventions, canonical story formats, modernist montage, and disciplinary purity. These films *already* use cinematic montage in ways Marcus calls for in the future but are also perceived as outside the ethnographic tradition Marcus addresses.[69] They are films with use-value for those of whom they speak; they come from women/natives/others; they reconfigure the imaginary geography of cross-cultural representation itself and place ethnographic film as one, marginalized, voice among many.

These films move beyond the challenge of developing a better way for ethnographers to vex one another with their precision. Instead they propose bold and innovative directions for cross-cultural representation in which others are no longer objects of study (however sensitive to needless perforation such study might be), no longer even equals in the production of work that will enlist their efforts in the redemption of Western anthropology. They are now themselves the founding voices—pioneers, provocateurs, and poets—of a discourse of their own making, made with full, sometimes painful awareness of what has come before and of the representational residue available for adaptation, rejection, or redress.

Some works such as Trinh's *Reassemblage* and *Naked Spaces: Living Is Round* or Sensiper's *Films Are Dreams* clearly address assumptions and conventions housed within the anthropological unconscious, but most do not. This large body of work displays a very different geography from the one imagined by most ethnography and offers a different answer to the question of whether it is possible to know difference differently. These works draw much of their inspiration from elsewhere, from other traditions, other forms, other perspectives and emphases. If other voices, speaking from other places, do not turn to ethnographic film as a primary source of inspiration, this should be occasion for pause. It invites "us" to reflect on the current state of, and discourse about, an ethnographic film tradition that has sought to represent others when, "we" have been told, they could not represent themselves.

5

PERFORMING DOCUMENTARY

Orientations

Consider these two scenes. They are the first sequences from two recent works and they indicate some of the ways in which the boundaries of documentary and experimental, personal and political, essay and report have blurred considerably.

The first is from *Sari Red* (Pratibha Parmar, U.K., 1988). Throughout the sequence hard-to-identify, pulsating, perhaps spiritual music plays. The frame shows nothing but the easy shimmer of blue-green water; the shot lasts at least fifteen seconds. A little girl dashes down an alleyway; she is arrested in a freeze frame. Laundry flutters from a clothesline. Two Asian women walk down a crowded urban street; behind them, a policewoman moves from left to right. The voice-over of a polished, female voice intones, "It was not an unusual day for November, bright, chilly." The voice tells us that three women were walking home after classes as we see a small group of young Asian women walk along the street. Two women, whom we see only from shoulders to waist, work on dressing in saris. The music continues. One of the women, now on a rooftop, pivots, the sari fabric swirling in the air like a veil. The image of water is superimposed; the two substances—fabric, fluid—play across the frame. A woman's hands knead dough in close-up. Two more Asian women work together in a backyard. A woman stands, dressed in a blue sari, until the film cuts to the close-up of a blue coffin handle. Chanting voices fade in: "Paki wog; Paki wog. . . ." As the scene cuts to a long shot of an apartment building with laundry fluttering from balconies, the same female voice-over continues:

> Invisible wings carrying words of hatred.
> This was not the first time. They had heard it before.
> The voices of hatred, the laughter of hyenas
> Taking pleasure in our pain.

The second scene is the pre-credit sequence from *Sights Unseen* (Jonathan Robinson, India/United States, 1990).[1] It begins with a quote from Jean Genet's *A Thief's Journal:* Traveling and border crossings are passage less into another country than "to the interior of an image." A slow-motion, close-up shot of an Indian woman fills the frame as she slowly turns to the right, away from the camera. Indian music accompanies the image as a male voice-over commences, "In his hotel room, the tourist dreams of the native quarter." In a dark, unidentifiable space, flames leap up from a small wood fire. The voice continues, "In the native quarter, he becomes nostalgic for the vacuousness of the hotel room." The Indian woman reappears. The camera tracks in slow motion to the right as she turns to the left, facing a European man who approaches her. The voice: "He has come for an entertainment which at every step risks becoming too intrusive, too threatening." The man brushes by her, but they do not embrace. Instead they gaze at each other, perhaps unsure of each other's reality. "He is the product of a culture that looks restlessly outside itself for its dream material." A radio beeping signal, similar to that used with the RKO logo, begins as the film cuts to the color image of a slowly revolving globe. Over the globe the film's title appears.

These two scenes suggest something of the texture and tone of what may well be a distinct mode of documentary representation: performative documentary. This essay attempts to explore the distinctive qualities and issues that come associated with this highly suggestive, clearly fabricated, referential but not necessarily reflexive form of documentary filmmaking.

A New Mode in Town

Things change. The four modes of documentary production that presented themselves as an exhaustive survey of the field no longer suffice.[2] The final mode, reflexive documentary, might be expected to return us to a modified version of the first, expository, mode, but this has not proven the case. Instead the reflexive mode as first conceived seems to harbor within it an alternative mode, a mode that does not draw our attention to the formal qualities or political context of the film directly so much as deflect our attention from the referential quality of documentary altogether. Films suggesting this alternative mode, which may be called performative documentary, include: *Sari Red* and *Khush* (Pratibha Parmar, U.K., 1988, 1991), *History and Memory* (Rea Tajiri, United States, 1991), *Unfinished Diary* (Marilu Mallet, Canada, 1983), *Our Marilyn* (Brenda Longfellow, Canada, 1988), *Sight Unseen* (Jonathan Robinson, India/United States, 1990), *Films Are Dreams* (Sylvia Sensiper, Tibet/United States, 1989), *I'm British But . . .* (Gurinder Chadha, U.K., 1989), *Unbidden Voices* (Pranja Parasher and Deb Ellis, U.S., 1989), *A Song of Ceylon* (Laleen Jayamanne, Sri Lanka, 1985), *Territories* (Isaac Julien, Sankofa Film and Video Collective, U.K., 1984), *Looking for Langston* (Isaac Julien, U.K., 1991), *Tongues Untied* (Marlon Riggs, U.S., 1989), *Forest of Bliss* (Robert Gardner, India/

United States, 1985), *The Body Beautiful* (Ngozi Onwurah, U.K., 1991), and *Naked Spaces: Living Is Round* (Trinh T. Minh-ha, West Africa/United States, 1985).

What such films have in common is a deflection of documentary from what has been its most commonsensical purpose—the development of strategies for persuasive argumentation about the historical world. If we place documentary within the framework proposed by Roman Jacobson's six aspects of any communication (expressive, referential, poetic, rhetorical, phatic, and metacommunicative), performative documentary marks a shift in emphasis from the referential as the dominant feature. This window-like quality of addressing the historical world around us yields to a variable mix of the expressive, poetic, and rhetorical aspects as new dominants. (Ever since *Night Mail* [Basil Wright and Harry Watt, Great Britain, 1936] and *Turksib* [Victor Turin, Soviet Union, 1929] documentary has exhibited these qualities; what is distinctive here is their function as an organizing *dominant* for the text.)[3] This shift blurs yet more dramatically the already imperfect boundary between documentary and fiction. It also makes the viewer rather than the historical world a primary referent. (These films address us, not with commands or imperatives necessarily, but with a sense of emphatic engagement that overshadows their reference to the historical world.)

One implication of this shift is the possibility of giving figuration to a social subjectivity that joins the abstract to the concrete, the general to the particular, the individual to the collective, and the political to the personal, in a dialectical, transformative mode. One risk, exemplified by the oxymoron "reality television"—meaning those shows like *I Witness Video, Cops,* and *FBI: The Untold Story* that are discussed in chapter 3—is the collapse of all questions of magnitude and social subjectivity into spectacle and a reactionary politics of law and order. This essay sets out to explore the consequences and implications of the performative mode of documentary representation in further detail.

A schematic summary of these five modes of documentary representation, suggesting how each attempts to provide redress for a deficiency in the previous mode while eventually presenting limitations of its own, would look like this (*see table*). Documentary arises, with Grierson and Dziga Vertov, in response to fiction.

Mode —Deficiency

Hollywood fiction
—absence of "reality"
Expository documentary (1930s): directly address the real
—overly didactic
Observational doc. (1960s): eschew commentary, observe things as they happen
—lack of history, context
Interactive doc. (1960s–'70s): interview, retrieve history
—excessive faith in witnesses, naive history
Reflexive doc. (1980s—formal and political): question documentary form, defamiliarize the other modes
—too abstract, lose sight of actual issues
Performative doc. (1980s–'90s): stress subjective aspects of a classically objective discourse
—possible limitations: loss of referential emphasis may relegate such films to the avant-garde; "excessive" use of style

In relation to performative documentary, the first four modes can be more readily seen to share a common emphasis on the referent. Performative documentaries may make use of these other four modes by inflecting them differently. (None of these modes expels previous modes; instead they overlap and interact. The terms are partly heuristic and actual films usually mix different modes although one mode will normally be dominant.) Expository qualities may speak less about the historical world than serve to evoke or poetically engage this world. Questions of authority may diminish in favor of questions of tone, style, and voice. *Reassemblage*, for example, effects such a shift through its poetic cadences of image, music, text. *Tongues Untied* opens with the mesmerizing call of "brother to brother, brother to brother," accompanied by images of black men at play and in relation to one another, followed by graphic video footage of police brutality against young black men at Howard Beach, and concluding with a slow, balletic dance by Marlon Riggs himself, in which he moves across a darkened, undefined space, his hands above his head, searching and protective, until he ends in the arms of another black man, Essex Hamphill.

Observational techniques no longer give the impression of "capturing" the referential realm itself, the historical world as it is, so much as lend stress to qualities of duration, texture, and experience, often liberated from intimate association with social actors giving virtual performances according to the expressive codes familiar to us from fiction. *Forest of Bliss*, *The Nuer*, and *Our Marilyn* share this characteristic, bringing to the fore a vivid sense of temporal duration and spatial location without establishing the dramaturgical propositions so common to classic observational works such as *Primary, High School,* or *Soldier Girls* (individuated characters, psychological complexity, and virtual performances).[4]

Interactive techniques, which traditionally incorporate the filmmaker within the historical world he or she films, now give greater emphasis to the affective dimensions of experience for the filmmaker, to the filmmaker's subjective position and emotional disposition. Diane Kitchen's *Before We Knew Nothing,* for example, gives remarkable priority to the experience of fieldwork itself for its practitioner; *Films Are Dreams* and *Before We Knew Nothing* insist on the mediations that come between field-worker and subject, in these cases, preexisting images, imaginary geographies, and projected desires.

Reflexive techniques, if employed, do not so much estrange us from the text's own procedures as draw our attention to the subjectivities and intensities that surround and bathe the scene as represented. Reflexiveness may draw attention to the performative quality of the film per se, heightening our awareness that it is the film which brings into being as if for the first time a world whose appearances and meanings we think we already know. *Khush,* for example, interposes a continuing motif of two women languorously embracing each other, a highly stylized and fictitious "event" that evokes the subjective dimension contained within the more traditional interviews that parallel it. Similarly, *I'm British But . . .* intercuts its interviews with shots of a Bangla music group standing on a rooftop performing a song that provides a reflexive commentary on the statements of the film's interviewees. (The interviewees begin by asserting their unhyphenated identity as Scots, Welsh, English, no longer a part of the older, less assimilated Pakistani community; the song reminds us of the colonial legacy and its racist continuation that cannot be so readily erased.) In a more formally complex and integrated way, *A Song of Ceylon* also remembers the colonial legacy by placing a ceremony devoted to curing a case of possession within a framework that suggests possession may be a form of political resistance that has particular resonance for women.

The Referents R Us

Performative documentary presents a distinct disturbance to ethnographic film. Such films have been classically bound together by a triadic conception of "the field": the academic institutions that support it, the geographic sites that host it, and the disciplinary forces that police it.[5] Further binding them together is a conception of realism and its apparent access to the historically real which performative documentaries devalue (but do not reject). Performative documentary suspends realist representation. Performative documentary puts the referential aspect of the message in brackets, under suspension. Realism finds itself deferred, dispersed, interrupted, and postponed. These films make the proposition that it is possible to know difference differently.[6] Realist epistemology comes into question and under siege. It is this suspension of representation as commonly practiced that authorizes Trinh to write, with breathtaking force, against that inevitable turn within the realist imperative when things are meant to add up, gather themselves to a conclusion, come to the point, or penetrate to the heart of the matter:

> Seeking to perforate meaning by forcing my entry or breaking it open to dissipate what is thought to be its secrets seems to me as crippled an act as verifying the sex of an unborn child by ripping open the mother's womb.[7]

The disturbance to ethnography is epistemological in magnitude. It is a disturbance as old as art itself but it operates in unexpected and disconcerting ways when located within the heart of the discourses of sobriety, among them documentary, and, among documentaries, ethnography more than most. What do we know and *how* do we know it? What counts as necessary and sufficient knowledge?

Such an epistemological shift poses questions of comprehension as well. To comprehend *Tongues Untied, Surname Viet Given Name Nam, A Song of Ceylon,* or *Territories* requires us to attend to the content of the form, in Hayden White's phrase. This may render them precariously close to incomprehensible within the institutional framework of documentary practice today and the discourses of sobriety it emulates. The sense of incomprehension is not literal—such films can be understood it seems—but categorical: they seem comprehensible more as fictions or formal experiments than as documentaries.

In short, performative documentary takes up the challenge proposed by Teresa de Lauretis but in a more dispersed perspective: de Lauretis argues that the principal challenge for a feminist aesthetics is to construct a feminist viewer position or subjectivity regardless of the actual gender or subjectivity of the viewer.[8] Performative documentary adopts a similar goal in relation to subjectivities that range from black or Pakistani British gay to that of the Spanish-speaking Chilean exile in francophone Montreal and the Afro-Caribbean children of the diaspora dislocated in contemporary Britain.

Performative documentary clearly embodies a paradox: it generates a distinct tension between performance and document, between the personal and the typical, the embodied and disembodied, between, in short, history and science. One draws attention to itself, the other to what it represents. One is poetic and evocative, the other evidential and referential in emphasis. Performative documentary does not hide its signifieds in the guise of a referent it effortlessly pulls from its hat. These films stress their own tone and expressive qualities while also retaining a referential claim to the historical. They address the challenge of giving meaning to historical events through the evocations they provide for them. Performative documentary eschews the conventional plots adopted by most historians (tragedy, comedy, romance, and irony) and the conventional, realist notions of historicality they sustain as well.

Their structure more closely approximates that call for figurability made by Fredric Jameson in his discussion of *Dog Day Afternoon.* Figurability, like Raymond Williams's notion of "structures of feeling," is an emergent category, a possibility that takes form in a liminal moment prior to any empirical gesture toward verification: Figurability addresses "the need for social reality and everyday life to have developed to the point at which its underlying class structure becomes *representable* in tangible form. . . . [T]he relationship between class consciousness and figurability, in other words, demands something more basic than abstract knowledge, and implies a mode of experience that is more visceral and existential than the abstract certainties of economics and marxian social science: the latter merely continue to convince us of the informing presence, behind daily life, of the logic of capitalist production."[9] Jameson calls for a sense of class consciousness in "vivid and experiential ways" that moves us into the domain of culture where representation finds itself suspended among "personal fantasy, collective storytelling, narrative figurability."[10] (These are precisely the modes combined in Marlon Riggs's *Tongues Untied* and Pratibha Parmar's *Khush,* and, though strongly referential, such works are at a considerable remove from earlier efforts to represent the experiential such as *Paul Tomkawicz, Streetcar Man* [Roman Kroitor, 1954], or *Drifters* [John Grierson, 1929], where a far more classic realism holds sway.)

Performative documentaries embody, through their form, an existential situatedness that is a necessary precondition for the type of class consciousness described by Jameson.

But such films remain true to the paradox mentioned a moment ago; the referential aspect of the message that turns us toward the historical world is not abandoned. Such works then, though expressive, stylized, subjective, and evocative, also constitute a fiction (un)like any other. The indexical bond, which can also prove an indexical bind for the documentary form, remains operative but in a subordinated manner.

In *Sari Red,* for example, the central "incident," in which three Pakistani women are run down on the sidewalk by a van containing several white males, retains its historical status, as does the murder in *The Thin Blue Line,* but its meaning is up for grabs. (This struggle over interpretation within the domain of the factual and historical has never been more evident, or fateful, than in the successful defense of the four white police officers who brutally beat Rodney King on the streets of Los Angeles. The first jury's acceptance of the defense's interpretation makes vividly clear how crucial questions of viewer and frame, or context, are.)

Sari Red locates the incident, associatively, within a nexus of class, race, nation, and memory, and the film's poetic/expressive/conative work is less directed at proving what "really happened" than in reframing what has been remembered, contextualizing it within a situated response of memory and collective affirmation. *Sari Red* seeks to promote a social subjectivity within the viewer that remains unattached to a logical explanation, a way of accounting for this brutal event that reduces the existential and visceral to the abstract and analytic. *Sari Red* departs from the search for a code, a master narrative, an explanatory principle within which to subsume the particular to the general. Instead it holds to the particular, the historicality of history, while rendering it within a framework that refuses to fetishize the mystery of the unrepeatable, the past and done, leaving it frozen in a timeless moment of mythology. This film, like other performative works, makes its target an ethics of viewer response more than a politics of group action or an analysis of the ideology of the subject. Its very form exemplifies such an ethic in its own responsiveness to what has been, and been done.

Unlike reflexive documentary, performative documentary uses referentiality less as a subject of interrogation than as a component of a message directed elsewhere. Performative work may have a defamiliarizing effect, in the spirit of the Russian formalists' notion of *ostranenie,* or of Brecht's concept of alienation, but less in terms of acknowledging the constructed nature of the referential message and more in prompting us to reconsider the underlying premises of documentary epistemology itself. Performative documentary attempts to reorient us—affectively, subjectively—toward the historical, poetic world it brings into being.

This shift parallels the notions in Charles Sanders Peirce's semiotics that give priority to the experiential quality of an individual's relation to signs.[11] What Peirce calls the "logical interpretant" might correspond to the tendency of performative documentary to dispose us to see our relation to the world anew, in less abstract, overly conceptualized categories. Peirce argued that the final effect of a sign is to dispose us toward action modified as a result of the experience of the sign, or, here, text. This is a level of engagement that serves to "make sense" of the world rather than to impose a pure logic. To defamiliarize a previous relation opens the possibility for a change of habit, a transformation of awareness, a "raised" consciousness in those visceral and existential terms that are part of figuration.

Evocation

The shift of emphasis toward the poetic, expressive, and rhetorical also reconfigures questions of validation. The process of identifying a problem and proposing a solution no longer has operative force. Our assessment and engagement, then, is "less in terms of [the message's] clarity or its truth value with respect to its referent than in terms of its performative force—a purely pragmatic consideration."[12] Questions of pragmatics shift the dominant from the work's referential relation, its indexical binding to fragments of the historical world, to its relation to its viewers. *We* are what such films refer to.

Stress falls on the evocative quality of the text rather than on its representationalism. Realism, of course, is quite capable of drawing upon expressive qualities. Subjective camera movement, impressionistic montage, dramatic lighting, compelling music: such elements fit comfortably within a realist style but, in documentary, they are traditionally subordinated to a documentary logic, which is governed, in turn, by the protocols of the discourses of sobriety.[13] Expressive qualities color, inflect, flavor, but seldom determine the overall organization of the text or the viewer's overall response to it.

Performative documentary, on the other hand, frees these expressive elements from their subordination to a logic. Such documentaries can therefore be more iconic than indexical, being less heavily dependent on an indexical authentication of what is seen and heard. (*The Thin Blue Line* offers vivid examples, perhaps none more so than the slow-motion flight of the vanilla ice-cream malt that sails through the night air in some of the reenactments of the crime.) Performative films rely much less heavily on argument than suggestion; they do not explain or summarize so much as imply or intimate. In *Reassemblage,* for example, Trinh insists that she will not speak about but only "speak nearby." She is good to her word when we see, for example, an elderly man weaving in a village. No comment occurs to anchor this "ethnographic detail"; instead images of weaving are themselves woven into a montage that evokes a sense of rhythm and quality of life without attempting to penetrate, isolate, or conceptualize what we see. In films like *Reassemblage* or *A Song of Ceylon,* we observe social actors who do not coalesce into characters (that fusion of actor and role that gains stability and psychological depth over the course of the [realist] narrative). In others works like *Films Are Dreams* or *Tongues Untied,* social actors take on the narrative coherence of a character; they approximate once more those forms of virtual performance that are documentary's answer to professional acting. But in either case, the stress is on the referential turn toward, not a historical domain, expressively enriched, but an experiential domain, expressively substantiated. It is the difference between description and evocation.

Some time ago David MacDougall offered eloquent testimony to the capacity of ethnographic film to describe everyday life and lived experience in a way distinct from written texts. This quality seemed well worth cultivating to MacDougall since it made use of film to render the texture of experience with such compelling detail. As he put it, film can render

> . . . the appearance of a people and their surroundings, their technology and physical way of life; their ritual activities and what beliefs these signify; the quality of the interpersonal communication, and what it tells of their relationships; the psychology and personalities of individuals in the society; the relation of people to their environment—their knowledge of it, use of it, and movement within it; the means by which the culture is passed on from one generation to another; the rhythms of the society, and its sense of geography and time; the values of the people; their political and social organization; their contacts with other cultures; and the overall quality of their world view.[14]

For MacDougall, this evocative potential seemed linked to a potential shift in epistemology, or at least a radical reconceptualization of the terms and conditions of ethnographic film so that it would no longer be seen simply as a colorful adjunct to written ethnography but offer a distinct way of seeing, and knowing, of its own. But MacDougall does not insist on this rupture. There is the lingering sense that the texture of life contributes to an economy and logic that are still fundamentally referential and realist. MacDougall also evokes a generic oneness ("the overall quality of their world view") which leaves the position, affiliation, and affective dimension of the filmmaker's own engagement to the periphery. Performative documentary seeks to evoke not the quality of a people's worldview but the specific qualities that surround particular people, discrete events, social subjectivities, and historically situated encounters between filmmakers and their subjects. The classic anthropological urge to typify on the basis of a cultural identity receives severe modification. (MacDougall's own films exhibit these performative qualities, to a greater extent than this quote, and may attempt to persuade traditional ethnographers to give greater attention to film but in a way that leaves traditional assumptions essentially intact.)

The break with the tradition of referentiality and realism that Dziga Vertov, Sergei Eisenstein, and Jean Rouch, among others, pioneered receives more forceful articulation in Stephen Tyler's call for a postmodern ethnography. (Unfortunately, Tyler's call addresses written ethnography; he seems unaware of how much his call has already been answered, but largely outside the domain of the ethnographic discipline itself.) Tyler writes, "[Evocation] defamiliarizes commonsense reality in a bracketed context of performance, evokes a fantasy whole abducted from fragments, and then returns participants to the world of commonsense transformed, renewed and sacralized."[15]

Since "sacralize" does not appear in the *Oxford English Dictionary,* I can only surmise that it is Tyler's attempt to convey the sense of spiritual renewal that evocation carries for him, more than the sense of altered consciousness and social transformation it holds for me. What does stand out in Tyler's call is the move away from empiricism, realism, and narrative;

his is a call for a defamiliarizing mode of expression that embodies a sense of a world brought into being between text and viewer that is remarkably close to the pioneering theories of Sergei Eisenstein.[16]

Genealogy

Performative documentary, like reflexive documentaries, does not propose a primary object of study beyond itself but instead gives priority to the affective dimensions struck up between ourselves and the text. It proposes a way of being-in-the-world as this world is itself brought into being through the very act of comprehension, "abducted from fragments," as Stephen Tyler puts it. Using the "dynamite of a tenth of a second" celebrated by Walter Benjamin, performative documentary burst the contemporary prison world (of what is and what is deemed appropriate, of realism and its documentary logic) so that we can go traveling within a new world of our own creation.

Films like *Tongues Untied* step beyond thick interpretation, beyond problems and their "solution," beyond explanation or spectacle. *Handsworth Song, History and Memory, Sari Red, Of Great Events and Ordinary People, Unbidden Voices* and *Sights Unseen* all find forms of historical horror that the text then surpasses by giving form to memory and social subjectivity, to remembrance and transformation. Such works offer figuration to alternative forms of social subjectivity and the human self—beyond the individual and his or her conscience, beyond the subject of Althusserian ideology, beyond the manifestations of an unconscious that reenacts its tales of a family romance. Such figuration possesses a dialectical quality. It moves between the particular, with its density and texture, and the general, with its power to name and conceptualize. It circulates between the body, with the knowledge resident within it, and history, where knowledge and power contend. Location, body, self: these elements of a world we thought we knew turn strange and unfamiliar in the landscape of performative documentary.

Among the genealogical precursors to performative documentary are:

1. Early Soviet cinema, including the work of Dovzhenko, Eisenstein, and Vertov, which developed a remarkable array of techniques to defamiliarize everyday perception and yet retain a vivid sense of historical consciousness.

2. Those early expository documentaries that were as much poetic as argumentative, such as *Night Mail* (Basil Wright and Harry Watt, Great Britain, 1936), *Turksib* (Victor Turin, Soviet Union, 1929), *Song of Ceylon* (Basil Wright, Ceylon/Great Britain, 1934), *The Bridge* (Joris Ivens, The Netherlands, 1928), *Listen to Britain* (Humphrey Jennings, Great Britain, 1942), *Louisiana Story* (Robert Flaherty, United States, 1948), or *The River*

(Pare Lorentz, United States, 1937). Such films gave the impression of discovering mystery and wonder in the world around us and resorted to poetic rhythm, montage, visual rhymes, and musical incantation to awaken such wonder in the viewer.

3. The avant-garde tradition that mediated between the "two materialisms" (of the cinematic apparatus itself and historical materialism), including the work of Godard, Jan Jost, and David Rimmer.[17]

4. The avant-garde tradition of autobiography that coincides in many aspects with the confessional quality of a number of performative documentaries, including Jonas Mekas, Kenneth Anger, Maya Deren, and, above all, Stan Brakhage.[18]

5. The ethnopoetics of Jean Rouch, who has consistently argued for, and embodied, a style of filmmaking that does not so much combine the subjective and objective poles of traditional ethnography as sublate them into a distinct form.[19]

6. The tradition of magical realism, specifically in the form discussed by Fredric Jameson, where it serves as an alternative to the postmodern nostalgia film. Magical realism, in this perspective, eschews the representation of the past by images and simulacra for a "different kind of past that has (along with active visions of the future) been a necessary component for groups of people in other situations in the projection of their praxis and the energizing of their collective project."[20]

7. Recent interactive and reflexive documentary (*Las Madres de la Plaza de Mayo, Cane Toads, Roses in December,* and *The Thin Blue Line*), where moments of performativity nest within the domain of a different dominant.[21] Performative documentary could be considered a reversal of priorities, or dominants, in this case, from a referential emphasis to a more expressive one.

8. Those recent works discussed in chapter 4 (*The Body Beautiful, Measures of Distance, History and Memory,* and so on) which combine elements of autobiography and the poetic in a documentary form to which a situated, embodied sense of political testimonial has been added. (What these films suggest is the significant degree to which certain avant-garde and documentary traditions have become blurred into a more singular enterprise, affording a perspective from which much of what we have called documentary might be reconsidered as experimental and much of what we have called experimental or avant-garde might be reconsidered as documentary.)

In addition to this cinematic genealogy, both a historiographic and a linguistic model provide suggestive affinities. Performative documentary moves toward those forms of historical explanation described by Hayden White as formist and contextualist but in a far more vividly dialectical fashion.[22]

Formist explanations favor the unique characteristic of situations and events; stress falls to "variety, color and vividness" (White, 14). The tendency is toward dispersal rather than integration, with lower regard for conceptual precision than other alternatives. "But such historians usually make up for the vacuity of their generalizations by the vividness of their reconstructions of particular agents, agencies, and acts represented in their narratives" (15). (And, I would add for performative documentary, the vividness of their evocation of the subjectivities that accompany these agents, agencies, and acts.)

Contextualist explanations also give low priority to generalization. They set events within a context but stop short of deriving laws, governing principles, or prevailing ideas as the mechanistic and organicist forms do. Contextualist historiography straddles the terrain between "the radically dispersive tendency of Formist and the abstractive tendencies of Organicism and Mechanism" (18). It settles for a relative integration of trends or general characteristics of a period or epoch. As White puts it, contextualism favors tacit rules for linking specific historical occurrences to a more inclusive domain: "these rules are not construed as equivalent to the universal laws of cause and effect postulated by the Organicist. Rather, they are construed as actual relationships that are presumed to have existed at specific times and places, the first, final, and material causes of which can never be known" (18).

Though sharing the preference for the local, the concrete, and the evocative, performative documentary also generally insists on the dialectical relationship between precisely this kind of richly and fully evoked specificity and overarching conceptual categories such as exile, racism, sexism, or homophobia. These latter are seldom named and never described or explained in any detail. They are tacitly evoked through juxtaposition and montage (Howard Beach footage in *Tongues Untied,* Chinese military occupation of Tibet in *Films Are Dreams,* police "riot control" in *Handsworth Songs,* for example), but the texts do not insist on specific linkages or explanations. This they leave, to a significant degree, to the viewer. (It is we who must discover that the specific instances we see share a family resemblance characterizable as racism, sexism, and so on.)

Performative texts thus avoid both the reductionism inherent to theory and the vacuous obsession with detail inherent to formism and contextualism. They are more properly, and fully, dialectical than a more abstract, theoretical account of dialectics could be. And as a dialectical representation, performative documentary addresses the fundamental question of social subjectivity, of those linkages between self and other that are affective as fully as they are conceptual.

A useful genealogical model here might be the ancient Greek use of the middle voice.[23] What seems most suggestive is the way in which the middle voice was originally positioned in relation to the active voice, with the passive voice serving a subordinate function. Middle voice addressed those situations in which an action took place within a subject or effected the nature of the subject, situations where the action envelopes the subject and the subject is immersed in the action. In active voice a subject, already constituted anterior to an action, acts (she persuades her friend). In middle voice the subject and her subjectivity is itself constituted in the process of acting (she obeyed her friend: in Greek, "persuade" and "obey" are the same verb used in the active and middle voices respectively).

The middle voice cuts through the dilemma constructed by the ancient debate of whether we are fully developed mortals responsible for our actions or the passive objects of divine activity. Middle voice is something of a linguistic response to the sense we may have that we are "immersed in the action in such a way that, at least at times, 'doer' and 'done to' become inadequate categories, drawing a sharp line, legislating a boundary, where none is felt. . . . "[24]

Social subjectivity would link not only the doer and the done to, in self-constituting action, but the state of "doer/done to" experienced by one and that experienced by others. Social subjectivity, like the social imaginary that it transcends, is a category of collective consciousness. It exceeds or surpasses the monadic desire by a preconstituted subject underpinning the dynamics of self/other, us/them dichotomies. Social subjectivity evokes a discourse of visceral, existential affinity. Social subjectivity transforms desire into popular memory, political community, shared orientation, and utopian yearning for what has not yet come to be. Like Marlon Riggs's dance upon a darkened stage in *Tongues Untied,* or the latent, both homoerotic and political energy of the sleeping, hammock-held sailors of *Battleship Potemkin,* this form of subjectivity gives physical embodiment to the power of collective, self-transformative action.

A Shift in Praxis: From Unity to Affinity

Performative documentary takes up those strategic locations called for by the shifting terms of identity politics and a postmodern disposition for cyborg affinities.[25] By relying on a dispersed, associative, contextualizing, but also social and dialectical mode of evocation, performative documentary is a particularly apt choice in a time when master narratives, like master plans, are in disrepute. They invoke an epistemology of the moment, of memory and place, more than of history and epoch. An altered emphasis, an alternative epistemology, but one that remains open, teleonomic and social. What Fredric Jameson describes as the "power and positive value of situation-specific thinking and speaking" could have been written with performative documentary itself in mind:

> . . . dialectical thinking and language—or a properly dialectical code as such—projects a synthesis of both, that is to say a thinking which is abstract and situation-specific all at once (or which, to use Marx's far more satisfactory formulation, is capable of "rising from the abstract to the concrete").[26]

But reality-transforming, affinity-building qualities remain at a premium. Without those aspects of performative documentary that evoke questions of magnitude, of a felt tension between representation and represented, evocation will collapse back into the solipsistic terms of a privatized consciousness. Social subjectivity will remain beyond the horizon of a text that affirms the personal vision and subjective experience of individual, poetic consciousness but little more. This question of magnitude as a domain of social subjectivity and historical engagement is what distinguishes performative documentary from a large portion of the traditional film avant-garde with which it otherwise shares so much.

And yet the passage from a transcendental but individual consciousness to a dialectical and social one is further compounded by the absence of a specifically political frame within which performative documentary might be received. The formalists' claim that there is no "there" there becomes joined to the Marxists' lament that there is no Left left. This is not quite true, though. It would be more accurate to say that the Left has taken a dispersed, decentered form, and that its absence is only perceptible when what we seek is the traditional Left of vanguard parties, united front politics, and a correct line. Political affinities are already dispersed across a wide field of organizations and issues; they overlap and coalesce in unpredictable and unstable ways. There is great cause for optimism in this movement toward a new magnitude of political organization and process, to which performative documentary contributes significantly, but an aura of nostalgic loss and misrecognition may also loom. This is, after all, a time of multinational if not global capitalism, of a new world order of command and control, of interactive but hierarchically organized communications, of a "late" capitalism that continues to discover ways to transform and perpetuate itself.

As this economic lion, or perhaps paper tiger, grows larger and larger, more globally interconnected and less locally responsible, the contrast between its power and scope and the apparent power of identity politics, makeshift alliances, and cyborg affinities may seem dwarfed out of all proportion. This is a perception that performative documentary sets out to revise. By restoring a sense of the local, specific, and embodied as a vital locus for social subjectivity, performative documentary gives figuration to and evokes dimensions of the political unconscious that remain suspended between an immediate here and now and a utopian alternative.

When, in Lizzie Borden's *Born in Flames* (1983), Adelaide Norris asks Zella Wylie about the political efficacy of united-front politics, Wylie offers a hypothetical choice: Which would you rather see, one big, powerful lion or five hundred mice pounce through the door? Wylie opts for the mice: "Five hundred mice can do a lot of damage."[27] Performative documentary is on the side of the mice.

6

EISENSTEIN'S *STRIKE* AND THE GENEALOGY OF DOCUMENTARY[1]

Strike
[*Stachka*] USSR. Dir/ed: Sergei Eisenstein; assist: G. Alexandrov, I. Kravchunsovsky, A. Levshin; script: Proletkult Collective (V. Pletnyov, Eisenstein, Alexandrov, Kravchunovsky); cinematog: E. Tisse, V. Khvatov; art dir: V. Rakhals; cast: Grigori Alexandrov, Maxim Straukh, Mikhail Gomorov, Alexander Antonov, Judith Glizer, Boris Yurtsev, I. Ivanov; prod: Goskino/Proletkult.

Bold, imaginative work by new Russian director Eisenstein. Short on plot, no star appeal, but full of kinetic editing and Marxist sloganeering. Could be limited hit if artsy quality doesn't drive politicos away. May show strong legs despite hints of weak bo. Best aimed at cult and midnight circuit.

—Nich

Breaking New Ground

By making the abstract incarnate *Strike* gives renewed vitality to the most impressive aspects of documentary today. Embodied, abstractions like class struggle or racism become more than categories of debate; they enter the realm of lived experience. They engage us body and soul. As *Shoah* discovers the incarnation of past experience in present behavior, as *The Thin Blue Line* reveals how memory shapes past events to serve present needs, as *Tongues Untied* gives embodiment to subjectivity and a politics of experience, *Strike,* an extraordinary first film by Sergei Eisenstein, makes dialectical consciousness incarnate. Here is a political, and documentary, style of filmmaking that blurs all our received notions of where the bounds of social representation lie.

Eisenstein clearly deserves the accolades he has gained for innovation, even if this praise often recruits him to a formalized history of cinema rather than treating him as a key combatant within the arena of social interpretation. More than any other active filmmaker, Eisenstein has discovered ways to represent not simply the external appearance of class struggle but its conceptual foundations as well: historical, class consciousness, and the materialist dialectic. And he does so with particular regard for the distinctive space between us, the movie screen, and the surrounding world. This is the space which Eisenstein infuses with dialectical consciousness; such space subsumes and transforms us. It reconfigures who we are and makes this new person incarnate, available to consciousness, disposed to action. It is as though Eisenstein chose to respond to Benjamin's challenge "to articulate the past historically [by seizing] hold of a memory as it flashes up at a moment of danger" by devising his own form of writing in lightning.[2]

As an exercise in rendering the abstract concrete, *Strike* could be considered as the first chapter in Eisenstein's long-promised adaptation of Marx's *Das Kapital* for the screen. It is, in fact, the first of a projected series of films on events leading up to the October Revolution, but this is a misleadingly limited goal for what Eisenstein has actually accomplished.[3] He has not told yet another story of individual conscience and collective struggle, in the same mold as other socially conscious narratives such as *The Molly MacGuires* (Martin Ritt, 1970), *Norma Rae* (Martin Ritt, 1979), *Chapeyev* (Sergei and Georgi Vasilyev, USSR, 1934), or even *The Battle of Algiers* (Gillo Pontecorvo, Algeria/Italy, 1965), where *individual* characters and their consciousness serve a classic identificatory function.

Eisenstein has not presented a didactic truth or moral message that characters announce or spectators carry away like apples in a lunch pail. Instead Eisenstein has fulfilled his own goal for what film can do in the representation of class, history, and revolution: "*to teach the worker how to think dialectically.* To show the method of the dialectic."[4] In commenting on this notation, made by Eisenstein in preparation for filming *Das Kapital*, Jacques Aumont astutely notes, "Finally, and contrary to what one might expect from what has gone before, the object privileged [by Eisenstein] in Marx's work is not the theoretical one, like any of the key concepts from *Capital*. It is at another level entirely that Eisenstein selects his true object—the Marxist method itself."[5]

> Our conception is that a person first of all researches the material, and then posed the question of how to give form to the material.
>
> Besides, material can be presented with

> or without a story. Storyless films still have a plot.[6]
>
> —Victor Shklovsky

Strike gives *figurative embodiment* to more than just a strike; it is not the documentary record of a real strike, or the true story of an imaginary one. *Strike* is not a fictional-story realm within which class struggle finds itself constrained by the formal demands of psychological realism and narrative closure. Eisenstein's concern with narrative form in his published writings has led critics to assign him to the ranks of fiction filmmakers, especially with the prescriptive Dziga Vertov setting forth an agenda for what we would call documentary that clearly excludes his work. The disputes between Dziga Vertov and Eisenstein that have been so widely reported in the West present a false temptation: consign Eisenstein to the dustbin filled with that bourgeois opiate, fiction, and elevate Vertov to the rank of *kino* pioneer. When writers stress Eisenstein's inventiveness, it is in the context of the ever-increasing maturation of the fiction film while Vertov's is in promulgating the founding principles of documentary.[7]

Neither Vertov nor Eisenstein, however, as honest critics readily admit, is so readily corralled. The square peg Eisenstein cannot be fit into the round hole fiction. Just as Meyer Shapiro's trenchant attack on Freud's psychoanalytic reading of Leonardo banished psychoanalysis from the disciplinary domain of what counts as good art history, so Dziga Vertov and all the film historians who have followed him have banished Eisenstein from the domain of what counts as good documentary.[8] They have done so, in part, by creating a doxa that insists on a difference between documentary and fiction in the first place and then pushing Eisenstein over to one side of the line and Vertov to the other. I prefer to treat fiction and nonfiction as a blurred or fuzzy boundary and to examine ways and means of addressing the real historiographically, as with Eisenstein, or in the present, ethnographically, as with Vertov.

In these terms, Eisenstein is a neither/nor figure: neither fiction as we have known it nor documentary as it has come to be defined locate his work effectively. Powerful as a fiction, *Strike* is also the most impressive achievement in documentary representation since *Who Killed Vincent Chin?*

> When a fact is taken as a brick for a construction of a another sort, the pure newsreel disappears. It is all a matter of montage.[9]
>
> —Sergei Tretyakov

Strike, in other words, doesn't teach us that strikes arise because of exploitative work conditions, the alienation of labor power, or the inhuman attitude of factory owners—although it makes no effort to deny these lessons either. Factual litanies of woes, authenticated catalogs of abuse, detailed chronicles of union struggle with their moments of success and loss, and biographic homage to those who personify defiance in the face of adversity—*Strike* exhibits none of these familiar, limited (but fully understandable) traits so abundant in documentaries on the working class.

Likewise, *Strike* does not present an idealized leader upon whom leadership devolves; it doesn't present events in strictly causal sequence or embellish them with scrupulous attention to historical details; it eschews the parallel plotting of romantic courtship with social adventure; it lacks those identificatory mechanisms that join viewer to characters with singular precision (psychological complexity, expressive acting styles, point-of-view editing); and, finally, the story world of the characters lacks the coherence or continuity customary to realist, and even expressionist, fiction. *Strike* remains poised to move in whatever direction, on whatever plane of reality suits its larger purpose. It exhibits none of the proclivities of the fiction film that Eisenstein vowed to analyze but not to imitate.[10] Neither fiction nor documentary satisfactorily describes the border zone Eisenstein so exuberantly occupies.

Warning: Dialectics at Work

Strike makes incarnate the space between. This is the space between spectator and screen, between social actors and individual consciousness, between ideology and actual conditions, between bourgeois consciousness and its social situation. *Strike* constructs between us and it a historical consciousness and a social subjectivity capable of carrying us beyond the film itself. It does so in the act of viewing itself. *Strike* engages us in the process of bringing into being a world where this very action prompts us to experience, *materially, viscerally,* the transformative potential of dialectical thinking. We enter a realm in which we actively coalesce an array of fragments to bring into imaginative being a world that does not yet have historical existence and is therefore incapable of empirical documentation. This is a Marxist form of modernist collage, or what Eisenstein himself termed dialectical montage.

If the final effect of a sign is to dispose us toward action modified as a result of the experience of that sign, as Charles Sanders Peirce suggested, *Strike* may be among the first films to render such an effect dialectically. The rhythms and evocations; the surveillance and subterfuge of the bosses, the resistance of the workers; the reverberations of what has come before within the context of what comes later; and the qualitative transformations wrought by a remarkably sensuous montage of attractions present a temporality that is not linear in arrangement nor teleological in progression but contingent and transformative, rich with that potential for excess that could be called *aufhebung,* or reality-transforming.

Strike is not another indictment or negation of the misery of capitalism. It is, instead, a negation of the negation, an embodiment or figuration of class consciousness, dialectical thought, and social praxis as it is lived and breathed by social actors. There are, for example, those thirty-three shots heard round the world with which the film concludes. These shots depart from any pretense at a literal historicity. From the moment the factory manager pounds on his desk, spilling black ink across the map of the workers' quarters, we enter a realm in which an array of fragments coalesce to bring into being a world that is not yet materially substantiated but is nonetheless real by dint of being represented as though for the first time.[11]

Motion matches motion: the pounding fist becomes the downward thrust of a butcher knife. This downward thrust transforms into the downward flight of workers as Cossacks pursue them in the woods where they had picnicked. The crosscutting builds in rhythmic crescendo, ending with the death of the ox and the slaughter of the rebellious workers. A long shot of proletarian bodies strewn across a meadow dissolves into soldiers marching back, from frame right to left, as though over the lifeless bodies of those possible selves who will no longer be. The camera continues this motion in the final shot of the sequence, panning right to left across the meadow and the bodies lying there.

After this massacre in thirty-three shots, Eisenstein adds a four-shot coda: (1) the word "Remember," (2) an extreme close-up of a frowning gaze, (3) the word "Proletarians!" and (4) an extreme close-up of these same eyes snapping to full attention. Here is the imperative that structures the entire film: re-member, re-construct, retro-spect; make the past your present as you struggle toward a future that could not otherwise be.

The entire sequence violates any sense of historical specificity to constitute that effervescent space, now, in which historical consciousness achieves materialization. Temporality itself is up for grabs. Eisenstein has, for example, imbued his male workers with a communitarian spirit that may even seem prelapsarian. They cavort and gambol, they frolic on the waterfront, conspire among abandoned locomotive wheels, draw up strike demands while picnicking in the woods.[12] They are as lively, robust, and strong-willed as Lang's workers are enervated and impressionable in *Metropolis.* These are not the downtrodden who have nothing to lose but their chains. Eisenstein has overcome the persistent handicap of those who exhort workers to unite: Why should workers join together as workers when it is *as workers* that they experience alienation and exploitation?[13] It is only when they are not workers that some small taste of a better life becomes possible (illusory, if they are ultimately still workers). These workers give suggestive embodiment to precisely this alternative way of being in a world not yet fully of their own devising.

Eisenstein has convincingly responded to Kenneth Burke's challenge to rethink the representation of workers: if it is not our ambition to *become* workers then we must represent workers in the process of becoming more than they have been without becoming the bourgeois subjects they oppose. Their representation requires a multiple valency and Eisenstein has provided one. The spies act furtively, constantly striving to pass as only workers, hiding their intentions and desires, remaining fully, and dangerously, closeted (in the language of gay pride). Eisenstein's workers, however, gambol exuberantly. Their zest and vitality, their defiance and wile, construct a fraternity of men (more than the icon of oppressed workers in a social stratum of splintered families). The representation is similar to that of a gay community. The homoerotic exuberance here, like the homoerotic languor of the Potemkin's sailors in their hammocks, makes these men workers who are more than workers, even as their transformative potential awaits full realization.

Astonishingly, the workers' gay abandon remains unrecognized. No history book refers to it. Almost no criticism identifies it.[14] It remains a representation with a vivid referent (a set of real social practices) but without a signified (a sign of community yet to be brought into social existence). The effects of signification has not yet risen to the level of conscious apprehension; the dialectic awaits completion. (Eisenstein makes his workers more than workers but he does not construct an erotics of power, authority, and domination. His tack is diametrically opposed to the fascist aesthetic of virile, striving bodies orchestrated into formal patterns and aimed at goals of domination.)

Eisenstein has effected his own version of the hysteron proteron (the reversal of a natural order, such as cause and effect) for which Vertov has been so keenly praised in *Man with a Movie Camera.*[15] Eisenstein gives embodiment, in the collective figure of the proletariat, to that form of historical, nonindividuated consciousness which has yet to come into being on the plane of history itself. No one worker embodies it, no one worker articulates it; in strict historical reckoning, it exists only as a possibility, as that which ought to be in distinction to what is. And it is this consciousness, shaped from the montage of attractions Eisenstein has set before us, that the film's final words paradoxically, or, more exactly, dialectically, urge us, no longer the wretched of the earth, to remember, and *see,* as though for the first time: "Remember, Proletarians!"[16]

Eisenstein has forged time, and history, into the figure of prolepsis. Such a figure befits a dialectical consciousness that activates the past in a present that is itself simultaneously past to a future of its own making. Unlike the conservative visions of *Metropolis* (Fritz Lang, Germany, 1926) or *Blade Runner* (Ridley Scott, 1982), *Strike* bestows dignity and vision upon its worker-heroes. They are neither pawns nor rabble, neither atmosphere nor cyborgs. If documentary offers perspective and commentary on the historical world, *Strike*'s perspective—of a world brought into being in the space between—"Remember, Proletarians!"—offers a radical, embodied revision of history, consciousness, worker, and cinematic form. No longer the lonely figure of alienation, the worker comes to embody, proleptically, the potential for being-in-action that hierarchy and hegemony strive to control or destroy.

Knowledge Incarnate

Strike attains that form of embodied knowledge that is so crucial to innovative work in documentary today. Eisenstein resorts to reenactment not to give us a pseudo-authentic impression of what events were really like but to give substantive form to the political unconscious and radical subjectivity itself. What is it like to share in a communitarian consciousness and what is it like to leave a film wanting to complete it, in fact, now? *Strike* gives us the closest thing we have to an answer.

In refusing to offer lessons so much as remembrance, Eisenstein aligns himself with the cinema of exile, diaspora, and dislocation. He breaks with the expository tradition and its classic problem/solution structure. Close to fiction, like *The Body Beautiful, Unfinished Diary, Khush,* and other similar films, *Strike* adheres to the particularities of time and place. Here, as in these other films, movement and travel are restricted. The workers are the constant target of surveillance; documentary images, realist *trompe d'oeil,* hidden cameras all serve the interests of the managers. Space and its representation are not yet their own. "Life caught unawares," in Vertov's phrase, is life betrayed.

And, like those luxuriating, hammock-held bodies filling the frame in the opening movement of *Battleship Potemkin* (1925), the workers in *Strike* constantly exude the potential energy of subjects whose very identity stems from their being-in-action. None of that sterile posing that freezes people into mythic icons,[17] none of that studied iconography of desire that renders actors into stars, none of that condensation of action and agency into the individuated figure of psychological realism that defines bourgeois narratives of fiction and documentary alike. Acrobatic, resourceful, determined, these workers remember, and are to be remembered, with open eyes and alert bodies, ready to spring into action with the collective force of five hundred mice.[18]

Strike, like several other recent films, among them *The Thin Blue Line, Surname Viet Given Name Nam, Of Great Events and Ordinary People, Shoah, History and Memory,* and *Roger and Me,* breaks out of the indexical bind. This is the bind created when documentary relies upon its stock in trade, its ability to portray what occurs in front of the camera with great fidelity, to the point of captivity (what occurs demands an authenticity in its portrayal that squeezes the filmmaker's own perspective from the historical event that precedes him or her; what has already occurred takes precedence over the dialectical process of remembering the past to transform the future). *Strike* refuses to offer an indexical pathway back to the past as the visible ruins of a congealed consciousness and meaning.

As in these other films, it is only *now* that we can see that what was can make a difference to what will be. (*Now* was that which was up for grabs rather than itself a source of historical consciousness; the struggle *then* to make a future other than what was is what we *now* can see, when we see, as Eisenstein allows us, dialectically.) *Strike* makes this dialectical process its final referent as it constitutes its subject both as theme (historical consciousness) and viewer (we are the subjects in which this abstraction becomes an active process).[19] Rather than forging a path back to the historical record via indexical linkages, *Strike*'s path is toward what it brings into being between itself and the viewer: a historical consciousness made manifest by form itself.[20] This is a cinema of attractions that does not "add up" at all but transforms itself by means of our apprehension that the whole is greater than the sum of the parts. Here is a demonstration of magnitudes of which most fiction (and much documentary) can only dream.[21]

Reviving Old Forms

Strike also revives a vital but neglected quality of early cinema: that tendency which Tom Gunning, drawing from Eisenstein's own writing, retroactively labels a "cinema of attractions." What Gunning describes is an alternative mode of representation that eventually became incorporated as a component of classic narrative: the impulse to show, to put on display openly and exhibitionistically rather than covertly and voyeuristically.

Gunning describes this process as it worked in pre-1906 cinema:

> To summarize, the cinema of attractions directly solicits spectator attention, inciting visual curiosity, and supplying pleasure through an exciting spectacle—a unique event, whether fictional or documentary, that is of interest in itself. . . .
>
> It is the direct address of the audience, in which an attraction is offered to the spectator by a cinema showman, that defines this approach to film making.[22]

In Eisenstein's cinema of attractions the totalizing effect escapes the limit Gunning sets for early cinema—of providing interest (only) in itself. Eisenstein exceeds the limits of the indexically bound documentary and realist-bound narrative. Eisenstein is indeed a *show*-man, and what he addresses to us directly is that gaze and those words that urge us, "Proletarians" (those viewing subjects constituted as proletarians by the film's own form), to "Remember." Here is showmanship of a special kind. Along with the constructivists, Eisenstein developed a kinetic art, not as an aesthetic experiment or exciting spectacle of interest in itself, but from a "passionate desire to incite the spectator to action."[23]

Final Things

When Eisenstein ends—but does not conclude—his *closing* act is a pair of eyes that spring open and urge us, as though with a suddenly dawning consciousness, to "Remember." This act exceeds indexical reference, allegorical meaning, or bland analogy. (His ending, of eyes snapping open, also contrasts radically with Buñuel and Dali's beginning, of an eye cut by a razor blade wielded by Buñuel in *Un Chien Andalou* [1928]. *Strike* does not assault but awaken; it does not associate the camera's view with violence but with re-vision.)[24]

Eisenstein also locates both the animal and human slaughter of the film's concluding sequence in the interior of social practices; both are grounded in institutional history, not the great intertext of artistic invention. The metaphor does not escape the historical domain for that of abstractions. These are the very social practices that produce consciousness as surely as class conflict, that produce the slaughter of workers as surely as butchered meat. It is the arena of social practice, not the aesthetic preferences of the director, that give shape to the attractions, and juxtapositions, Eisenstein chooses to show. (This is what distinguishes him so vividly from Fritz Lang in *Metropolis* and Ridley Scott in *Blade Runner* where non-dialectical consciousness prevails.)

Eisenstein's workers no longer make commodities for those who steal their labor. They make themselves. They make themselves over, using material that is not "out there" but is instead the stuff of materialist consciousness itself. They are not only touched but constituted by the production of signs for which the signified is not a history lesson or external referent but a will to transform that brings into being the utopian moment hitherto repressed in the political unconscious.[25]

Eisenstein's workers are us. It is we who remember what they have experienced. It is we who act, who continue and complete what they began, who exceed that form of consciousness contained by narrative or expository form.

The means to transform "the end" are at hand. They involve the reconfiguration of what has now been figured: they involve the praxis of negating the negation. As Walter Benjamin put it speaking of fashion where fashion could stand for the standardized flow of novelty and repetition that defines the conventional bounds of both fiction and nonfiction cinema,

> Fashion has a flair for the topical, no matter where it stirs in the thickets of long ago; it is a tiger's leap into the past. This jump, however, takes place in an arena where the ruling class gives the commands. The same leap in the open air of history is the dialectical one, which is how Marx understood the revolution.[26]

The blur of boundaries inaugurated by Eisenstein comes, in part, from the act of leaping itself. To be-in-action is to blur all notions of a subject who is before she leaps.

7

PLEASE, ALL YOU GOOD AND HONEST PEOPLE
FILM FORM AND HISTORICAL CONSCIOUSNESS

Of Time and Dialectics

> The memory of past time depends on the present project of the subject: the intentionalization of the past changes with the intentionalization of the future.
>
> —Anthony Wilden, *System and Structure*[1]

If the future, like the past, is made and remade in terms of our present situation, it cannot be known in advance and made subject to dicta, dogma, or any other teleological imperative. And yet the future cannot be abandoned as merely unknowable. It is the ceaseless dialectic of past, present, and future that sustains historical consciousness for the social *actor* as well as the historical spectator, and it is the construction of such actors within a viewing context that provides the present focus. It is a question of form and the content of this form.[2] Political art needs to "convey the sense of a hermeneutic relationship to the past which is able to grasp its own present as history only on condition it manages to keep the idea of the future, and of radical and Utopian transformation, alive."[3]

Images, as we know, are always present tense. Their referent, what they re-represent, may be elsewhere, but this absent referent seems to be brought to life in the present moment of apprehension, over and over. Does this only further erase a fading sense of the historical in postmodernity, or does it leave open possibilities for historical representation beyond those of the written word? Something is clearly different. Historical consciousness requires the spectator's recognition of the double, or paradoxical, status of moving images that are present referring to events which are past. This formulation involves viewing the present moment of a film as we relate to past moments such that our own present becomes past, or prologue, to a common future which, through this very process, we may bring into being.

This chapter examines such hermeneutic relationships in four texts that, among them, invite meditation on uses of the image in the construction of an idea of history, historical consciousness, and the future. The texts are: *JFK* (Oliver Stone, 1991), *Who Killed Vincent Chin?* (Renee Tajima and Chris Choy, 1988), *Dear America: Letters Home from Vietnam* (Bill Couturie, 1987), and various programs and reports constituting television coverage of the Gulf War in 1991 (termed the "Gulf War text" hereafter).[4] (This chapter will also allude to a fifth film, *Land without Bread* [Luis Buñuel, Spain, 1932], as precursor. *Land without Bread,* like *Strike,* belongs to a genealogical pantheon separate and distinct from those heralded works of early documentary that no longer contribute full measure to a transformed future.)

This choice of texts has the advantage that, in most instances, at least one text will challenge or refute claims or possibilities marked out by the other three. This chastening element of qualification will help make clear the degree to which formal solutions to historical dilemmas are always only partial. Just as both formal and political forms of reflexivity operate in texts, so, too, the strategies argued as most promising here can serve more than one political purpose, depending on more specific aspects of the text itself, its contextual placement, and the viewer's response.[5]

The present approach to historical consciousness borrows from what Freud called *nachträglichkeit* and Hayden White called "willing backward": "willing backward occurs when we rearrange accounts of events in the past that have been emplotted in a given way, in order to endow them with a different meaning or to draw from the new emplotment reasons for acting differently in the future from the ways we have become accustomed to acting in our present."[6] (This is the act to which Anthony Wilden's epigraph also refers.) Ultimately, I want to try to connect the idea of rereading with a *form* that heightens the necessity for doing so in the belief that this linkage opens up possibilities for engendering a historical consciousness. (Specifically, I focus on collage, but, as *Land without Bread* reminds us, other forms that stress fragmentation, strange or irreconcilable juxtapositions, and the necessity for a retrospective form of reading are also possible.) I want to distinguish this process and the form that engenders it from traditional modes of realist representation.

Nachträglichkeit joins squarely with the question of modernism posed by Hayden White and of postmodernism posed by Fredric Jameson.[7] More than merely a phenomenon of "reading comprehension," retrospection or rereading functions dialectically, in the form of a feedback loop. As we retrospect, we model a future on the basis on our present situation as it is mediated by how we *now* understand our past situation. As we retrospect, we construct a story (*histoire*) from our present perspective but mediated by what we now understand of past events in the plot to which we contribute, in "the story so far."[8]

The search for a form commensurate with this mode of consciousness will clearly not produce a formulaic solution. The uses and effects of form can no more be guaranteed than the future foretold. But if some forms lend themselves to certain subjectivities and interpretations more than others, this particular search will be for forms that intensify the need for retrospection, that require recall in order to grasp the pattern they propose, that heighten the tension between a representation and its historical referent, that invoke both past and present in the dialectic of constructing a future. Such a search will necessarily carry us to the borders of realism, if not beyond. The idea of omniscient narration, individuated psychology, linear causality, and temporal closure will be put at risk, if not subverted. Time itself, the existential time of lived experience and textual encounter, takes an active role, allowing for temporal organizations that "may be synchronic, diachronic, mythical, repetitive, ostensibly circular, actually spiral or structured (but not read) as a mosaic."[9]

Working the blurred border zones of realism has fundamental importance to documentary representation and historical consciousness. Within this border zone the paradoxical status of realism as a mode of representation that attests to knowledge of the world and affords aesthetic pleasure for the senses, that evidences a capacity to speak about the historical world and to please us with its rhetoric, or style, remains acute. To resolve this paradox in either direction so that a text is made transparent to the world, as unmediated knowledge, or rendered opaque, as a realm of disinterested, aesthetic engagement, is to dull the very edge that gives realism its power and continuing use-value.[10] Realism alone will not suffice. A border zone beyond the territory of classic realism requires exploration. The moment when realism spoke with the clarion voice of truth is "no longer our own."[11]

The hermeneutic relationship at issue involves the paradoxical or, better, dialectical link between form and knowledge. Inasmuch as dialectical time is *lived* time, this involves embodied knowledge. We are moved to ask what lies beyond the text, what action remains yet uncompleted, what enigmas remain in need of resolution. This is a different form of question and response from believing what we see, or even from believing and disbelieving what we see all at once. It is to understand at one and the same time that texts of historical consciousness are what they are and that they exceed themselves. This dialectic demands a divided consciousness, one attendant to past, present, and future, to signifier, signified, and referent, to the particular and the general, the strange and familiar, knowledge and pleasure, form and content.[12]

This understanding cannot settle into the empirical certitude of appearances or into the abstract profundity of deep structures without doing serious damage to dialectical consciousness itself. It is the both/and quality that allows for an existential engagement with time, of a past now present, that provides an armature to the future harbored within the political unconscious. In this way, what has been can indeed serve as prologue to a future yet to be brought into being.

The challenge is to untrack narrative without destroying it. Retardations, delays, slippages, diversions, incomplete reasoning, unfinished arguments, partial proposals, competing claims, jarring or strange juxtapositions, fissures, gaps, or other peripeteias mark this strategy. It approximates what we customarily attribute to collage in the effect it produces (although *Land without Bread* reminds us that surrealism, another key part of the modernist moment, provides a different angle of incidence on this array of effects).

Historical consciousness, collage, surrealism: they differ markedly from postmodern amnesia, ossified forms of montage, or classic realism. Strange juxtapositions and unexpected fissures require us to fit fragments within a shifting, often tacit field of reference. As Robert Burgoyne puts it, "In short, historical narrative [what I here term "collage"] is seen as a performative discourse, a product of the same kinds of actions that produce historical events; the investing of the world with symbolic meaning."[13]

Put more strongly, historical representation, and collage, becomes a form of cartography quite distinct from its Cartesian predecessors: the assumption of a fixed reference point or even the determination of a fixed location "on the map" no longer has the commonsense cogency that was once taken for granted.

The contemporary search for alternative forms of representation parallels a waning of historical consciousness itself. It accompanies a new dimension to historical questioning. The modern event (massively demonstrated in what might have once been called the sublime and brought to yet sharper focus in disasters, catastrophes, and social holocausts) eludes traditional historical understanding. Questions arise that traditional storytelling techniques cannot answer. Too much of that excess magnitude we invoke by saying "history," too much noise or dissonance, too many loose ends and dangling uncertainties remain. The (narrative) center will not hold:

> But not only are *modern* accidents more horrific than anything that earlier generations could possibly have witnessed, the photo and video documentation of such accidents confirms the impossibility of representing them as elements of a story or narrative and, moreover, of being able to derive explanations of their occurrence from the observation of the recorded images themselves.[14]

The desire for and the impossibility of explanation are precisely what *Land without Bread* mocks and celebrates. Less literally historical than *JFK*, *Who Killed Vincent Chin?*, or *Dear America*, it nonetheless examines that cross-cultural temporal divide that operated within the anthropological unconscious of the 1920s and '30s: They were Our more primitive selves.

But the images Buñuel presents defy the explanations provided. And the explanations defy reason. A "logic of misery" prevails that throws back into the face of Western humanism the very images it uses to explain itself. No "accident," anthropological expeditions and travel adventures bring back, in Buñuel's hands, images that defy explanation on their own terms or those our guiding commentator provides.[15]

Such a mode of representation foreshadows the *endless* fascination with the type of images referred to by White such as the Zapruder footage of President Kennedy's assassination. Likewise, *Land without Bread* sardonically foreshadows the remarkable plenitude of explanations for and interpretations of Gulf War footage that revealed, quite clearly, nothing. The questions that can be asked of the use of the image in an age of historical amnesia and cybernetic simulations are manifold. Some of the most pressing ones—part of the dissonance or noise within traditional historiography—involve the border zones of realism and the figures of subjectivity and consciousness we find inhabiting them.

Madness, Mood, Voice, and the Event

All four texts examined here isolate specific events: the assassination of President Kennedy, the murder of Vincent Chin, the coming home (via letters) of Vietnam War vets, and the Gulf War. None sets out to paint the broader sweep of history within which such events might be embedded. The very singularity of such events provides a surface upon which various meanings can be inscribed. And yet this surface lacks the "grit," the points of attachment that hold it securely within a given context and explanatory matrix. To re-present the event is clearly *not* to explain it. Multiple interpretations and meanings seem to explode outward. The event—up for grabs, decontextualized or de-realized, burdened by the specter of death—produces a crisis for representation. The surface mirrors back assigned meanings dutifully, disdainful of any obligation to closure or truth. Like gender itself, the event becomes party to a social contract, available for representation but incapable of confirming any one epistemology or ontology. What White says of modernism applies to the problematic of all four texts:

> Modernism thereby effects what Fredric Jameson calls the "de-realization" of the *event* itself. And it does this by consistently voiding the event of its traditional narrativistic function of indexing the irruption of fate, destiny, grace, fortune, providence, and even of "history" itself into a life (or at least into some lives) "in order to pull the sting of novelty" and give the life thus affected at worst a semblance of pattern and at best an actual, transocial and transhistorical significance.[16]

The type of poetic, descriptive, but essentially linear and causal historical narrative traced by Ken Burns's *The Civil War* suffers forfeiture. The Big Picture remains out of view. These four texts struggle to achieve—or in the Gulf War text, evade— the imperative, "Only connect." But they do so in relation to the event as the paradoxical category that can deflect all meanings as well as point to those semblances of pattern that, rather than "fate" or "destiny," might be called historical materialism.

All four texts pose the risk of sliding toward a discourse, not of expository sobriety, but delirium. The fraying away of the event from an explanatory frame; the logical impossibility of explaining the whole by means of the part; the reluctance to name the framework in which apparent disorder now assumes pattern and meaning (intensified by an aversion to "master narratives"); the analytic impossibility of determining causality, intentionality, or motivation from the visual record; the heightened intensity brought to bear on the event itself as though it *ought to* yield up its secret meanings—what it portends for a future to which it remains mysteriously bound; all these factors burden the interpretation of the event with an excess that threatens to explode in pure delirium.

In *JFK*, particularly, speculation, conjecture, inference, and even fantasy abound. Abandoning the ironic mode of *Land without Bread*, *JFK*, *Dear America*, and the Gulf War text seem overinvested in the image and what it might or should mean. They exhibit signs of an emotional (over)identification that is strikingly akin to the overinvestment in the image attributed to women characters in 1940s films as described, for example, in Doane's *The Desire to Desire*.[17] Questions of hysteria or paranoia hover at the border zones of realism.

The changed nature of the event corresponds to a changed form of discourse. We search for an alternative epistemology, on the one hand, and, on the other, find our search approaching paranoia in its resort to suggestion, inference, faulty syllogisms, and leaps in logic in order to extract pattern, and meaning, from overdetermined and inexhaustible events.

What *JFK*, for example, then highlights are alternative tenses and modes to those we normally associate with expository, nonfictive, and historical discourse. Instead of a straightforward past tense ("Oswald shot Kennedy") we encounter subjunctive tenses ("Kennedy would have jeopardized the military-industrial complex if . . . ") and conditional tenses ("Oswald might have been exactly what he said he was, a patsy"). In these texts, historical representation falls under the sign of performative documentary.

There is an honesty here that could be misinterpreted as subjective impressionism, unlicensed fictionalizing, or even coercive manipulation. What *JFK* suggests is a return to modes of historical investigation commonly associated with pre-nineteenth-century notions of rationality, objectivity, and *non*narrative, terms which, in fact, are themselves a legacy of the (vigorous but failed) effort to separate fact from fiction cleanly. In three of these texts (excluding the Gulf War text), the imaginative dimension to historical representation, and action, takes precedence over an empirical logic foreclosed to utopian transformation.

One final commonality needs mention before examination of each text separately: There is both a remarkably diverse set of modes (subjunctive, performative, conditional),[18] tenses (past, present, future), and voices (active, passive, and middle), and an equally complex array of source material.

Webster's *Third New International Dictionary* defines subjunctive as "a set of verb forms that represents an attitude toward or concern with a denoted act or state not as fact but as something entertained in thought as contingent or possible or viewed emotionally (as with doubt, desire, will). . . ." Such a definition is entirely in keeping with the dominant stress of performative documentary and historical fictions like *JFK*.

The performative mood would be those utterances that deflect our attention away from the referential claims of the text to the more expressive, poetic, or rhetorical dimensions of the text per se. This deflection does not draw attention to the organizational properties of the text as surely as formal or political reflexivity would do; it is, instead, an insistence on the expressive gesture itself. There is a strongly performative quality to the opening minutes of *Who Killed Vincent Chin?*, for example, where various types of source material kaleidoscopically invoke the social milieu (Detroit, 1982) without feigning any transparently realist depiction of this milieu. The performative mood is more than stylistic flourish. In my view it approximates/counters one possible source of ideological effect in a text: instead of surreptitiously substituting a sign system (realism, for instance) for the historical referent such a system appears to capture or present, the performative mood heightens our awareness of how referential meanings are themselves produced without dispensing with the meanings so produced entirely.

The conditional mood, devoted to matters of supposition, and the ablative absolute case, specifying "time, cause, or an attendant circumstance of an action," also propose themselves as linguistic models for the types of text/event/viewer relations (hermeneutic relations) discussed here. The move away from conventional declarative structures appears to correspond to a move away from "rationality," or linear causality, and toward something closer to chaos theory (the discovery of pattern within apparently entropic processes by reframing or recontextualizing them). This is distinct from classic notions of "deep structure" or "structuring absence" where what is not seen or given materially can still be specified within a routine linguistic protocol. (It can be named or specified even if it cannot be represented.)

Middle voice originates in Greek grammar and refers to those verb forms that indicate an effect on the subject occasioned by the action described by the verb. "I take," for example, may become "I choose" in middle voice, carrying with it a sense both of affect and of heightened moral consciousness. Similarly, during certain interviews and collage patterns, our sense of involvement may shift from "I see" to "I witness," or "I realize." Such changes lack the linguistic markers that the middle voice would have in writing and remain more speculative; nonetheless, I believe this concept to be an apt one for the type of effect produced by *Land without Bread*, *JFK*, and *Who Killed Vincent Chin?*

The use of source material is equally complex. *Who Killed Vincent Chin?*, for example, turns to home movies, interviews shot by the filmmakers, interviews conducted by others and reused by the filmmakers, photographs, "behind the scenes" observational footage of network news coverage, the reproduction of broadcast news, cartoons, advertisements, and press conferences. *JFK* relies on a set of sources whose authenticity is often clearly meant to be subject to question: a fictional enactment of Jim Garrison's investigation in the present tense, fictional reenactments of what "might have been" the case in the past tense of the assassination and events leading up to it (who exactly "remembers" or recounts these episodes remains conjectural through much of the film), home movies, archival footage (usually film or television news coverage from the early '60s), press conferences, and interviews that reconstruct disclosures based on historical records.

Dear America: Letters Home from Vietnam utilizes its soundtrack to represent the authentic content of letters written by U.S. soldiers in Vietnam (although this content is "performed" by well-known actors). *Dear America* also relies on home movies shot by soldiers during their tour of duty, archival footage and television newscasts related to the war, and graphic titling (particularly a running count of the number of U.S. troops in Vietnam and the number of dead and wounded among them during each year of the war).

The Gulf War text, although it organizes its dispersed set of sources in a different manner, nonetheless presents a remarkable array of source material in the course of its flow: "live" coverage on the scene, live reports from a studio setting of occurrences elsewhere (often with split images using monitors, sometimes with maps, graphic inserts, sync sound, and sound off all at once), visual material from the Gulf presented on a time-delay basis (partially to avoid the enemy's use of simultaneous information for military purposes, particularly on CNN's round-the-clock, live coverage), Pentagon and network "file" footage of weapons and their performance, Pentagon footage of air strikes (including images transmitted by "smart bombs" and bombers as they hit their targets), graphic titling and subtitling, interviews with experts, interviews with officers and non-officers by anchors and reporters, and, at least in a few cases, conditional-mood representations of what might have happened had U.S. bombing been less effective.[19] Finally, of course, there are the medley of "station breaks," announcements, and ads that differentiate the flow of one news stream (about war) from another (about consumer products and services).

This complex arrangement of diverse source material suggests some of the ways in which the representation of the modern event eludes capture by the linear, realist narratives of yesteryear. Even in the Gulf War text where a classic rationality tends to prevail at an overt level, the very form of the representation suggests the tug of a strong undertow in other directions (toward, for example, the derealization of the event itself, the replacement of the bodies of social actors—troops, be they friend or foe—with the bodies of televisual personalities—reporters, authorities, and "anchors"—and the dissolution of the historical referent into the media-text that represents it).[20] The exact direction in which each text aims is different. This diversity of aim is the subject to which we now turn.

Kennedy: A Man and His Body

All four texts could be regarded as basically expository (with stress on a poetic modality in *Dear America* and a fictional one in *JFK*), but three (all but the Gulf War text) incorporate a considerable number of performative qualities as well. All three give stress to expressive, poetic, and rhetorical aspects of their message; all three engage questions of subjectivity and the body with appreciable force. Like Errol Morris's *The Thin Blue Line,* none of these films adopts the classic problem/solution formula of expository documentary. They favor a mode of explanation that is less frontal, less beholden to a careful, clear enumeration of causal factors bearing consequences for which a solution can be proposed. Instead, all three prefer to evoke a sense of the milieu against which the event to which they attend arose: the rise of a military-industrial complex in *JFK,* the racial and class tensions in the Detroit of the early '80s in *Who Killed Vincent Chin?,* and the popular memory of the war in Vietnam for *Dear America.* This reframing of events functions similarly to contextualist historiography: it establishes a new, retrospective frame within which the inchoate becomes comprehensible by dint of the larger, implicit pattern to which it now belongs.[21]

JFK devotes its first twenty-five minutes to a gradual accumulation of situations and events that provide, obliquely, not only a beginning but an implicit frame or "embedded explanation"—an explanation that precedes the remainder of the film's effort to assign agency and determine guilt. In this prelude we see and hear: former President Eisenhower's warning of the danger to democracy of a growing military-industrial complex; President Kennedy's inauguration and a montage of 1960s political iconography from Fidel Castro and the Cuban revolution to Martin Luther King, Jr., and the civil rights movement; Kennedy blaming the CIA for the Bay of Pigs fiasco; Kennedy declaring the fight in Vietnam unwinnable; a woman's body being pushed from a moving car (one of the first of many imaginative reenactments, we return to her complete story much later); Kennedy arriving in Dallas and the start of the fateful motorcade; the woman pushed from the car in a hospital warning those attending her that "They'll kill Kennedy" (but our knowledge of her is no different from her attendants'; only retrospective knowledge makes her warning prophetic and its dismissal tragic); a gradual musical crescendo builds as the motorcade continues; in another reenactment, in black and white, a man, apparently suffering an epileptic seizure, diverts attention along the parade route; individual figures, including a child, are isolated in the crowd; a rifle fires, the screen goes black; then, in a metaphoric trope similar to the balloon that drifts upward when a child is murdered in Fritz Lang's *M,* pigeons fly skyward.

Walter Cronkite appears on screen, in archival footage of his actual news bulletin, to announce that President Kennedy has just been shot in Dallas. The focus shifts to Jim Garrison in New Orleans as we move through a similar mix of enactment, reenactment, and archival material tracing the aftermath of the shooting. Thirteen years later, the events still obsess Garrison. One fitful night, he awakes to proclaim, "It's incredible." Within moments, Garrison has launched the investigation that will consume the remainder of the film.

Like Eisenstein's reliance on a montage of attractions in *Strike, JFK* engages us in the process of bringing into being a world constituted from shards, fragments, a series of facts and events, viewed in conditional or subjunctive form and capable of infinite permutation. (If we argue that Eisenstein liberated documentary from the requirement to provide authentic images of historical events through unrehearsed and unstaged filming, Oliver Stone—like Jean-Luc Godard, Dušan Makaveyev, Werner Herzog, Trinh T. Minh-ha, Raul Ruiz, Jill Godmilow, Errol Morris, and many others—is clearly one of his successors.) More coherent and concise than Garrison's own investigation, this opening passage nonetheless signals the associative method by which Garrison will proceed and the conclusion at which he will arrive: Kennedy threatened the very military-industrial complex of whose power Eisenhower warned; a network of schemers and doers carried out the deed, using Oswald as a patsy, installing Johnson as president and guaranteeing the continuation of the status quo.

But no one and nothing says as much. It remains for the viewer to arrive at this conclusion from the juxtaposition of elements Stone provides. Like Eisenstein and Buñuel, who relied heavily on montage or strange juxtaposition as a fundamental source of pattern and meaning, Stone falls subject to attack for manipulation. (The strongly montage-driven *Who Killed Vincent Chin?* which offers equally complex layers of sound and image juxtaposition would no doubt come in for the same criticism if it received comparable coverage in the mainstream press.) My contention is that

Stone's project is not manipulative at all but highly suggestive, adopting unconventional moods and voices to imply what, if stated, could only be distorted. Because he does not spell out his argument in a "rational," problem-and-solution manner, because it appears as the content of the form, as an implicit frame or embedded explanation, he triggers, in some, a profound discomfort. A "meaning-effect" occurs, but its source is not identifiable enough (for "rational" analysis, assessment, and debate). (Profound discomfort with *JFK* is similar to nervous laughter at *Land without Bread:* we *experience* a jostling or jarring of conceptual frames rather than a reasoned explanation within the terms of one such frame; the visceral effect of this experience spills out as discomfort, feelings of being manipulated, or nervous laughter.)

Paradoxically, just as Stone retrospectively reframes the assassination within an explanatory web, he also dwells on this singular event obsessively. Part of the traumatic nature of the modern event (of which this assassination is representative and for which the Holocaust may well be the ultimate example in Western consciousness) is precisely that it does not fold into a larger historical frame readily. It resists narrativization. Questions of agency, responsibility, causality, and consequences elude determination. They may be *mu* questions—questions posed or addressed within the wrong frame. Alternative frames are called for. Much of the impetus behind Hayden White's article "The Fact of Modernism" is to reconsider modernist art as a way of escaping *mu* questions posed within a traditional realist framework that explains discrete events by their placement within a linear, causal chain in order to address the modern event as, precisely, an event unlike any other.[22]

The repetition compulsion that marks a fixation on isolated events from the Hindenburg disaster to the Challenger explosion, from the Holocaust to famine in Ethiopia, from Kennedy's assassination to the events of Tiananmen Square, or the Gulf War, can, like realism, only be understood within a both/and, potentially paradoxical frame. On the one hand, the impulse is to fix and memorialize, to insist on the distinctiveness and the fetishistic importance of the event itself. On the other, the impulse is to extract meaning, to make use of this event in a dialectic of past, present, and future that retains the hope of radical transformation. The dialectic swings between a state of fixation and a project of existential transformation. The tone of *JFK* can therefore be described as both nostalgic and transformative anger, the strange coupling of arresting and galvanizing impulses.

It would be possible, in hermeneutic terrain such as this, to introduce the psychoanalytic notion of paranoia as analogue for the tone, tenor, and voice of these texts, especially *JFK.* What Stone, or the character Jim Garrison, attempts, in his obsessive retrieval and reassembly of facts (including the Zapruder footage), is to *make* images speak. This frozen, arrested moment (rendered mute and undecipherable for this very reason) demands a story. It demands insertion in "the story so far" whereas its frozen quality shifts it into the domain of "once upon a time." Images and memories must be made to move, to take time, to trace a path from then to now, to reenter the historical narrative from which they have been excised. This proves only partially successful.

The past returns via speech and words—from confessional interrogations (David Ferrie) to revelatory disclosures (Mr. X)—to which Stone, or Garrison (we cannot always say which), adds images (shadowy figures plotting murder, debaucheries gilded with plans for a coup d'etat, bullets slipped onto passing gurneys, etc.), or as images—centered on that fateful moment when shots rang out—to which Stone, or Garrison, adds words (the incantation of "back and to the left" that Garrison speaks in sync with the Zapruder footage to prove his theory).

But speech added to images is like captions added to pictures: they steer us toward one understanding and away from others within an arena of social interpretation where meaning is inevitably up for grabs. No guarantees can be issued, no certainties obtained. And illustrative or imaginative images added to speech only heighten frustrations: they add an "image too many"; they produce an impossible multiplication of a historical event by attempting to illustrate (unseen, unknown) aspects of its specificity. Moreover, the spoken accounts, like conflicting oral histories, do not jibe. Vested interest and its "willing backward" that obfuscates more than it reveals are all too apparently at work. More conclusive proof than speech is wanted.

By making an obsession and a fetish of the event, Stone (and Garrison) can never see what he wants to see most of all: the causally determined Big Picture, the organizational flowchart tracing every line of responsibility, or even the exact way in which Kennedy died. At the trial, Garrison's repetitive screening of crucial frames from the Zapruder footage as he intones "back and to the left, back and to the left" acts like a magical incantation, striving to make verbal repetition a causal agent that will compel mute images to speak the truth. It, too, fails. The film cries out, "Conspiracy," but Clay Shaw goes free. Despite its affinities with collage, implicit frames, and embedded meanings, there is also an undercurrent of obsessive, nostalgic longing for the explanatory power and precision of realist narrative and causal frames. *JFK* may finally impede the very call for historical consciousness and transformative agency that it simultaneously embodies and brings into (partial) being.

As with the modern event generally, this obsession with the singular, arrested event speaks to a crisis of agency. The loss of linear chronology and classic, realist narrative, the rise of a modernist, and postmodernist, sensibility, threatens to collapse time into an eternal now, the now of the event (signaled vividly in the Gulf War text and its next of kin, reality TV shows generally). The event becomes obsessively repeated in the hope that it might be sprung into a temporal trajectory where causality and agency return. Meanwhile, possible agents—from the CIA to Oswald—are both everywhere and nowhere. Both Stone and Garrison prove the truth of Brecht's dictum that a photo of a Krupp munitions factory tells us nothing. Rather than anchoring or guaranteeing anything, adding speech or words only multiplies meanings. Stone and his character want things to *make* sense in the same strong, reflexive sense in which narratives *take* place. But just who is there to do this making or taking? Who *is* responsible? Delirium, and paranoia, are in the air.

When he wrote his seminal essay "The Paranoid Style in American Politics," Richard Hofstadter identified the key moment in social paranoia as the refusal to acknowledge mediating factors within the social milieu.[23] Issues, no matter how carefully or even obsessively assembled the facts may be, suddenly polarize into black and white. All types of mediating complexity fall away, leaving only the great Manichean battle between Them and Us. Polarizing processes of denial and projection, so precisely described in Sartre's *Anti-Semite and Jew,* operated routinely in anti-Catholicism, anticommunism, homophobia, the anti-Masonic movement, the witchcraft trials, and other cases of paranoid style.

In her study of postwar American "women's movies," Mary Ann Doane relies primarily on psychoanalysis to account for the spectators' psychic investment in the female characters in these films. She devotes a chapter to paranoia. Following Freud's argument that paranoia stems from the denial of homosexual wish fantasies by men for their fathers, Doane notes a similar polarizing process at work on the individual level as Hofstadter finds on a social level: "Paranoia, in its repudiation of the Father, allies itself with the dyadic structure of narcissism, the imaginary, the pre-Oedipal."[24] It's Them against Me, this time, and the psychic paranoid, like the social movement paranoid, becomes obsessed with evidence, interpretations, and all the attendant questions of causation: who, how, why. . . . (Paranoids can master an awesome array of facts but will simultaneously mash these facts into astonishingly oversimplified dichotomies.) Doane continues, "Thus the delusion is a desperate attempt on the part of the paranoiac to compensate for the absence of the paternal signifier."[25]

Combine "paternal signifier" (the phallus) with "social mediation" (male loyalties and bonding, class alliances and dependencies, the state and hegemonic process) and we are back in the realm of *JFK* with its extraordinary combination of political analysis, on the one hand, and a (seemingly unnecessary) cabal of homosexual "perverts" and assassins, on the other. Oliver Stone offers a textbook version of Freud's argument that paranoia stems from the fear that a member of the same sex who has played a formative emotional role now has sexual designs on you. Rather than acknowledge the sexual charge to emotional bonds with a member of the same sex (classically the father), the paranoid refuses to admit to any attraction whatsoever. Instead he projects evil designs onto others.

What *JFK* suggests is that Stone, like many other Vietnam vets, feels that his country, his father land, has turned against him. The good father lies slain. The evil father holds the upper hand. This source of threat and evil is represented, through projection, in the figure of scheming homosexuals. The resulting homophobia generates the image of Clay Shaw, a cartoon exaggeration of the decadent, sadistic homosexual, who is casually disloyal to his country and indifferent to the murder of his president.

In this paranoid vision, everything sinister gets loaded onto the figures of furtive plotters from Pentagon officials to David Ferrie. Political conspiracy and homosexuality spiral around each other in a (paranoid) pattern of guilt by association. Kennedy and Garrison become equally exaggerated visions of purity, decency, and integrity. Their obsession is not with sex but with truth. Stone's films are routinely about the exploits of men who combat the actions of evil, sexually sinister father-figures while women characters look on supportively, or in dismay. Gays become the central part of a figuration of paranoid fear and loathing that is (unfortunately) intimately tied to a profound sense of betrayal by one's country, one's government, and those covert forces that set a coup d'etat in motion.

Kennedy dies a hero and martyr in *JFK,* and Jim Garrison walks out of the courtroom into a field of dreams, hand in hand with wife and son, at film's conclusion. His is the good family to Shaw's, Bannister's, Lyndon Johnson's, and David Ferrie's corrupted ones. In this light, one of the most overdetermined lines in the entire film may well be male hustler Kevin Bacon's quip to Kevin Costner's Jim Garrison, "You don't know shit because you haven't been fucked in the ass."

Like the paradoxes of realism (and their exaggeration in surrealism) which require, for comprehension, holding two (incompatible) ideas in mind at once, an understanding of *JFK* requires holding the social and psychic together at once. A steady emphasis on psychoanalytic symptomatology may lose sight of mediating, social factors necessary to bring individual biography into the realm of social history. Vivid enough grounds exist for paranoia in terms of a global economy and alienation, social amnesia, and the loss of the historical not to require us to make a Freudian reduction to the pathologies of the nuclear family (the *reduction* to, not the *inclusion* of personal and familial mediations). As Anthony Wilden puts it, "It is not the women that men cannot 'satisfy'; WHAT MEN CANNOT SATISFY ARE THE MACHINES: technique, technology, production, performance."[26]

What Jim Garrison cannot satisfy are the machines of knowledge he himself sets in motion. He becomes caught up in the "technologies of knowledge" that bring multiple family romances (Clay Shaw's, John F. Kennedy's, his own) into play alongside a national tragedy and the shibboleth of domestic fascism.[27] At film's conclusion, as he walks into the distance with wife and children, it is quite possible to say that Jim Garrison still doesn't "know shit," but this may not be quite so true for us.

What we have learned, via these juxtapositions and their paradoxical injunctions, may be termed *JFK*'s oblique subject. Less obtuse than Barthes's "third meaning" and also less obvious than the traditional notion of a theme in classic realism, the oblique subject is that retrospective frame within which the past enters into a historical project aimed at a transformed future.[28] The oblique subject is that which *makes* action and event possible—in the strong, reflexive sense—retroactively. It constitutes the range of the possible without determining it once and for all. In *JFK,* the oblique subject reveals that glimmer of pattern, and meaning, that makes an altered future foreseeable through the process of reassembling fragments from the past in the moment of viewing (the story so far).[29] Paranoia, though, obscures this glimmer of a pattern for another, more arresting one. Fixation, fetishism, and paternal signifiers, on the one hand, social catastrophe, loss, and a compulsion to redress the ensuing void, on the other, both pivot around the figure of paranoia. Willing backward in order to move forward and wishing backward in order to regain in fantasy something lost in fact remain thoroughly in tension.

JFK struggles toward the vision of a transformative future, dragging with it, like the pianos, donkeys, priests, and other accoutrements of bourgeois family romance offered up in Buñuel and Dali's *Un Chien andalou,* a compulsion to repeat. In *JFK,* social and individual paranoia become fetters to a historical consciousness still in the process of coming into being.[30] The oblique subject reveals the symptoms of both potential transformation ("It's up to you") and paralysis (the fixation on that moment in Dallas, the mythic, well-nigh Norman Rockwell iconography cloaking the figure of Jim Garrison). *JFK*'s collage effects may be less than perfect; Oliver Stone's, and Garrison's, relation to the "paternal signifier" may betray distorting elements of both Freudian and social paranoia. The array of idealized and demonized identifications, and their paranoid motivations, sop up energies that might have otherwise turned to excess, to those magnitudes that exceed the text, which we can still glimpse imperfectly, in the content of this film's form.

The White Blind Spot and Film Form

Like *JFK* and *The Thin Blue Line, Who Killed Vincent Chin?* also rejuvenates the "who done it" suspense genre into the stuff of epistemological and political inquiry.[31] My claim is that viewing *Who Killed Vincent Chin?*—the most important political documentary of the 1980s—establishes a present moment of viewing in relation to what has gone before, in the film, such that our own present becomes past, or, more conventionally, prologue, to a future, outside the film, which, through this very process, we may bring into being.

The murder of Vincent Chin by Ronald Ebens, who apparently mistook Chin, a Chinese American, for Japanese and blamed him for the loss of his job in the auto industry, presents the traces of an absent, past, dead subject. It is one of many films that put at their center an absent subject. (*Hotel Terminus: The Life and Times of Klaus Barbie* [Marcel Ophuls, 1988], *Roger and Me* [Michael Moore, 1989], *Far from Poland* [Jill Godmilow, 1984], *He's Like* [John Goss, 1986], *Roses in December* [Ana Carringan and Bernard Stone, 1982], *Sari Red* [Pratibha Parmar, 1988], and *Waiting for Fidel* [Michael Rubbo, Canada, 1974] are a few others.) This tactical choice reinforces the sense of absence or loss in a productive way. The traces that remain (photographs, archival footage, testimony from others, letters, and other documents) lack the "grit" that could contain a life. To re-present a life, and, here, the murder of a now absent person, is clearly *not* to explain it. Multiple interpretations and meanings seem to explode outward.

Who Killed Vincent Chin?—with its superficial resemblance to an MTV visual style—poses the risk of sliding not toward a discourse of expository rigor but toward a flailing, wild hysteria. Through a collage of moods, tenses, voices, and sources, though, *Who Killed Vincent Chin?* achieves a distinct linkage between the general and particular. It evokes the general but does not name it. Writing of Bertolucci's *The Conformist,* Robert Burgoyne comments, "Moments of struggle are recoded in such a way that local, historical events acquire a secondary referent. The double-coding can be understood as a kind of shift in perspective, manifested through the temporal and point of view structure of the film."[32] Choy and Tajima adopt a different type of recoding from Bertolucci, involving much more radical shifts in spatial and temporal perspective.

Their approach also differs sharply from that of Oliver Stone. If *JFK* seeks to find a frame that, in retrospect, will prove a fascist conspiracy behind Kennedy's assassination at the risk of sliding into paranoia along the way, *Who Killed Vincent Chin?* invokes a retrospective framing of its murder precisely in terms of those mediations that paranoia denies or represses.

Like *JFK,* this film also begins with an implicit frame or embedded explanation built from a welter of fragments. Like *JFK,* this opening establishes an initial violence (murder) but also tacitly proposes the associative form that will allow us to interpret and understand this event. The opening succession of shots include: topless dancers describing their jobs; a policeman recounting how Robert Ebens and his stepson, Michael Nitz, beat Vincent Chin to death with a baseball bat in a McDonald's parking lot near the "Fancy Pants" bar; Mrs. Chin on the *Phil Donahue Show,* choking back tears at the loss of her son; neighbors of Ebens saying he and his family are "good people" and it (the murder) was "just one of those things [that] could happen to anyone"; Ronald Ebens, on a local TV show, denying that he has ever been a racist; men streaming out of a Detroit auto factory with a black quartet singing "Get a Job" on the soundtrack; shoppers at a mall listening to groups sing ditties about "their city," Detroit; a friend of Ebens describing his and Ebens's ethic, "You work hard and you play hard."

The collage of material continues: Mrs. Chin, against a background of traditional Chinese music, recounts the shocks, hardship, and racism she discovered in America such as being driven from the Detroit baseball stadium by (white) fans who refused to tolerate the presence of Asians; Ronald Ebens tells of his own courtship, marriage, and move to Detroit as the black quartet now croons "How sweet it is to be loved by you . . . "; and a group of auto workers go from work to a bar where they talk about how the Japanese sell cars cheaply by paying workers less for their labor. (This entire segment takes less than ten minutes of screen time.)

What this opening does is imply linkages that remain unstated. There is no voice-over commentary to orient us; scenes exhibit that "peculiar dispersal of documentary across a heterogeneous series of objects" without the guiding hand of a narrator.[33] Heterogeneity grows in intensity, signaling a double refusal: the film will neither play a surrealist game with the historically real (through an insistence on the irreconcilable strangeness of its juxtapositions) nor uphold realist epistemology (through the organizing unity of verbal commentary or continuity editing). To some extent Choy and Tajima's style undercuts my claims. Its rough-hewn, pounding, industrial tone may fit the scene of the crime, but it also enacts a commentary that aims at an emotional and moral level, which, once discharged, may run response to ground in a manner not entirely dissimilar from reality TV. The structure or form addressed here opens up other dimensions of response which are less easily discharged within the film's own frame.

Who Killed Vincent Chin? searches for a frame greater than a strict sequence of events with their presumably inexorable causality. The film seeks out a frame that cannot be named, at least not without the risk of making the apparently paranoid leap that dooms Jim Garrison in *JFK*. As Garrison himself says, "It's up to you" (ostensibly to the jury but with eyes aimed at the camera, and, by extension, us); *Who Killed Vincent Chin?* creates a structure that measures our response to such a challenge. It pivots, dialectically, between past and present, present and future, and among race, class, masculinity, sex, work, pleasure, and death. This pivoting upholds a tension between the local and the historical, the particular and the general, the need for abstract or conceptual knowledge and the desire to impart a knowledge rooted in the body. *Vincent Chin*'s investigative action embodies an epistemological genealogy that brings embodied and disembodied knowledge together without blending them into a unity.

Disembodied and embodied knowledge arise from different levels: from realist representations of aspects of the event, and from the interstices, the gaps, leaps, contradictions, and strange juxtapositions produced by a modernist assembly of these representations, respectively. If Vincent Chin's murder is to be understood in relation to the more abstract categories of class, race, and gender (already thoroughly embedded in the opening sequence), it must also be understood in all its specificity. And if it is to be understood in its specificity (down to the graphic descriptions of Eben's repeated blows to Chin's head), it must also be understood in the wider, more abstract frame that the film provides without naming, withholding the reifying alibi of a name from that which would otherwise lull us with the comfort of a false concreteness.

Even the actual murder is never spelled out at any one place in the film. Any realist description of the murder becomes part of the story (*histoire*) we construct from what the plot places before us. I resort to such a description here since my goal is not to replicate the form and structure of the film; the effect of this account, however, is quite distinct from the effect produced by the film.

The fatal exchange between Ebens and Chin as retroactively constructed by the viewer from the fragments offered in the text:

> Ron Ebens shouts encouragement to a black stripper, Starlene, at the "Fancy Pants" club, but Vincent Chin makes a derogatory comment. They start to argue with each other about the dancer's merits. Both are sitting along the bar on which Starlene dances.
>
> Ebens: "It's because of you little motherfuckers that I'm out of work."
>
> Chin: "Don't call me a fucker."
>
> Ebens: "I'm not sure if you're a big fucker or a little fucker."
>
> A fight ensues. Chin knocks Ebens down and leaves. Ebens tracks Chin down and beats him to death with multiple blows from a baseball bat while his stepson holds on to Chin.

This exchange suggests a complexity that the film's own tacit insistence on racist antipathy does not exhaust. A considerable amount of the argument's intensity seems to have arisen over the opposite evaluations of Starlene's performance. A fatal brew of sexism, machismo ("big" and "little" fuckers), *and* racism may have produced a result that none of these oppositional hierarchies would have produced alone.

The viewer also can bring together those comments by Ronald Ebens, dispersed through the film, that amount to his reflections on the fateful event and its consequences:

> I felt like a real jerk, being in jail, knowing the next day was Father's Day.
>
> If you want to construe that [his "motherfucker" remark] as a racial slur, I don't know how you could do that, but I didn't say that.
>
> It was like this was preordained to be, I guess; it just happened.

> It's not something you plan on happening, but it happens.
>
> I've never been a racist. And God is my witness, that's the truth.
>
> [Protest by the American Citizens for Justice] is selfish, a way for Asian Americans to get ahead, overcome their alleged plight, alleged because I know very few Asians, very few.

Ebens's statements represent a knowledge all too fully embodied, all too totally tied to immediate, personal experience and local context. Like Sartre's anti-Semite, Ebens wishes

> to be massive and impenetrable . . . not to change. Where, indeed, would change take [anti-Semites]? We have here a basic fear of oneself and of truth. What frightens them is not the content of truth, of which they have no conception, but the form itself of truth, that thing of indefinite approximation. . . . They do not want any acquired opinions; they want them to be innate.[34]

The shadow of paranoia seems to cloak "the bigot's reduction"—the segregation of Us from Them across the social imaginary—but the passionate urge to question and know, the addiction to an epistephilia that compels the paranoid's account of why They act as They do, vanishes from Ronald Ebens's world. If anything, we approach the failure to make an imaginative leap toward uncertainty and speculation at all. This leap catapults the social paranoid beyond the facts, details, and other minutia he or she collects as avidly as any bona fide historian (in Richard Hofstadter's view) and beyond the imaginative but unnamed leaps that *Who Killed Vincent Chin?* itself requires of its viewers. The paranoid leaps toward irreversible certainty, *Who Killed Vincent Chin?* toward indefinite approximation: resolution or redress are for us to bring into being, beyond the text.[35]

Ebens's refusal of the metaphorical dimension of language, his need to cling to the literalism of metonymy (of what is physically present rather than the alternatives that could replace it), fits more precisely with the profile of classic schizophrenia than paranoia (and again contrast radically with the metaphorical work of collage evident in the film as a whole). He who has admitted killing another man uses as his means of defense a *refusal to see* (to frame, to bracket, to contextualize) that *Who Killed Vincent Chin?* makes almost impossible for its viewers. For Ronald Ebens retrospection, willing backward, reinforces a profound sense of non-agency. Events took place in which he can no longer recognize himself as agent. "It was like this was preordained to be, I guess; it just happened."[36]

This may be Ebens's perspective, but it is clearly not the film's. Choy and Tajima take a position not of nostalgic passivity but of passionate revision. Ronald Ebens clings to the literal model of the chronicle, unwilling to make the leap beyond an ahistorical sense of destiny. The film, however, invites bold conjecture with every cut, every new juxtaposition, every shift and change of frame. Choy and Tajima reject the monad-centered, judicially required demand for *a guilty individual*. Unlike *El Chacal de Nahueltoro* (Miguel Littin, Chile, 1969) and *Death by Hanging* (Oshima Nagisa, Japan, 1968), Choy and Tajima take no interest (not even skeptical interest) in inculcating an acceptance of personal responsibility for crimes by those who commit them. Without letting Ebens off the hook, they avoid the sense of global conspiracy a paranoid view of racist violence might entail and the debilitating sense of victimization as an "ideological effect" of institutionalized bias that an Althusserian structuralism might produce.

The oblique subject brought into being by the viewer, by means of the collage principle at work here, clearly involves race, class, and gender, three words *not* spoken in the film itself but omnipresent in what the collage *shows* to be at work (in the space between shots and scenes). Willing backward, *nachträglichkeit,* means aiming toward a future state in which these terms achieve the full expressivity of embodied knowledge, where the meaning and effect of such terms are liberated from the chains of abstraction and implanted in the heart.

The *experience* of the text, then, is integral to grasping the content of the form. *Who Killed Vincent Chin?* proposes an alternative form of knowledge that may have recourse to abstractions such as "race" or "class" but that builds its knowledge from a return to the concrete, the felt and active experience of *making sense* of what we see and hear. A comment by Leslie Devereaux, intended for a different context (debates within anthropology), has application here:

> The conventions of scientific writing work against the portrayal of experience in favor of elicited systems of thought, and observed regularities of public behavior, usually reported *as* behavior, that is, with the emphasis on action rather than interaction, and prescription rather than contingency, which amounts to grave distortion of human actuality. In this rhetorical form it becomes hard not to render people homogenous and rule following [or breaking], no matter the disavowals we utter about this. Our scientized standards of evidence privilege speech over feeling and bodily sensation, which is assimilated to the personal. The personal, the putatively private, is an indistinct category of suspicious character.[37]

Who Killed Vincent Chin? circumvents the conventions of scientific writing, and of juridical procedure, moral judgment, and Marxist analysis. Feeling and bodily sensation occupy a central place in this alternative strategy of collage and retrospection. What concepts and abstractions arise do so by dint of passage through a more experiential domain, and the knowledge that ensues may well be of a different order.

The film's dynamic editing dedicates itself to bringing such a possibility into being for the viewer. The film overtly sustains that cry for justice which the judicial system has yet to hear. More obliquely, it presents as its subject a white racism that cannot speak its own name. White racism recognizes no name for itself insofar as it can be subsumed within the domain of what "was preordained to be."

Approximating the Marxist call to rise from the abstract to the concrete, and charged with the intensity Jameson associates with existential historicism where the past retains a "vital urgency," *Who Killed Vincent Chin?* approximates many aspects of George Simmel's model of a web of conflict, but without its implicit conservatism.[38] The oblique subject of race, class, and gender clearly constitutes the range of possible actions without determining them, but the question of agency itself remains problematic. Ebens's petty-bourgeois aspirations; his masculinist sense of pride and chauvinism; the reinforcement of friends; and work and social milieu (where, in one instance, people take turns bashing a Japanese car with a sledge hammer in a televised spectacle of frustration and anger) all clearly impinge on what happened. Choy and Tajima juxtapose these elements in ways we, if not Ebens, cannot fail to apprehend. It required all these factors, acting in concert, through the "medium" of Ebens, to achieve a result that in another time and place would be unthinkable.

Like contemporary notions of the divided and split subject, identity politics and shifting affinities, Simmel's conflict theory renders classic concepts of a binary class struggle chimerical. Where, then, does agency reside? Everywhere and nowhere. To place it *in* abstracted classes or monadic agents would reify; to place it in "what's preordained to be" would mystify. Instead, *Who Killed Vincent Chin?* situates agency within the web of conflict itself, in the space between, in the (invisible) frame for thought and action. Such a web consists of relationalities more than things. "Things happen," but less because of providence than because of shifting alignments of forces at strategic moments and critical points.

Such models call for the concept of a dominant—that specific concatenation of factors that transforms existing, conflictual relations decisively. The artistic dominant of strange juxtapositions or collage operates analogously to a political dominant of making sense, in a retroactive process of historical intentionalization, from those fragments of a global economy (transnational, postmodern, late capitalism) that we encounter in seemingly inchoate or random display. The randomness becomes an alibi for Ronald Ebens that *Who Killed Vincent Chin?* does not allow its viewer. Mrs. Chin's final, choking plea (after Ebens's ultimate acquittal) offers to us the possibility of social agency as both historical viewers and social actors. We are called upon to complete elsewhere "the story so far" begun by the film: "Please, all you good and honest people. . . ."

Dear America: The Desire in Men's Bodies

Dear America: Letters Home from Vietnam begins the slide away from the linkage of historical consciousness and transformative vision that the Gulf War text carries yet further.[39] And yet, it is a work of considerable power, capable, as many war-related films appear to be, of prompting favorable response across the political spectrum it appears simultaneously to transcend. Unlike the mix of arrested and transformative anger or passionate re-viewing that function, in *JFK* and *Who Killed Vincent Chin?* respectively, to locate the viewer within a charged political process, *Dear America* speaks in a voice of nostalgic (and fetishizing) humanism. Like the previous two works, it lacks a voice-over commentator who speaks on behalf of the film. Instead, a disparate array of visual source material (from "home movies" by soldiers in Vietnam to graphic titles announcing the number of American dead year by year), coupled to the voice-over narration of actual letters home from Vietnam soldiers by accomplished actors, builds from a mosaic of impressions the story *Dear America* seeks to tell.

This work, commissioned by Home Box Office and presented theatrically as well as on television, comes quite close to classic narrative form. A sense of closure and assumptions of individual agency bring the event back within the folds of a larger, narrative history. Not only is each letter like a short story, the letters fall into a pattern that tells a classic coming-of-age story. Like a number of Hollywood films, *Dear America* addresses a masculinity suspended at the brink of manhood.[40] It differs in this regard from works like *The Best Years of Our Lives* (William Wyler, 1946) or *Coming Home* (Hal Ashby, 1978) in turning away from the hardships of traumatized soldiers turned civilians.[41] The sense of conflict and contradiction is itself attenuated. *Dear America* does not explore the nature of war trauma, the politics of the Vietnam War, or the gulf between civilian and military as much as it strives to achieve healing and reconciliation by means of narrative form.

Dear America takes shape as a personal *bildunqsroman* orchestrated from the arrangement of letters home by numerous soldiers and rendered, thereby, into an allegory of national reconciliation. The emphasis is very emphatically on the personal and individual. What propels events on any larger scale seems to belong to that category of destiny that Ronald Ebens identifies in *Who Killed Vincent Chin?:* things just happen.

Like Ronald Ebens, these soldiers fail to understand why things happen. But they are also presented as the innocent mediums through which large, impersonal forces act (an innocence *Who Killed Vincent Chin?* refuses to grant). The problem of agency, of how to posit causal relations to the forces at work (unevenly, in contradiction, within a mode of production), becomes the trauma of events without agency, "the horror, the horror" of the modern event itself. *Dear America* dwells, with humanistic compassion, on the trauma such events pose to individuals who seek to retain the notion of subjecthood at the very moment when any sense of personal agency (or responsibility) vanishes. The conservative solution posed here lies in the transformation of global, historical power relations into personal, psychic trauma for which therapeutic remedies remain available.

This transcendental therapy depends on remembering the war within a personalist frame. Reminders of the larger forces, of destiny and the pain of history, add poignancy more than retrospective comprehension. Like the famous saga of World War II told by the *Victory at Sea* series (Henry Salomon, 1954), *Dear America* addresses those who have already lived the Vietnam War and do not seek new understanding, a re-vision of what they know, so much as commemoration, a way of making sense of what they do not yet understand (by framing, narrativizing, and compulsively repeating arrested memories as talismanic fetish). The images and rock music grafted onto the voice-over recitation of the letters call out, "Remember this." The juxtapositions seldom pose a perturbing strangeness or demand an active effort to make connections (sense) of what they show.

Even though a personalist frame prevails (without the paranoid dimensions of *JFK*), an undertow nonetheless disturbs the tone of reminiscence. These images and music remind us of the incommensurateness between the one and the many, the individual and the nation-state, the rhetoric of unity and the eulogy of loss, the claims of victory and the crises of (masculine) identity that war relentlessly presents. Repeated clips of General Westmoreland making informal morale-boosting visits among his troops, for example, could be juxtaposed with other statements, for other audiences, that urge us to re-frame and revise our understanding of his function in a larger though implicit frame. But even as presented, his stock responses to the fears and anxieties he encounters contribute to the undertow that permeates the personalist frame: the Father, he who bears the phallus most visibly, cannot console his sons, those who fear losing it most totally. His consolations and words of encouragement are not what these men want to hear: he cannot console when it is the missing voice of maternal comfort these men want to hear most of all. The film, however, will provide what the general cannot. It will offer us this full and final measure of redemption, and it is this offering that brings the film within the circle of conventional history and classic narrative form.

Compared to the more properly dialectical use of collage in *JFK* and *Who Killed Vincent Chin?*, *Dear America* moves closer to pastiche. But whereas Fredric Jameson characterizes pastiche as a postmodern tendency to recycle elements of past stories, styles, and histories in ways that drain them of affect, *Dear America* mixes pastiche (or a conservative mode of collage) with the affective force of traditional realism. What remains intact, despite the "dispersal" of the film itself across a heterogeneity of letters, places, times, and source material, is the individual person (the author of the letters that organize the film). (This form of dispersal is what the Gulf War text also manages to contain so impressively through the trope of the entire nation as a person.) Heterogeneity of source material (the collage of television news coverage, home movies, photographs, military footage, press conferences, graphic titles, and voice-over recitation) throws us all the more forcefully, not toward a means of giving figuration to an abstract web of conflict and power, but toward the individual psyche that remains, remarkably enough, intact at the center of this modern Babylon.

These letters provide our primary source of orientation toward the psychic maelstrom war engenders. Like many performative documentaries, *Dear America* underplays the referential aspect of its sounds and images. The images presented here most often act iconically to trigger generic types of memory ("patrol," "recreation," "arrival," "eating," etc.) rather than to specify a given time and place indexically. They give the viewer something to feel attached to rather than something in need of completion, something not yet fully brought into being. What this film stresses is a phatic link between letters and those who hear them, between what has happened and what needs to be done (not to transform the future but to suture up and heal the past).

Distinct from a sense of embodied *knowledge,* these voices convey a sense of embodied emotion that prefers consolation to knowledge. As compensation for the collapse of questions of magnitude into longings for redemption, *Dear America* offers vivid feeling tones of dislocation, male bonding, fear, trauma, anxiety, desperation, and bereavement.

These feelings are seldom more vivid than in their references to absence: the enemy and home are nowhere to be seen. What the home movies suggest, and the letters convey, is a profound desire to see what cannot be seen, and to be where one cannot be. Vietnam itself figures essentially as an absence, its people targets of distrust or, on occasion, charity, its culture unfathomed, and its language reduced to a handful of instrumental commands (of which the most reflexively compelling is *Didi mow*—Get out of here).

Rather than a compulsion to make images speak, to wrest from them the truth, *Dear America* sets out to find voices that might heal the breach in masculinity that war has ripped asunder.[42] What the film requires is a voice that will bring sound and image back into the unity from which they have fallen. The discovery of such a voice becomes the oblique subject of the film. What *Dear America* requires is reunification, a resolution to the traumatic crisis in masculinity produced by war. (Whether such trauma might affect Vietnamese soldiers is never considered by the film.) Discovering such a voice can occur only after the passage of time (the film was made over fifteen years after the end of the war). It is a nostalgic voice of mourning but not a retrospective one; it is engaged in wishful hindsight more than radical re-vision.

This unifying requirement is met in the final scene.[43] The final sequence presents us with: the voice of an actress reading the letter a mother left at the Vietnam War Memorial, the names of fallen soldiers inscribed on the memorial's black marble, a dissolve to superimposed photographic images of soldiers and other names, and the final image of a soldier (presumably the mother's son) upon which the camera zooms in until his face fills the frame and the mother concludes her moving letter:

> Jim told me how you died, for he was there and saw the helicopter crash. He told me how your jobs were like sitting ducks. They would send you men out to draw the enemy into the open and *then* they'd send in the big guns and planes to take over. He told me how after a while over there instead of a yellow streak the men got a mean streak down their backs. Each day the streak got bigger and the men became meaner. Everyone but you, Bill. He said how you stayed the same happy-go-lucky guy that you were when you arrived in Vietnam. And he said how you of all people should never have been the one to die. How lucky you were to have had him for a friend. And how lucky he was to have had you.
>
> They tell me that the letters that I write you and leave here at the memorial are waking up others to the fact that there is still much pain left from the Vietnam War. And this I know: I would have rather to have had you for twenty-one years and all the pain that goes with losing you than never to have had you at all.
>
> Mom.

Rather than serving to cast a judgment on the present, the past serves to effect a final, unconditional reconciliation. Between the image of the fallen son and the voice of the grieving mother, the film achieves a union that erases loss, pain, and social history. All the previous letters, *from* soldiers in Vietnam *to* those back on the home front, have prepared for this one letter of response, this voice *from home, from mother,* that makes incarnate the fantasy of the maternal voice as the enveloping, soothing, embracing voice of mother to child.

Kaja Silverman quotes a revealing passage from Michel Chion on this fantasy:

> In the beginning, in the uterine night, was the voice, that of the Mother. . . . One can image the voice of the Mother, which is woven around the child, and which originates from all points in space as her form enters and leaves the visual field, as a matrix of places to which we are tempted to give the name "umbilical net." A horrifying expression, since it evokes a cobweb—and in fact, this original vocal tie will remain ambivalent.[44]

Not the least of the ambivalence stems from the myth of total unity on the one hand and the derealization of all things masculine on the other.

This voice *dissolves* difference. It permeates the space necessary for identity (and opposition) within the imaginary realm which in turn prepares men for their positions of autonomy and independence within the symbolic order. But it is (often) a dissolution devotedly wished, as, for instance, in citizen Kane's nostalgic yearning for "something he lost." What the fantasy of the maternal balm dissolves is history and historical consciousness (the dialectic of separation and linkage among past, present, and future). Little wonder that the images of womb and cobweb lie so close together (and that Vietnam represented a "quagmire" our leaders so astutely avoided in the blitzkrieg victory against Iraq).

Traumatic experience, so corporeally registered in the terrors of war, threatens to annihilate body and self.[45] The maternal fantasy promises reconciliation, restoration, and redemption from whole cloth, from the myth of the eternal acoustic envelope that replaces the time and place of historical encounter. What better, more classic story of Oedipal restoration could one desire than this?—particularly if it means redeeming in fantasy lives already consumed by the forgotten history of a lost war.

Into the Gulf: The Technologies of Simulation

"Forget history." This could be the motto of the Gulf War text if historical consciousness means anything like the intentionalization of the future by the past proposed here. This is not to say there is no sense of history in the Gulf War coverage, only that it is not part of a project aimed at keeping the idea of "radical and Utopian transformation alive." In the historical folds of the Gulf War text time is on our side, but it is the non-dialectical time of a preordained teleology: what was manifest destiny for one generation of politicians is a new world order for another. Names change but the nation's mission and destiny do not.

Time once again becomes that seamless ribbon of temporal and spatial progression that describes classic realist narratives in which consistent, responsible characters move inexorably toward their final destiny and the resolution of the oft-told tale of "Once upon a time." A collective act of international redemption unfolds, with the United States as savior to a fallen world. Like the Invisible Hand that ensures the common good amid the chaos of the marketplace, America's role as leader of the free world establishes harmony amid the Babylon of lesser nations. Like an Amen chorus, the Gulf War text confirms this role. Like a fundamentalist sermon, it divides the world into Manichean halves: the children of light and children of darkness, leaders as prophets of redemption and leaders as fallen renegades. The Gulf War text's audience is but one remove from the messianic position of those leaders who act as agents of a greater cause. It is not a question of passive viewers and active leaders but of concentric circles of proximity to the invisible, intangible mission meant to absorb us all.

The Gulf War text, a composite text to be sure, is necessarily disjointed. The same organizational pattern of disparate sources and strange juxtapositions occurs but turned to different ends. The events treated clearly qualify for Hayden White's definition of the modern event, but the Gulf War text strives to belie White's claim that such events "do not lend themselves to explanation in terms of the categories underwritten by traditional humanism, which features the activity of rational or irrational but at any rate 'agents' conceived in some way to be *responsible* for their actions and the possibility of discriminating clearly between the causes of historical events and their effects over the long as well as the short run in relatively commonsensical ways."[46]

The collision of ads promoting the safety of Chrysler's cars with images of the mass destruction of Iraq's tanks and the juxtaposition of a rainbow coalition of men and women in shades of black, white, red, and yellow to celebrate the U.S. Armed Forces in a Boeing ad with footage of a "smart" bomb descending down the air shaft of military headquarters in Baghdad evoke no implicit frame, convey no embedded explanation opening onto a transformative historical consciousness. The commentary of reporters and anonymous touts neutralizes the potential for transformation such juxtapositions contain. Amid the ruins and debris of such unholy linkages, these guides to history-in-the-making persistently focus on the qualities and characters required by traditional humanism. (This is precisely what *Land without Bread* denies us, leaving its strange juxtapositions to rattle and disturb.) Neither ads nor networks "make" the news, these voices feign, only leaders and their subordinates can do that; the network news teams tirelessly assure us that agency remains alive and well.

This channeling effect in the midst of an extraordinary array of disparate levels and types of discourse enacts a classic, commonsense move: when confronted with conflicting or contradictory reports, eliminate those that might confound the (already) prevailing view. The result is to confirm a sense of unity, a social imaginary and social subjectivity without flaws or seams. Of one piece, this realm nonetheless bifurcates effortlessly into agents of evil and doers of good. Launched, like most classic tales, by an act of violence, and resolved by the restoration of equilibrium, the story of the Gulf War *takes* time, *takes* place, and *makes* sense by dint of the very form used to describe it.[47] It is a form that wills from sight evidence of disorder and artifice, the entirely unnatural clashes and dissonance, the remarkable disjunction of spectacle and banality that underpin the Manichean, melodramatic tale it has to tell.

Unlike *JFK*, where delirium flirts with paranoia, the delirium of the Gulf War text slides into the channels of consumption already laid out by the mode of production it epitomizes. (Reality TV is, of course, its next of kin, enacting on a quotidian level what the Gulf War text enacts as epic.) This text is in familiar company with spectacle. As spectacle, it contains fixations and arresting moments that might pose a threat to narrative progression within an economy of signs that gives pride of place to the act of consumption, even the consumption of horror, death, and history alongside ordinary commodities. Spectacle may be a form of historical arrest but it is also the fulfillment of a consumerist fantasy. The subjunctive and conditional moods that characterized *JFK* and *Who Killed Vincent Chin?*, and, to a lesser degree, *Dear America,* slide toward the iterative tense: given the teleological frame, the cascade of events can be reduced to a repetitive litany of America's march toward victory and the liberation of Kuwait made available for its viewing audience for immediate consumption.[48]

Rather than a compulsion to repeat which might be seen, as it is in *Dear America,* as an attempt to resolve or master the trauma of loss, this repetition of battles, bombs, and bromides operates not *beyond* the pleasure principle but wholly within it. Like Ronald Ebens, the Gulf War text can only reiterate the mantra of Destiny: "Make it so," as Captain Jean-Luc Picard would say aboard the Starship Enterprise. What follows are but iterations of that command in the instrumental language of military action and network coverage. Neither racism nor neo-imperialism intrude upon a consciousness reliant on metonymic iterations at the points where conceptual leaps to different frames and contradictory meanings might occur. No process of retrospective consciousness raising takes place on the part of the viewer as it does in *JFK* or *Who Killed Vincent Chin?* Stock phrases that could be unpacked and reframed to explore the transformation of the military-industrial complex into a media-business-government oligarchy, such as "We'll be right back after these messages," instead slide past in unexamined innocence.[49]

The concept of an oblique subject to the Gulf War text becomes quite dubious given how patently it wears its messages on its sleeve. Themes of nationalism, militarism, masculinism, and the construction of a social imaginary around patriotism and America's global mission abound. If there is something more oblique it may reside in how the melodramatic narrative of banality and spectacle implodes all questions of magnitude into the textually contained pleasures of vicarious experience. In its interminable but repetitive rhythms nothing exceeds the text. The historical referent remains, but it squares entirely with the signifieds of the text itself. (The sense of a referent produced by the text is a referent that matches, like a shadow, the signifiers of the story as told.)

Excess and history as an open-ended, transformative project fade from sight. The absorption of historical materialism, and of the material reality characterized by face-to-face encounter, may be the oblique subject of a text that is so reluctant to heed the demands of *habeas corpus.* All four of these texts clearly confront the psychic traumas posed by bodily injury or death, but only the Gulf War text addresses this issue by denying the existence of the damaged or destroyed body. Early on the Pentagon announced that this time, in contrast to the Vietnam War, it would not provide a "body count." The implications escaped attention, but this meant the dematerialization of the bodies of men at war (and women, who suffered their own, still unexamined trauma both as prisoners of war and as comrades in arms).

The Gulf War's General Schwarzkopf does not occupy the position of maternal consoler assigned to Vietnam's General Westmoreland in *Dear America.* Instead he presents himself with casual but ithyphallic assurance at podiums and before maps on which he can march and maneuver colorful signifiers of battles waged in what might as well have been distant galaxies. As removed from battle as the audience he addressed, the general underwrites the concept of war without bodies, battle without trauma, that promised to make this The Best War of Our Lives.

Bodies do abound in this report on the war, but they are the bodies-once-removed of Pentagon spokespeople, "behind the lines" generals, geriatric experts, and the press itself. It is TV's body that comes to replace that of the missing G.I. and the unseen enemy. (Television becomes the home away from home that erases the haunting sense of absence pervading *Dear America.*) One day, near the end of the war, Dan Rather, on prime-time news, guides us through an enemy bunker in liberated Kuwait City, inviting us to imagine with him the havoc gunners here might have caused to our troops as they poured across the beaches "just over there." Bernard Shaw and Peter Arnett report, live from Baghdad, the nightmarish effects of the early bombing runs on the city. Arthur Kent, with fighter planes ascending into the desert sky behind him, reports on the war he cannot see, controlled from command centers he cannot enter. Shot/countershot between anchorpeople in studios and reporters in the field replace the absent scene of bombardment, mayhem, and death. TV's body, in the guise of a living room appliance, reporter surrogates, and the text as simulacrum, occupies the space that would otherwise be available to historical actors. (In this sense, the Rodney King videotape reveals the battered body of the apparent "enemy" that the Gulf War text so insistently denies.)

TV's body presents one more iteration that contributes to the cancellation of history: it reiterates the Command/Control/Communication model (CCC) developed by the military to cope with, if not engender, the modern event. CCC operates in virtual time and space to yoke all elements into a single social imaginary. It depends on the hierarchical, Manichean (and often paranoid) melodrama of good and evil in which this war, like the Cold War it supersedes, unfolds. No sense of mediation remains outside the network that holds this sum of parts together. Inside, agency, responsibility, and subjectivity assume the positions the mission and destiny of the CCC system assigns. Outside is only Them, the fallen and dangerous ones, disembodied, demonized, dematerialized. Mediating the space between is the umbilical net spun by media representation. The maternal voice emanates from television's simulacrum of a body that is not one.[50]

Coda

We have moved from the urgent challenge of *JFK,* "It's up to you," and the impassioned "Please, all you good and honest people" of *Who Killed Vincent Chin?,* through the grieving acceptance, "I would have rather to have had you for twenty-one years and all the pain that goes with losing you than never to have had you at all," of *Dear America,* to the implosive and unreflexive *gerede* (empty talk) of the Gulf War text, "We'll be right back after these messages." Empty but embracing. This form of text evades, even mocks, Hayden White's assertion that the unrepresentability of the modern event has acquired its counterpart in the "story events" of a modernism that can render what happens "unsusceptible to historical explanation" and to "narrative representation."[51] *This* counterpart, the Gulf War text, gives every appearance of historical explanation and narrative representation. It adopts some of the collage-like trappings of modernism but none of its effect, none of its resistance to story telling as coherence and mastery.

Brian Henderson, discussing the work of Godard, compares collage to montage well: "In regard to overall form, [collage] seeks to bring out the internal relations of its pieces, whereas montage imposes a set of relations upon them and indeed collects or creates its pieces to fill out a preexisting plan."[52] The surface similarity of all four works in their pronounced heterogeneity of objects, sources, and codes does not extend to more fundamental levels of effect. The Gulf War text works to reduce the strange effects its form might induce through a mimicry of the military's Command/Control/Communication model (most masterfully in its substitution/displacement of the traumatized historical body with the soothing voice of television's own virtual body). *Dear America* is closer to the humanistic montage of classic Hollywood where a string of disparate scenes, actions, or events are yoked together by an underlying notion of process (here, represented as masculine crisis and consolation) that repeats trauma in order to master it. But *JFK* and *Who Killed Vincent Chin?,* each in its own way, dissolve event and agency away from their realist pillars without reducing them to nothingness. Centered around the absent but not repressed body of those who were the targets for the "accidents," the incomprehensibleness, of modern events, these two films leave social justice and historical explanation in suspension. *JFK* and *Who Killed Vincent Chin?* push their search for form into the border zone between realism and modernism occupied by collage.

Collage is less a process of "fleshing out" on the part of the text than "filling in" on the part of the viewer. The sense of partial knowledge and suspended closure, the sense of incompleteness and the need for retrospection, makes of the text what we must make of history: the site of an active, continuous struggle within representation to bring into being those radical and utopian transformations that exceed any text.

NOTES

1. Embodied Knowledge and the Politics of Location

1. Leslie Devereaux, "Cultures, Disciplines, Cinemas," Leslie Deveraux and Roger Hillman, eds., *Alternative Visions: Essays in Visual Anthropology, Cinema and Photography* (Berkeley: University of California Press, 1995).

2. Hayden White, *The Content of the Form* (Baltimore: Johns Hopkins University Press, 1987), 53.

3. Linda Williams, "Mirrors without Memories—Truth, History, and the New Documentary," *Film Quarterly* 46, no. 3 (Spring 1993): 17, 18.

4. Jean-François Lyotard, *Heidegger and "the Jews"* (Minneapolis: University of Minnesota Press, 1990), 26.

5. Trinh T. Minh-ha, *Woman, Native, Other* (Bloomington: Indiana University Press, 1989), 89.

6. Marianna Torgovnick, *Gone Primitive: Savage Intellects, Modern Lives* (Chicago: University of Chicago Press, 1990), 231.

7. Walter Benjamin, "Theses on the Philosophy of History," *Illuminations* (New York: Schocken, 1969), 255.

8. Rigoberta Menchu's *I, Rigorberta* and Cherríe Moraga's *Loving in the War Years* are excellent examples of written testimonials that parallel many of the preoccupations of Mallet's *Unfinished Diary*.

9. The intensity with which Hara seeks to retrieve a past, the obsession with its hold over him, and the ways in which his past has become someone else's (Miyuki's) present send up echoes of film noir. Hara's own relation to what he films (subjection, humility, debasement, and the concomitant need to control [mastery through repetition]) also has echoes of what Kaja Silverman terms "male masochism." She quotes Reik, ". . . in no case of masochism can the fact be overlooked that the suffering, discomfort, humiliation and disgrace are being shown and so to speak put on display . . . one feels induced to assume a constant connection between masochism and exhibitionism" (197).

Silverman links masochism to a crisis in masculinity where men no longer experience an imaginary relation of fullness and completeness to the phallus; they attempt to renegotiate this imaginary fullness through repetition of that which produced their trauma. The repetition also places them in (imagined) peril once more, as embodied, say, in the nightmarish qualities of film noir, or the literal nightmare of Fred Derry (Dana Andrews) in *The Best Years of Our Lives* (1946). Insightful and suggestive as this is, I am not sure I can locate the historical trauma at work in Hara (born 1945). Feminism itself might seem a candidate but this risks transposing a U.S.-based feminist critique to Japan and making insupportable assumptions about the social actor, Hara, as we see him in the film. Whether his trauma stands in for that of a larger male cohort as noir heros apparently do for returning G.I.s also remains unclear. I have reservations about shifting to a psychoanalytic plane when it is then so exceedingly difficult to return to a historical one. Silverman's work is exemplary in this regard; a comparable treatment of documentary issues has yet to be attempted. Kaja Silverman, *Male Subjectivity at the Margins* (New York: Routledge, 1992). See pp. 54–65 in particular.

10. Hara Kazuo, quoted in Laura Marks, "Naked Truths: Hara Kazuo's Iconoclastic Obsessions," *Independent* 15, no. 10 (1992): 26.

11. This conception of knowledge and wisdom is strongly indebted to Gregory Bateson. See, for example, his "Conscious Purpose versus Nature," *Steps to an Ecology of Mind* (New York: Ballantine, 1972).

12. Leslie Devereaux, "Cultures, Disciplines, Cinemas," *Alternative Visions* (Berkeley: University of California Press, 1995).

13. I have explored this question in two previous, related essays, "Questions of Magnitude," in John Corner, ed., *The Documentary and Mass Media* (London: Edward Arnold Publishers, 1986), 107–22, and "History, Myth and Narrative in Documentary," *Film Quarterly* 41, no. 1 (Fall 1987): 9–20.

14. Teresa de Lauretis, "Semiotics and Experience," *Alice Doesn't* (Bloomington: Indiana University Press, 1984), 182–83.

15. Ursula K. LeGuin, "Bryn Mawr Commencement Address (1986)," *Dancing at the Edge of the World* (New York: Harper and Row, 1989), 152.

16. Ursula LeGuin, "Bryn Mawr Commencement Address," 148, 149.

17. Nancy Chodorow, *The Reproduction of Mothering* (Berkeley: University of California Press, 1978), 169.

18. Teresa de Lauretis, "Semiotics and Experience," *Alice Doesn't* (Bloomington: Indiana University Press, 1984), 183.

2. The Trials and Tribulations of Rodney King

1. Quoted in Bill Carter, "Story Rights for Crimes Certainly Pay," *The New York Times,* June 19, 1992, D1.

2. See Peter Wollen, *Signs and Meaning in the Cinema* (Bloomington: Indiana University Press, 1972), for a useful discussion of Peirce's semiotics.

3. See, for example, his *The Evil Demon of Images* (Sydney: Power Institute Publications, 1988).

4. Some of the headlines to stories in *The New York Times* that followed this dramatic curve were: "Rodney King Testifies on Beating: 'I Was Just Trying to Stay Alive,'" March 10, 1993; "Rodney King Unsure on Beating Details," March 11, 1993; "A Video Image becomes Flesh," March 12, 1993; "U.S. Rests Its Case against Policemen Accused in Beating," March 16, 1993; "Blows Saved Rodney King's Life, Officer Testifies," March 25, 1993; "Los Angeles Prepares to Prevent Repeat of '92 Riots," March 30, 1993; "Jury in Police Beating Trial Hears a Stark Final Defense," April 10, 1993; "As Los Angeles Tenses for Verdict's Aftermath, Some Fear for Civil Rights," April 10, 1993; "An Edgy Los Angeles Awaits a Jury's Verdict," April 11, 1993; "Officers in Los Angeles Say They Feel Better Prepared for Unrest," April 12, 1993; "Trial-Induced Anxiety in Los Angeles," April 13, 1993; "2 of 4 Officers Found Guilty in Los Angeles Beating: Tension Eases as Residents Hail the Verdict," April 18, 1993; "Fear Subsides with Verdict, but Residents Remain Wary," April 19, 1993; "Experts See Little Room for Appeal in King Case," April 21, 1993; "Batons in the Jury Room: The Reaching of a Verdict," April 24, 1993.

5. Hayden White differentiates between a linguistic study of texts that attempts to adjudicate the proper and improper utilization of a given code, and a semiotic study of texts that bypasses the question of the referent to ask how certain meanings are produced "by the establishment of a mental set toward the world in which certain systems are privileged as necessary, even natural, ways of recognizing a 'meaning' in things and others are suppressed, ignored, or hidden in the very process of representing a world to consciousness." He continues, "This is to shift hermeneutic interest from the content of the texts being investigated to their formal properties . . . as a dynamic process of overt and covert code shifting by which a

specific subjectivity is called up and established in the reader, who is supposed to entertain this representation of the world as a realistic one in virtue of its congeniality to the imaginary relationship the subject bears to his own social and cultural situation." I find White's description generally accurate. It does not, however, take adequate account of sign systems based on indexical images such as photography, cinema, and video, where the remains of the referent persist to a far greater extent than in written languages. In these cases, the image as raw evidence and the effort to preserve it as a datum, or pearl, within an interpretive frame become a singular process of considerable importance. Hayden White, *The Content of the Form: Narrative Discourse and Historical Representation* (Baltimore: Johns Hopkins University Press, 1987), 192, 193.

6. The official name for these clubs is the PR-24 baton. The use of terminology to mask the brute reality of what this object is belongs to a larger pattern of one-dimensional operationalism that I discuss at greater length in relation to the testimony of defense witnesses.

7. Among these sources are Sgt. Stacey Koon, with Robert Deitz, *Presumed Guilty: The Tragedy of the Rodney King Affair* (Washington, D.C.: Regnery Gateway, 1992); Stephen Brill, "In Praise of Justice in Simi Valley," *The American Lawyer* 14, no. 5 (June 1992): 5–6; Roger Parloff, "Maybe the Jury Was Right," *The American Lawyer* 14, no. 5 (June 1992): 7, 78–80; *The American Lawyer* and Court TV co-production, *Video Trial Report:* California v. Powell: *A Defense against a Videotape,* 1, no. 4 (June 1992): 60-minute videotape; Court TV, *The "Rodney King" Case: What the Jury Saw in* California v. Powell (1992): 2-hour videotape. The videotapes are particularly valuable since they contain portions of the verbatim testimony by the officers themselves and by various witnesses.

8. A basic aspect of the defense, that Mr. King's traffic violations or other behavior constituted a felony, therefore warranting the prone position that Mr. King failed to assume, is passed over in the limited coverage of the trial I have reviewed. Sgt. Koon, in his account of the events, describes the traffic violations King committed as felony violations, but his description of speeding, running stop signs, ignoring stop lights, and perhaps other violations do not seem, singly, to be felonies. Even if they are felonies, having the suspect assume a prone position is treated as a mandatory part of police procedure even though not all felons are so treated. It is also not clear which of these violations, other than speeding and failing to stop for the CHP, were clearly known to the officers at the time of the arrest. Why Mr. King was not given a traffic citation (as well as a DUI breath test) is not at all clear. Sgt. Koon and other defense witnesses tell their stories as though Mr. King were definitely a felony suspect and a threat to their safety from the very outset. (This is done partly through guilt by association in which the case is made that high-speed pursuits almost always involve more than speeding and usually involve unrelated felonies. When it later turned out that Rodney King was on parole and would have been sent back to prison for another felony violation, this argument seemed all the more convincing, but this is reasoning backward and irrelevant.) Without more concrete detail it is difficult to tell if this is a reasonable conclusion that would be applied to any driver who did what Mr. King allegedly did, or if this conclusion, from which so much of the event follows, is not itself an indication of racially motivated assumptions.

9. Sgt. Stacey Koon, *Presumed Guilty,* 30.

10. Koon, *Presumed Guilty,* 32.

11. Koon, *Presumed Guilty,* 31. Further citations from Koon's book are given as page numbers in the text.

Of course, were Mr. King white and in sports clothing, other conclusions might have been that he had the torso of an athlete or a body builder. A large, black male, confronted late at night, however, prompts the conclusion that this particular evidence, inscribed in the very bulk of Mr. King's body, identifies him as an ex-convict.

At another point, however, Koon does resort to a sports metaphor. He claims that Rodney King assumed a "cocked" position, like "a football lineman getting in position to blitz an opposing tackle" (32). This analogy presents itself to Koon even though King's "gibberish" and failure to follow orders might also suggest that he is far too disoriented to assume any tactically significant position, let alone act with the precision of a blitzing lineman.

12. My own narrative summation of this aspect of the trial (based on the [condensed] videotape recordings of the trial and Sgt. Koon's own book) is a classical narrative in its own structure. For that very reason, it is a distortion of how such narratives get constructed during a trial. Neither a witness nor a lawyer may "tell a story" from beginning to end during the argumentative portion of a trial (at the beginning and end statements or summations by the lawyers that do so are permissible, but such statements are impermissible during the middle, as witnesses and other sources of evidence are introduced).

All narrative accounts must develop through the classic question-and-answer, call-and-response form enacted between lawyer and witness. The jury, and spectator, must then construct the story—a coherent, chronological, causally linked series of actions, motivations, events, and effects—retrospectively. This task resembles the work of drawing a single meaning from a collage structure. It also resembles the derivation of meaning from a mixture of theater (calculated performances, strategies of deference and resistance within the *form* of testimony and cross-examination); everyday conversation (question/answer, the assembly of an overall impression from fragments modified by protocols and institutional constraints) and the confessional (the dynamics of attempting to extract a truth of which the subject may be unaware, the effort to offer rewards of salvation, or a clean conscience, in exchange for the truth, the role of lawyer as confessor, using interrogatories to extract this truth that no one person ever fully contains). For the jury and spectator, the end result is strongly retro-spective, and it is marked by a very sharp distinction between the *syuzhet,* or plot—the actual sequence in which events become revealed through testimony—and *fabula,* or story—the whole story or "whole truth" in which chronology yields to causality, motivations become assigned, effects measured, and responsibility or guilt determined. For further reflections on the peculiar form of narrative embodied in court trials, see James Clifford, "Identity in Mashpee," *Predicaments of Culture: Twentieth-Century Ethnography, Literature, and Art* (Cambridge: Harvard University Press, 1988).

13. Rodney King apparently had a blood/alcohol level of approximately .19 at the time of his arrest when the legal limit is .08. This is based on the level obtained several hours later during hospital tests.

14. In narrating the sequence of events that occurred that night, Sgt. Koon argued that he followed the prescribed policy of escalating and de-escalating in the use of force. He explains how he went through the following series of attempts to gain control: (1) physical presence (intimidation), (2) verbalization (commands), (3) "swarming" King (when four officers tried, unsuccessfully, to wrestle him to the ground and handcuff him), (4) use of the TASER (twice), (5) baton blows (aimed at his torso and limbs), (6) baton blows (aimed at his ankle, knee, and elbow joints). This, the point of no return beyond which lies only "deadly force" (the choke hold, baton blows to the head, spine, or groin, or the gun) was the point at which King

was finally handcuffed. By turning to this level of empirical detail, and by hinging police response to King's alleged control of the situation, larger contextual issues were removed from the jury's overt consideration, especially when the prosecution found no effective means of introducing them.

15. *The "Rodney King" Case: What the Jury Saw* videotape.

16. For further discussion of punctuation as a semiotic category, see Gregory Bateson, "The Logical Categories of Learning and Communication," *Steps to an Ecology of Mind* (New York: Ballantine, 1972).

17. Roland Barthes, "Diderot, Brecht, Eisenstein," *Image, Music, Text* (New York: Hill and Wang, 1977), 73–74.

18. Herbert Marcuse, *One-Dimensional Man: Studies in the Ideology of Advanced Industrial Struggle* (Boston: Beacon Press, 1964).

19. These comments are transcribed from *Video Trial Report:* California v. Powell and from *What the Jury Saw.*

20. *Video Trial Reports* videotape. In *Presumed Guilty,* Koon refers to this same moment, "At minute 3.36.12 on the tape, it clears and shows the officers standing back. They are evaluating the effect of their blows, as they had been trained to do. This explained to the jury the pulsating use of force, the moving in and hitting, then moving back to assess. It showed them that the officers weren't casually taking turns hitting the suspect, but carefully following policies, procedures, and training" (183).

21. *Video Trial Reports* videotape. In Koon's reply Briseno's role as active agent drops out. He sees a "stomping motion" but not the individual who produced it. This perception of actions without agents blocks any attempt to examine motive or intention. We enter instead a world of robotic forces and cybernetic feedback loops in which police officers become "black boxes" that process and respond to informational input with physical output based on training in specific procedures.

In his book, Sgt. Koon continues this use of subjectless language in which "stomping motions" are "applied" but individuals no longer appear as agents. He refers to a videotape of Rodney King during an interview after his release from police custody. Koon notes, "There was no indication that the fingers, which are easily broken, had suffered any trauma, much less been power-stroked with a metal baton" (157). The passive voice ("had been power-stroked"), together with the choice of "power-stroke" rather than "smashed," "hit with full force," or other terms less likely to evoke the precision, dexterity, and perhaps grace of an athlete's swing (itself free from the intent to cause harm), and the use of "baton" for a two-foot length of galvanized steel pipe, all serve to evacuate the action of human agency and violent intent. It was not Powell or Wind who beat Rodney King; it was a police protocol for which these men were but the means of application.

22. *Video Trial Reports* videotape.

23. All Powell's statements are from *Video Trial Reports* videotape.

24. *The "Rodney King" Case: What the Jury Saw* videotape.

25. Prosecutor Terry White often challenged defense witnesses by expressing incredulity when he did not get the answers he wanted. He asked Officer Powell, for example, a series of questions to demonstrate that Powell's remark that a domestic incident involving an African American household earlier that night had been "right out of *Gorillas in the Mist*" was racially motivated. He clearly hoped to imply a similar motivation in the beating of Rodney King. But White's persistent questioning never elicited the admission he sought. Officer Powell continuously denied what White suggested. White's questions may have begun to seem like badgering to the jury. In the condensed version of the trial, *The "Rodney King" Case: What the*

Jury Saw, White devotes over fifteen separate questions to this one remark. He never corners Powell successfully.

> *White:* Now this call that involved African Americans, was it in a jungle?
> *Powell:* In a what?
> *White:* A jungle.
> *Powell:* No.
> *White:* Was it at the zoo?
> *Powell:* No.
> *White:* Were there any gorillas around?
> *Powell:* No.
> *White:* This is a movie, *Gorillas in the Mist,* is that correct?
> *Powell:* Yes.
> *White:* Was there any wildlife around at all, during this call?
> *Powell:* Not that I saw.
> *White:* Other than these individuals who were African Americans, is that correct?
> *Powell:* No, I wouldn't call them wildlife.

The questioning continues but Prosecutor White fails to extract any damaging admissions from Officer Powell. White's questions, by baiting Powell, allow him to avoid the bait with yes/no answers rather than compelling him to explain his own remark.

26. Suzanne Espinosa, "Inside LAPD—Violence and Survival on the Beat," *San Francisco Chronicle* (June 1, 1992): A1, 4. Ms. Espinosa minimizes overt racism as an issue, describing her informants' attitudes as centered on questions of respect and control primarily. The bulk of her informants, however, are described as members of minority groups, who, perhaps understandably, present distinct problems for minority groups who regard the police as an army of occupation. Espinosa also does not pursue what seems to be the other key underlying factor: the machismo that makes the dynamic of intimidation and deference such a crucial measure of personal success as a cop. Justified by stories of cops killed because they acted too leniently or trustingly, this "king of the mountain" mentality becomes self-perpetuating at the same time, particularly when the citizens cops confront share a similar ideology of masculine identity.

27. The prosecution, too, sought to present the videotape as raw evidence when it, in fact, confirmed preexisting assumptions and the interpretive frame these assumptions generated. The prosecution chose to accept the same general interpretive frame as the defense. Its intent, though, was to show that these four officers exceeded procedural limits and acted with the intent to cause harm rather than effect an arrest. Here, an expert witness for the prosecution, LAPD Commander Michael Bostick, locates the exact moment when the beating of Rodney King became excessive and therefore criminal:

> *Bostick:* "Stop the video there." (The tape is at 3.43.22. Bostick must instruct Prosecutor White, who controls the playback of the videotape, while he stands in front of a monitor.)
> "Back up a couple of frames." (The video has advanced further, to 3.45.15, and is then reversed.)
> "Stop right there. [3.40.01.] Go forward, slowly, a couple of frames." (The tape advances to 3.40.15. The videotape report of the trial makes a quick dissolve to a later point in the exercise; the counter is now at 3.43.07.)
> "Back up about two or three frames." (The tape goes back to 3.42.22.)
> "Little bit more." (The tape goes back further.)

"Right here." (The counter shows 3.42.20.)

"In my opinion . . . from this point forward, based on my understanding and my viewing of this videotape, and my viewing of the police reports, the sergeant's log, and the Singers' statements, I believe, from this point forward, it is outside the policy of the Los Angeles Police Department."

Video Trial Reports videotape. The quick dissolve, or edit, in the middle of this passage suggests it may have been even more tedious, only increasing the likelihood that this attempt to fix the instant at which excessive force began backfired. The other videotape, *The "Rodney King" Case: What the Jury Saw,* also effects an invisible edit but does so to allow Commander Bostick to move from his first request to stop, at 3.43.22, to his final determination of where excessive force began, at 3.42.20, in one fell swoop. These two documentary reports of the trial overlay different interpretations, with different degrees of impact, through the contextualizing commentary and editing techniques used to report Bostick's testimony. The attempt to discover the pearl of truth that interpretive procedure itself creates could not be more plain. The videotape's impact, its indexical whammy, depends, though, on rawness, on the sense that what it shows is self-evident, in need of no interpretation. In this instance the prosecution mimics the interpretive mode favored by the defense, giving the impression that what we see is not self-evident, that experts, utilizing close analysis and procedural knowledge, can precisely identify the (invisible) boundary between policy and excessiveness. Such testimony may have undercut the prosecution's own, overconfident position that interpretation was unnecessary.

28. In his book *The Content of the Form,* Hayden White asserts that the content of a given discourse *is* its form as much as whatever information it carries and that to change the form is to change the meaning assigned this information if not the information itself ("The Question of Narrative in Contemporary Historical Theory," 42). This somewhat familiar point in film criticism has taken longer to penetrate the realms in which truth claims have long held sway such as historiography, science, or the law. Nonetheless, White offers a succinct description of what the ideological aspect of a text is: "specifically those 'metalinguistic' gestures by which [the text] substitutes another sign system for the putatatively extralinguistic referent about which it pretends to speak or of which it pretends to be a straightforward, objective, or value-free description." My argument here is that the "other sign system" includes the meanings assigned to the Holliday videotape that are meant to represent it as raw evidence, as duplicating properties of the extralinguistic referent, or as the actual event itself. Hayden White, "The Context in the Text: Method and Ideology in Intellectual History," *The Content of the Form* (Baltimore: Johns Hopkins University Press, 1987), 192.

29. The appearance of logic often derives from faulty syllogisms such as Sgt. Koon's conclusion that King was an ex-con because he was "buffed out" (heavily muscled). The thinking is: "Ex-cons are often buffed out; this man is buffed out; therefore, this man is an ex-con." This is faulty logic equivalent to saying, "Communists question authority; this man questions authority; therefore, this man is a Communist." What helps make it stick is the claim that "street smarts" support the conclusion. (Being buffed out is presumably more likely to signify a criminal record than athletic ability among the people Sgt. Koon encounters in the line of duty.)

This opens up the highly loaded issue of what I call the "algebra of probability," which forcefully classifies individuals according to statistical likelihoods that function both as stereotyping and as a form of tacit knowledge. (The origins of this as an *algebra,* a formal and socially shared body of knowledge, may derive from Malthusian theory on populations; when combined with power and hierarchy, such an algebra allows for the wholesale treatment of groups on the basis of predetermined characteristics.) The greatest value to this algebra comes from the ways in which "street smarts" plays an operationally useful function; the greatest danger from its proximity to guilt by association, stereotyping, and the elimination of due process.

30. Patricia Greenfield and Paul Kibbey, "Picture Imperfect," *The New York Times* (April 1, 1993): A15. Who counts as an expert is also at issue here. Ms. Greenfield is described as a professor of psychology and Mr. Kibbey as "a second-degree black belt in aikido." Neither is described as having any special expertise in cultural study, semiotics, hermeneutics, film and video study, or the law. This would be laughable were it not printed as the opinion of experts alongside government officials, noted columnists, and civic leaders.

31. Philip M. Gollner, "Batons in the Jury Room," *The New York Times* (April 24, 1993): 9.

32. I refer to Lawrence Kasdan's film *Grand Canyon* (1991), in which a white motorist strays from the L.A. freeways, gets lost in an area strikingly similar to South Central Los Angeles, faces certain attack by a gang of black males, and is rescued from this terrifying predicament by the "good black," tow-truck driver Danny Glover. After many complications, misunderstandings, and earnest efforts to bridge social, class, and racial chasms, the main characters celebrate a newfound commonality as they gaze at the wonder of nature from the rim of the Grand Canyon.

33. For an extremely instructive discussion of the continuities among television, freeways, and shopping malls, see Margaret Morse, "An Ontology of Everyday Distraction: The Freeway, the Mall and Television," in Patricia Mellencamp, ed., *Logics of Television* (Bloomington: Indiana University Press, 1991).

34. The hidden biases addressed by the question "What do you expect?" receives remarkable treatment in Anna Deavere Smith's one-woman play, *Twilight: Los Angeles, 1992*. Presented at the Mark Taper Forum in downtown Los Angeles, within a stone's throw of city hall and the federal courtrooms, the play consists of verbatim, but edited and carefully juxtaposed, interviews with twenty-six of the nearly 150 people she interviewed, ranging from former Chief of Police Daryl Gates to founder of Mothers Reclaiming Our Children, Theresa Allison, and from an anonymous (white) talent agent to the Park family, Korean shopkeepers. One of the most memorable of these portrayals is of "Maria," the only juror in the second, federal trial to grant an extended interview on the jury's deliberations.

What "Maria" (a pseudonym) reveals is an extraordinary process that seems to have very little to do with issues of evidence and argument. She describes how the first days of deliberation circled around and around. Jurors claimed they were tired and wanted to retire to their hotel in mid-afternoon. Jurors broke out in spontaneous eruptions of animosity for one another. Jurors squirmed to live up to or deny the stereotypical images they imagined their peers might have of them. One wealthy white woman urges anyone who might write a book about their experience not to mention anything personal about herself and then proceeded to divulge a torrent of confidences about her family life. One juror, a black male, came down with a severe case of hives and had to be taken to a hospital.

These dynamics are what "Maria" calls the jury's "AA meeting." It was not until emotional tensions that lingered below the surface were released that the jury could address the evidence and arguments themselves. As long as jury members acted out but did not acknowledge their own feelings of white guilt, racism, classism, and so on, "Maria" suggests, these unacknowledged (repressed) feelings dominated their interactions. Once these feelings were acknowledged, they no longer had to be acted out. They could be put aside.

This revelation complicates many of the arguments made here which assume an oversimplified, rational process of jury deliberation. Such deliberations have an entirely different style from the public part of the trial. They aim for consensus, not adversarial point/counterpoint. They are dialogical and free form in ways that court testimony is not. They are confidential and need not be explained, whereas the prosecution and defense make their arguments publicly and take considerable effort to explain the logic of their position. For additional comments on jury deliberations as a vestige of oral culture in the midst of a legal system that reflects the "logic of literacy," see James Clifford, *The Predicaments of Culture* (Cambridge: Harvard University Press, 1988), 328–29.

35. *The "Rodney King" Case: What the Jury Saw* videotape. This statement has been, like the rest of the trial, edited down to a shorter length by the producers of the two-hour tape. The statement transcribed here is the entirety of Michael Stone's summation as it is presented in the *What the Jury Saw* videotape.

36. Prosecutor Terry White's own summation was more a display of indignation than rhetoric. At one point he steps from the podium to point an accusing finger at Officer Powell. The judge must order him back to the podium, but not before White may have impressed the jury with his own abusive "attack" on the unsuspecting Powell. Almost certainly a calculated ploy, it seemed, like the rest of the prosecution's case, to assume the guilt that it was required to prove beyond a reasonable doubt. If nothing else, the defense succeeded precisely in establishing just such doubts.

37. Parloff, "Maybe the Jury Was Right," 79.

38. Koon, *Presumed Guilty,* 137.

39. Koon, *Presumed Guilty,* 139–40.

40. Koon, *Presumed Guilty,* 144.

41. Louis Althusser, "Ideology and Ideological State Apparatuses," *Lenin and Philosophy and Other Essays* (New York: Monthly Review Press, 1971), 127–86.

42. Koon, *Presumed Guilty,* 22–23.

43. Mike Davis, *L.A. Was Just the Beginning* (Westfield, New Jersey: Open Magazine Pamphlet Series, 1992), 5.

44. Davis, *L.A. Was Just the Beginning,* 7.

45. Davis, *L.A. Was Just the Beginning,* 7.

46. Fredric Jameson, *Postmodernism* (Durham: Duke University Press, 1991), especially pp. 38–45. Jameson highlights the Bonaventure's architecture of simulation that reflects back the surrounding city, disguises its own portals and entrances, and then offers up, within its hermetic and disorienting interior, emblems and tokens of movement proper (elevators and escalators). He then comments, "this alarming disjunction between the body and its built environment . . . can itself stand as the symbol and analogon of that even sharper dilemma which is the incapacity of our minds, at least at present, to map the great global multinational and decentered communicational network in which we find ourselves caught as individual subjects" (44). The architecture works all too well, on Jameson: He reads its effect with a defeatist tone, or with the pragmatism of someone who admits to a lack of maps for the global economy. In this reading Jameson misses the uncanny parallel between buildings like the Bonaventure and the smaller but similar spaces of gay culture: bars that reflect back the surrounding environment, disguise their linkage with it, and offer a disorienting, disjointed simulation of an alternative future within. (The parallel suggests how form does not yield a singular content when contextual frames are taken into account.)

Jameson also reads buildings like the Bonaventure far too much on their own terms, or those of the world traveler/tourist, rather than the dispossessed and displaced from whose perspective Mike Davis writes in *City of Quartz* (New York:

Random House, 1992, pp. 228–40, for example). From this perspective, the Bonaventure exhibits none of the playfulness or alterity of gay bars but plenty of the arrogance and willfulness of a world order that is anything but unmappable to the dispossessed. The politics of spatial segregation make maps far less necessary than transport.

3. At the Limits of Reality (TV)

1. Special thanks to Jane Gaines for offering an extended critique to a previous draft of this chapter.

2. Walter Benjamin, *Illuminations* (New York: Schocken, 1969), 220.

3. I have not provided the dates for the episodes from which these epigraphs are taken. Such detail would promote a spurious sense of specificity when what is at issue is the loss of a temporal dimension into a perpetual "now." This perpetual "now" clearly relates to Raymond Williams's discussion of flow as the central characteristic of television in *Television Technology and Cultural Form* (New York: Schocken, 1974). A less essentialist, more historically specific discussion of flow, clearly pertinent to my analysis here, is Rick Altman, "Television/Sound," in Tania Modleski, ed., *Studies in Entertainment* (Bloomington: Indiana University Press, 1986).

4. Extensive interest in the nature and function of existing social institutions, self-consciousness about the story-telling and interpretative process itself, openness to the possibility of evidential discrepancies, recourse to complex reasoning, and an acknowledgment of possible indeterminacies seldom comes into play. These absences help define the ideological reduction as such even though reality TV shares with much politically reflexive work a heightened sense of the constructedness of representations and frequently calls attention to its own devices, laying them bare in the parlance of Russian formalism. It does so, however, within an undisturbed framework of power and control that remains consistently attached to the narrating agency (the program or network).

5. See chapter 4, "The Ethnographer's Tale," for a further discussion of nausea and cultural norms.

6. I discuss these modes in considerable detail in *Representing Reality* (Bloomington: Indiana University Press, 1991). My purpose here is less to survey the actual modes and more to highlight the basic characteristics of documentary representation in order to compare and contrast them with reality TV's mode of representation. These characteristics are also discussed at length in *Representing Reality* in the three chapters grouped under the heading "Documentary: A Fiction (Un)Like Any Other."

7. Vivian Sobchack, "Inscribing Ethical Space: Ten Propositions on Death, Representation, and Documentary," *Quarterly Review of Film Studies* (Fall 1984): 287. Adopting a similar sense of narrative containment to the one developed here, Sobchack also notes, "It is in our cinematic fictions that 'sudden,' 'discontinuous,' 'violent,' 'inappropriate,' and 'atrocious' deaths find their current representation. Safely contained by narrative, in iconic and symbolic signs and structures, they titillate and offer a mediated view which softens their threat and real ferocity. Our documentary films, on the other hand, avoid the representation of death. Indexical in code and function, they observe the social taboos surrounding 'real' death and generally avoid reference to it" (286). I do not think the avoidance of death in documentary is as pronounced as she argues (to me it is a fundamental, recurring theme), but I would only point to the Rodney King videotape as evidence of the threat and ferocity that narrative contains. (How the defense lawyers followed such

a containment strategy in the first trial of the four LAPD officers is examined in the previous chapter.)

8. The concept of magnitude receives extended discussion in chapter 8 of *Representing Reality,* "Representing the Body: Questions of Meaning and Magnitude." It is defined there as "a tension between the representation and the represented as experienced by the viewer" (232).

9. Network news refers to more ephemeral items (sports scores, Olympics results, stock market data) when it can do so briefly and to unusual occurrences when it can do so dramatically (rocket launches in Florida, famine in Africa, "riots" in Los Angeles, and so on).

News of the nation-state need not submit to a visual imperative: attention-grabbing images are less crucial than instant coverage and immediate placement within a larger, continuing story such as the state of the economy or America's commitment to democracy around the world. For example, the woeful lack of dramatic images did nothing to deter the networks from providing endless coverage of an unseen Gulf War waged in the name of national security, Kuwait's liberation from tyranny, and a new world order for all. This was news that could still be covered as a dramatic battle between the benevolent father, President Bush, and the evil tyrant, Saddam Hussein.

By contrast, the decay and ruin of inner-city schools in America receives no mention on the news. Though visually dramatic, it does not appear to qualify as ephemeral or unusual and its larger story—the economic decline of America, the widening gulf between rich and poor, and the racist practices of geopolitical apartheid achieved with zoning, school districting, bank redlining, and police patrols—has not begun to be told on network news.

10. Some basic aspects of television news are covered in Bill Nichols, *Ideology and the Image* (Bloomington: Indiana University Press, 1981) and in William Gibson, "Network News: Elements of a Theory," *Social Text* no. 3 (Fall 1980): 88–111. Others have since offered elaborations on these concepts, including Peter Dahlgren, "Making Sense of TV News: An Ethnographic Perspective," *Working Papers in Communications* (Montreal: Graduate Program in Communications, McGill University, 1983); Margaret Morse, "Talk, Talk, Talk," *Screen,* 26, no. 2 (1985): 2–15; Elayne Rapping, *The Looking Glass World of Nonfiction TV* (Boston: South End, 1987); and Robert Stam, "Television News and Its Spectator," *Regarding Television,* E. Ann Kaplan, ed. (Frederick, Md.: University Publications of America, 1983), 23–43.

11. The appeal of reality TV approximates that of snuff movies, but tailored to the codes of taste required by prime-time broadcasting. The sober-minded trappings of respectable hosts and corporate sponsors, of documentary details and eyewitness reports, successfully deflect anger away from this perverse mode of production itself, allowing reality TV shows to prompt a discharge of anger and amazement at people who can be so extraordinary. "How could this happen?" we ask of what we see rather than of what produces what we see.

12. This format has a ring of the familiar to it not only as a primal recipe for spectacle or for its own banality. It also cannibalizes many of the melodramatic elements of the morality plays of early films such as Edwin S. Porter's *The Life of an American Fireman* (1902) and *The Great Train Robbery* (1903); Cecil Hepworth's *Rescued by Rover* (1905); or D. W. Griffith's *A Corner in Wheat* (1909), *The Lonely Villa* (1909), *The Lonedale Operator* (1911), and *The Musketeers of Pig Alley* (1912). Characters are quickly sketched out in stereotypic fashion, playing roles that frequently recapitulate those of the nuclear family: strong and benevolent patriarchs, earnest sons and respectful suitors, devious rivals and underhanded villains, honorable but vulnerable women, corrupted women of the night, innocent children, and devoted

mothers. Conflict centers around the struggle between good and evil, between virtuous Abels and immoral Cains, in domestic wars on drugs, robbery, theft, kidnapping, murder, gambling, and cruel confidence games.

Reality TV, however, absorbs melodrama, like documentary, perversely. Its purposes may still allow us to think of these forms in terms of class (they both speak to the precariousness of a world order when perceived from a middle-class point of view), but seldom in terms of domestic drama, the affective domain of women's experience, the maternal dilemma imposed on women of choosing either self-fulfillment or sacrifice, or in terms of the use of stylistic excess to draw our attention to the very force of repression itself.

13. See Raymond Fielding, *The American Newsreel: 1911–1967* (Norman: University of Oklahoma Press, 1972), for a useful account of the blurred boundaries and social purposes of early news reporting. During the Spanish-American War, the Battle of Santiago Bay, for example, was reenacted on movie lots more than once, in one case using cutout photographs of the actual warships.

14. The reference here is to Hayden White's *Metahistory,* in which he argues that historiographic writing undergoes prefiguration as its authors opt for various modes of narrative representation. These choices then establish the moral tone of historical accounts that use reference to "what happened" in a sort of *trompe d'oeil* move in which it now seems that the historical world itself has authorized this particular tone, this particular understanding of history. Reality TV, since it does not offer narratives on the level of historiography, also does not choose among prefigurative options. Its function and effect rely on its implosive quality: it does not so much account for the historical world as subsume it into a world of its own.

15. Tania Modleski, "The Rhythms of Reception: Daytime Television and Women's Work," in E. Ann Kaplan, ed., *Regarding Television* (Frederick, MD: University Publications of America, 1983), 74.

16. "How to" shows are another genre, testing another boundary. They, too, substitute vicarious participation for face-to-face encounter but also allow for viewers to "follow along," as they learn how to imitate what their mentors do. Cooking, home renovation, and gardening shows also activate a sense of the referent beyond and promise of easy passage to it. This *ease* of passage (no budget or bills, no issues of ownership or privacy, no questions of crime or poverty intrude) allows for everyday experience to effortlessly transform nature into culture, the raw into the cooked. The patrol-car duties performed elsewhere provide the guarantee for this ease.

17. Modleski, "The Rhythms of Deception," 71.

18. Michel Foucault, *The History of Sexuality,* vol. I (New York: Vintage Books, 1980), 61–62.

19. Foucault, *The History of Sexuality,* 45.

20. For a superb sketch of the backdrop to Hollywood melodrama of the 1940s and '50s in the eighteenth- and nineteenth-century novel, see Thomas Elsaesser, "Tales of Sound and Fury," *Monogram,* no. 4 (1972): 2–15, reprinted in Bill Nichols, ed., *Movies and Methods,* vol. II (Berkeley: University of California Press, 1985).

21. See Fredric Jameson's *The Geopolitical Aesthetic: Cinema and Space in the World System* (Bloomington: Indiana University Press, 1992) for an extended discussion of representations of paranoia, particularly in Western cinema.

22. The variable, historically contingent linkage between subversion and form is made quite succinctly by Judith Butler in an interview: "There is no easy way to know whether something is subversive. Subversiveness is not something that can be gauged or calculated. In fact, what I mean by subversion are those effects that are incalculable. I do think that for a copy to be subversive of heterosexual hegemony it

has to both mime and displace its conventions. And not all miming is displacing." Interview with Liz Kotz, "The Body You Want," *Artforum* (November 1992): 84.

23. Margaret Morse, "Talk, Talk, Talk—The Space of Discourse in Television," *Screen* 26, no. 2 (March–April 1985): 15.

24. The panopticon was a prison system devised by Jeremy Bentham. It featured circular tiers of cells without a fourth wall. Instead of a wall, this side was left barred but open so that someone stationed in a central tower could look into each and every cell at will. Michel Foucault has seized upon this idea as a metaphor for a type of social control based on the internalization of a pervasive system of surveillance. Knowing that guards *may be* watching, the prisoners act as if they *are* being watched, policing themselves under the (potentially) watchful eye of those who occupy the central, panoptic tower. See "The Eye of Power," in Colin Gordon, ed., *Power/Knowledge: Selected Interviews and Other Writings by Michel Foucault,* 1972–1977 (New York: Pantheon Books, 1980).

4. The Ethnographer's Tale

1. The countries cited after film titles are first, the country where it was shot, and second, the filmmaker's country of origin, if different. Where no country is cited, it is understood to be the United States.

2. Clifford Geertz, "Thick Description: Toward an Interpretative Theory of Culture," in *The Interpretation of Cultures* (New York: Basic Books, 1973).

3. Jean-Paul Sartre, *Anti-Semite and Jew* (New York: Schocken Books, 1965), 19, and Geertz, "Thick Description," 29.

4. Trinh T. Minh-ha, *Woman/Native/Other* (Bloomington: Indiana University Press, 1989), 74.

5. This body of work is primarily feminist in emphasis. Representative works include: Teresa de Lauretis, *Alice Doesn't: Feminism, Semiotics, Cinema* (Bloomington: Indiana University Press, 1984); Doane, Mellencamp, Williams, eds., *Re-Vision: Essays in Feminist Film Criticism* (Frederick, Md.: University Publications of America, 1984); Gaines and Herzog, eds., *Fabrications: Costume and the Female Body* (New York: Routledge, 1990); Annette Kuhn, *Women's Pictures: Feminism and Cinema* (London: Routledge, 1982); Laura Mulvey, "Visual Pleasure and Narrative Cinema," in Bill Nichols, ed., *Movies and Methods,* II (Berkeley: University of California Press, 1985); Kaja Silverman, *Male Subjectivity at the Margins* (New York: Routledge, 1992); and Gaylan Studlar, *In the Realm of Pleasure: Von Sternberg, Dietrich and the Masochistic Aesthetic* (Urbana: University of Illinois Press, 1988).

6. Laura Mulvey, "Visual Pleasure and Narrative Cinema," in Bill Nichols, ed., *Movies and Methods,* II (Berkeley: University of California Press, 1985), 308.

7. Ken Feingold, "Notes on *India Time:* The First in a Series of Videotapes," *CVA Newsletter* (May 1988): 16–22.

8. This term is discussed further in Nichols, *Representing Reality: Issues and Concepts in Documentary* (Bloomington: Indiana University Press, 1991).

9. Asen Balikci, "Anthropologists and Ethnographic Filmmaking," in Jack Rollwagen, *Anthropological Filmmaking: Anthropological Perspectives on the Production of Film and Video for General Public Audiences* (New York: Harwood, 1988), 33.

10. Arrival scenes are discussed in revealing detail in Mary Louise Pratt, "Fieldwork in Common Places," in James Clifford and George Marcus, eds., *Writing Culture: The Poetics and Politics of Ethnography* (Berkeley: University of California Press, 1986).

11. For further discussion of the modifications and shifts in tone and purpose that occurred in making *The Hunters,* see John Collier, "Visual Anthropology and

the Future of Ethnographic Film," in Jack Rollwagen, *Anthropological Filmmaking,* 87, where he details some of the changes wrought by Robert Gardner's editing of Marshall's footage; R. Gordon, "People of the Great Sandface: People of the Great White Lie," *CVA Review* (Spring 1990): 30–34; Karl Heider, *Ethnographic Film* (Austin: University of Texas Press, 1976), 31–32; and Keyan Tomaselli, "Myths, Racism and Opportunism: Film and TV Representations of the San," in Peter Crawford and David Turton, eds., *Film as Ethnography* (Manchester: Manchester University Press, 1992), 205–21, where he refers to Marshall's admission that aspects of the film were staged in the field or fabricated in the editing. The gist of the criticism is that the final film presents a romanticized view of an "untouched" people who possess both endearing charm and a disconcertingly irreverent regard for nature as the West has reconceived it.

12. David MacDougall, "Beyond Observational Cinema," in Nichols, ed., *Movies and Methods,* II, 278.

13. Marianna Torgovnick, *Gone Primitive: Savage Intellect, Modern Lives* (Chicago: University of Chicago Press, 1991), offers an extended account of the central, allegorical role played by the tale of Odysseus in Western travel narratives ever since, including ethnographic ones.

14. Valuable discussions of this point include: Kathleen Biddick, "Uncolonizing History in Cyberspace: Memory, Artificial Memory, Remembering," unpublished ms. delivered at the Second International Conference on Cyberspace, UC Santa Cruz, April 1991; Peter Bishop, *The Myth of Shangri-La* (Berkeley: University of California Press, 1989); and Edward Said, *Orientalism* (New York: Vintage, 1978).

15. Chandra Mukerji, *From Graven Images: Patterns of Modern Materialism* (New York: Columbia University Press, 1983), explores this gradual shift in detail.

16. In *Ethnographic Film,* Karl Heider promotes ethnographicness as a criterion of ethnographic films. He states that "films which attempt to achieve ethnographicness must share this quality of rational, explicit methodology" (46) but does not consider how to probe anthropology's own unconscious. All of his categories therefore remain susceptible to the very impediments that his methodological rationality and explicitness set out to counter.

17. Jay Ruby, "Eye-Witnessing Humanism: Ethnography and Film," *CVA Review* (Fall 1990): 16.

18. Jack Rollwagen, "The Role of Anthropological Theory in 'Ethnographic' Filmmaking," in Rollwagen, ed., *Anthropological Filmmaking,* 294.

19. Jay Ruby criticizes the tradition of amateur ethnography (work done by "fellow travelers," those who are often aware of anthropological tradition but without formal training in the discipline) in "Eye-Witnessing Humanism."

20. James Clifford, "Introduction," *Writing Culture,* 13.

21. Trinh T. Minh-ha, *Woman/Native/Other,* 136.

22. Kathleen Kuehnast, "Gender Representation in Visual Ethnographies: An Interpretivist Perspective," *CVA Review* (Spring 1990): 24.

23. James Clifford, "Introduction," *Writing Culture,* 20.

24. George Marcus, "The Modernist Sensibility in Recent Ethnography: Writing and the Cinematic Metaphor of Montage," *SVA Review* 6, no. 1 (1990): 4.

25. Deborah Gordon, "Writing Culture, Writing Feminism: The Poetics and Politics and Experimental Ethnography," *Inscriptions,* no. 3/4 (1988): 17.

26. Jon Olson, "Filming the Fidencistas: The Making of *We Believe in Nono Fidencio,*" in Rollwagen, *Anthropological Filmmaking,* 260.

27. George Klima, "Filming as Teleological Process," in Rollwagen, *Anthropological Filmmaking,* 228.

28. David Bordwell, *Narration in the Fiction Film,* 35.

29. The Twelfth Annual Nordic Film Festival revolved around the question of whether ethnographers could construct their work in accord with the narrative traditions and conventions of the cultures they study. The results were suggestive but inconclusive. The proceedings of the conference, at which an earlier version of this chapter was presented, are published in Peter Crawford and Jan Simonson, eds., *Ethnographic Film Aesthetics and Narrative Traditions* (Denmark: Intervention Press, 1992). David MacDougall has explored the extent to which Western conventions such as the canonical story format inform not only the films but also the selection of cultures to be studied in "Complicities of Style," in Peter Crawford and David Turton, eds., *Film as Ethnography*. Trinh's book, *Woman/Native/Other*, also discusses alternative story forms at length, especially in her final chapter, "Grandma's Story."

30. George Marcus, "The Modernist Sensibility in Recent Ethnography." Canonic story form and virtual performance, as aspects of the anthropological unconscious, become underexamined elements producing familiarity in relation to the strangeness carried by the unfamiliar aspects of another culture.

31. Trinh T. Minh-ha, *Woman/Native/Other*, 124, 123.

32. Christian Hansen, Catherine Needham, Bill Nichols, "Pornography, Ethnography, and the Discourses of Power," *Representing Reality* (Bloomington: Indiana University Press, 1991).

33. Michel Foucault, *The History of Sexuality* (New York: Vintage, 1980).

34. Linda Williams, *Hard Core: Power, Pleasure and the 'Frenzy of the Visible'* (Berkeley: University of California Press, 1989), 279.

35. Interestingly, those engaged in the creation of virtual realities (computer-based worlds that simulate our experience of this world) find that it is difficult for subjects to locate or orient themselves without some representative of themselves in virtual space. Programmers often design "default heads," visual representations of a human head, that will perceive and move through virtual reality in the same manner as the subject would if she or he were physically, as well as perceptually, "there." These guides or "tricksters" take cognizance of our inability to act if we cannot locate our own body in relation to the world around us. When limited to a head, such figures would seem to offer one more example of an imaginary geography where the mind/body split of Western civilization prevails. The mind enters into a strange and exotic realm, attaching itself to the guidance of a default head, while the physical body, left at the threshold, splits the mind's consciousness between two different streams of contradictory sensory input, leading, quite possibly, to nausea. As one participant at a recent conference remarked, there is considerable need for "default bodies" that locate the entire self with a virtual reality. Our experience and accountability within a distinctly different perceptual world depends on taking full account of our bodies and our selves, not just our mind and its theories.

36. Alison Jablonko, "New Guinea in Italy: An Analysis of the Making of an Italian Television Series from Research Footage of the Maring People of Papua New Guinea," in Rollwagen, *Anthropological Filmmaking*, 175–76.

37. Harald Tambs-Lyche and Kjellaug Waage, "Intimacy, Recognition and Nausea: Reflections on the Perception of Ethnographic Film by Norwegian Youth," *CVA Review* (Fall 1989): 32.

38. Italo Svevo, *The Confessions of Zeno* (New York: Vintage, 1958).

39. Tambs-Lyche and Waage, "Intimacy, Recognition and Nausea," 32.

40. Wilton Martinez, "Critical Studies and Visual Anthropology: Aberrant v. Anticipated Readings of Ethnographic Film," *CVA Review* (Spring 1990): 34–47. Martinez offers a more elaborated commentary on the very significant implications of his studies of audience response for visual anthropology in "Who Constructs

Anthropological Knowledge? Toward a Theory of Ethnographic Film Spectatorship," in Crawford and Turton, eds., *Film as Ethnography:* 131–61.

41. Martinez, "Critical Studies and Visual Anthropology," 41.

42. Asen Balikci, "Anthropologists and Ethnographic Filmmaking," in Rollwagen, ed., *Anthropological Filmmaking,* 42–43.

43. Vivian Sobchack, "Inscribed Ethical Space: Ten Propositions on Death, Representation, and Documentary," *Quarterly Review of Film Studies* 9, no. 4 (1984): 283–300.

44. Alison Jablonko, "New Guinea in Italy," in *Anthropological Filmmaking,* 175.

45. Marianna Torgovnick, *Gone Primitive,* 16–17. She draws on Frances Spalding's biography, *Roger Fry: Art and Life* (Berkeley: University of California Press, 1980), for some of her detail about Fry. Sources for European conceptions of African art include William Fagg and Margaret Plass, *African Sculpture* (London: Durton, 1964); Jean Laude, *The Arts of Black Africa* (Berkeley: University of California Press, 1971), and Frank Willet, *African Art: An Introduction* (New York: Praeger, 1971).

46. Radikha Chopra, "Robert Gardner's *Forest of Bliss,*" *SVA Newsletter* (Spring 1989): 2.

47. Jay Ruby, "The Emperor and His Clothes," *SVA Newsletter* (Spring 1990): 11.

48. Julia Kristeva, *Desire in Language* (New York: Columbia University Press, 1980), 98.

49. Sarah Williams, "Suspending Anthropology's Inscription: Observing Trinh Minh-ha Observed," *Visual Anthropology Review* 7, no. 1 (1991): 12.

50. Williams, "Suspending Anthropology's Inscription," 9.

51. Marcus Banks, "Experience and Reality in Ethnographic Film," *Visual Sociology Review* 5, no. 2 (1990): 32.

52. Trinh T. Minh-ha, *Woman/Native/Other,* 48–49.

53. The professional or clinical gaze as well as the interactive mode of documentary filmmaking is discussed more extensively in my *Representing Reality.*

The single most important work on phenomenology and film in English is Vivian Sobchack, *The Address of the Eye* (Princeton: Princeton University Press, 1992). Dudley Andrews introductory texts on film theory, *The Major Film Theories* (New York: Oxford University Press, 1976) and *Concepts in Film Theory* (New York: Oxford University Press, 1984), are useful primers.

54. Alison Jablonko, "New Guinea in Italy," in *Anthropological Filmmaking,* 182.

55. David MacDougall, "Complicities of Style," in *Film as Ethnography,* 97.

56. Discussions of the use-value of phenomenology to a feminist theory of gender suggest something of its relevance to ethnographic film interpretation as well. Judith Butler, for example, argues, after Merleau-Ponty, for a conception of gender in which the body is "a historical idea" that renders gender specific through individual acts that are also socially indicative. These acts accumulate into a "legacy of sedimented acts" that constitute the self in a continuously open-ended yet stable fashion (274). Such acts, and their sedimentation over time, of course, are the very stuff of ethnographic film. Judith Butler, "Performative Acts and Gender Constitution: An Essay in Phenomenology and Feminist Theory," in Sue-Ellen Case, ed., *Performing Feminisms: Feminist Critical Theory and Theatre* (Baltimore: Johns Hopkins University Press, 1990).

57. Stephen Tyler, "Post-Modern Ethnography: From Document of the Occult to Occult Document," in Clifford and Marcus, eds., *Writing Culture,* 125.

58. John Collier, "Visual Anthropology and the Future of Ethnographic Film," in Rollwagen, *Anthropological Filmmaking,* 88-89.

59. Heider, *Ethnographic Film,* 35.

60. Bill Nichols, *Ideology and the Image* (Bloomington: Indiana University Press, 1981), 252.

61. Jon Olson, "Filming the Fidencistas," in Rollwagen, *Anthropological Filmmaking,* 271.

62. Kathleen Kuehnast, "Gender Representation in Visual Ethnographies," 25.

63. Deborah Gordon, "Writing Culture, Writing Feminism," 16.

64. James Clifford, "Introduction," *Writing Culture,* 21.

65. The direct usefulness of films to those about whom they are made also raises, by extension, a variation on the question that has reverberated through the museum world for some time now: Should film footage be repatriated to the culture where it was shot? Significant differences obtain when what is taken away are recorded sounds and images rather than one-of-a-kind artifacts, but the use-value of these materials, perhaps rushes and discarded footage even more than finished films since they bear a weaker imprint of the ethnographer's tale, may well be considerable. The time when their repatriation becomes a serious question is at hand.

66. Stephen Lansing, "The Decolonization of Ethnographic Film," *SVA Review* 6, no. 1 (1990): 13–15, 81.

67. The issue of the use of the present tense as a distancing device, a mechanism of power, a rendering of the Other as outside of time, or a trope guaranteeing the generalizing power of the ethnographer's claims is taken up in Clifford and Marcus, eds., *Writing Culture,* Johannes Fabian, *Time and Order: How Anthropology Makes Its Object* (New York: 1983), and George W. Stocking, Jr., "Maclay, Kubary, Malinowski: Archetypes from the Dreamtime of Anthropology," in George Stocking, Jr., ed., *Colonial Situations: Essays on the Contextualization of Ethnographic Knowledge* (Madison: University of Wisconsin Press, 1991). These issues are not so entirely one-sided, of course. Several recent articles explore how the use of the present tense can be efficacious, especially when this element of style is made more fully part of a conscious stylistic repertoire. See Helen Callaway, "Ethnography and Experience: Gender Implications in Fieldwork and Texts," John Davis, "Tense in Ethnography: Some Practical Considerations," and Kirsten Hastrup, "Writing Ethnography: State of the Art," in Judith Okely and Helen Callaway, eds., *Anthropology and Autobiography* (New York: Routledge, 1992).

68. Recurring through *I'm British But . . .* is a pop tune sung in Punjabi by a Pakistani-British rock group standing on the rooftop of a small neighborhood store. The lyrics, printed in intertitles to make the point more clear, are a vivid reminder of roots and the price of dislocation. One verse, referring to the massacre, goes:

> Recall that it was these same foreigners
> That took their rifles to us
> Innocent, fair flourishing lives
> How they stood and destroyed us
> And every corner bears witness
> At Jallianwala Bagh
> (*refrain:*)
> And you, my friend, come to England
> Leaving your Punjab.

69. Marcus, "The Modernist Sensibility in Recent Ethnography."

5. Performing Documentary

1. When a film shot in one country is by a filmmaker based in another country, I have listed the country where it was shot first.

2. I discuss these four modes in detail in *Representing Reality* (Bloomington: Indiana University Press, 1991).

3. "Dominant" is used in the Russian formalist sense as the formal organizing element of a work that orchestrates or regulates the function of all other elements. The dominant can range from a musical rhythm to a set of genre conventions. See Kristen Thompson, *Eisenstein's Ivan the Terrible: A Neoformalist Analysis* (Princeton: Princeton University Press, 1981), for an excellent discussion of this and other formalist concepts.

4. For a discussion of virtual performance see *Representing Reality,* 122.

5. Sarina Pearson presents this trichotomy in her thesis videotape, *The Field* (UC Santa Cruz, 1992).

6. Sarah Williams makes a call for this possibility in her critique of the anthropological criticism of the films of Trinh T. Minh-ha. Sarah Williams, "Suspending Anthropology's Inscription: Observing Trinh Minh-ha Observed," *Visual Anthropology Review* 7, no. 1 (Spring 1991): 7–14.

7. Trinh T. Minh-ha, *Woman/Native/Other* (Bloomington: Indiana University Press, 1989), 48–49.

8. Teresa de Lauretis, "Rethinking Women's Cinema," *Technologies of Gender* (Bloomington: Indiana University Press, 1987).

9. Fredric Jameson, "Class and Allegory in Contemporary Mass Culture: *Dog Day Afternoon* as a Political Film," in Bill Nichols, ed., *Movies and Methods,* II (Berkeley: University of California Press, 1985), 719.

10. Ibid.

11. The implications of Peirce's semiotics for feminism are treated in Teresa de Lauretis's "Semiotics and Experience," *Alice Doesn't* (Bloomington: Indiana University Press, 1984). I have extended her argument to fill a more inclusive frame.

12. Hayden White, "The Question of Narrative in Contemporary Historical Theory," *The Content of the Form* (Baltimore: Johns Hopkins University Press, 1987), 39.

13. I discuss "documentary logic," "narrative coherence," and the "discourses of sobriety" at greater length in *Representing Reality,* 118–25, and 3–4, 5 for discourses of sobriety.

14. David MacDougall, "Prospects for the Ethnographic Film," in Bill Nichols, ed., *Movies and Methods,* I (Berkeley: University of California Press, 1976), 146.

15. Stephen Tyler, "Post-Modern Ethnography: From Document of the Occult to Occult Document," in James Clifford and George E. Marcus, *Writing Culture: The Poetics and Politics of Ethnography* (Berkeley: University of California Press, 1986), 126.

16. A quite useful discussion of Eisenstein's thought in relation to how montage evokes a "fantasy whole abducted from fragments" is Jacques Aumont, *Montage Eisenstein* (Bloomington: Indiana University Press, 1987), especially chapter 4, "Montage in Question."

17. Jean-Luc Godard: *Vivre sa vie* (1962), *Numero Deux* (1975), *Six fois deux* (1976); David Rimmer: *Variations on a Cellophane Wrapper* (1970), *Real Italian Pizza* (1971); Jan Jost: *Speaking Directly: Some American Notes* (1974); Yvonne Rainer: *The Man Who Envied Women* (1985). The political significance of this work and the work cited in the next footnote (the autobiographical avant-garde) is nicely elaborated in David James, *Allegories of Cinema: American Film in the Sixties* (Princeton: Princeton University Press, 1989).

18. Jonas Mekas: *Diaries, Notes and Sketches* (1964–1969), *Reminiscences of a Journey to Lithuania* (1971); Kenneth Anger: *Fireworks* (1947), *Inauguration of the Pleasure Dome* (1954), *Scorpio Rising* (1962–63); Maya Deren: *Meshes of the Afternoon* (1943), *Ritual in Transfigured Time* (1946), *The Divine Horsemen* (1947, completed 1977); Stan

Brakhage: *Desistfilm* (1953), *Window Water Baby Moving* (1963), *Scenes from under Childhood* (1969), *The Act of Seeing with one's own eyes* (1971).

19. Of particular importance are *Les maîtres fous* (1954), *Jaguar* (1954–67), *Moi, un noir* (1957), *Chronique d'un été* (1960). The most complete discussion of Rouch is Paul Stoller, *The Cinematic Griot* (Chicago: University of Chicago Press, 1992).

20. Fredric Jameson, "On Magic Realism in Film," *Signatures of the Visible* (New York: Routledge, 1990): 137. Jameson provides a valuable series of references on the use of the term in relation to Latin American literature and sets his own usage in this context, stressing, however, slightly different points, particularly the combination of a historical orientation, the use of color photography in a way distinct from what he terms postmodern "gloss" (139–44), and the reduction of narrative dynamics by means of an increased attention to violence (this is in relation to fiction films). He concludes this characterization: "All [these films] . . . enjoin a visual spell, an enthrallment to the image in its present of time . . ." (130) which he distinguishes from the usual dynamics of the gaze and from any ontology of the real. He goes on to theorize that magical realism addresses those historical moments when disjunction, or the clash of modes of production, is central (138). There is, then, a historical root for the magical aspect of realism. "[T]he articulated superposition of whole layers of the past within the present (Indian or pre-Columbian realities, the colonial era, the wars of independence, caudillismo, the period of American domination . . .) is the formal precondition for the emergence of this new narrative style" (139). The close linkage of performative documentary with history and memory in relation to issues of race, class, and gender in a postcolonial world order gives resonance to this affiliation with magical realism.

21. The shift from these documentaries to performative ones is a matter of degree, and heuristics. (Some, like *Las Madres,* might readily be recruited to the ranks of the performative if we wish to stress the linkages to magical realism and to issues of historical disjunction, or struggle.) I have described these more expressive and poetic moments in terms of subjectivity and identification in *Representing Reality,* 155–60.

22. See White, *Metahistory* (Baltimore: Johns Hopkins University Press, 1973), especially pp. 13–21. Further references are cited as page numbers in the text.

23. My interest in this concept stems from informal discussion with Hayden White, who gave a talk on this subject and has an article on it in progress.

24. John Peradotto, *Man in the Middle Voice: Name and Narration in the* Odyssey (Princeton: Princeton University Press, 1990), 133. See also L. R. Palmer, *The Greek Language* (Atlantic Headlands, NJ, 1980), 292. Another key reference to the middle voice is Roland Barthes, "To Write: Intransitive Verb?" in Richard Macksey and Eugene Donato, eds., *The Language of Criticism and the Sciences of Man: The Structuralist Controversy* (Baltimore: Johns Hopkins University Press, 1970), 134–44. The potential relationship between middle voice and Freudian concepts such as sadomasochism would prove a fruitful avenue of exploration which is deferred here. A suggestive beginning, however, might be Mikkel Borch-Jacobsen, *The Freudian Subject* (Stanford: Stanford University Press, 1988); Borch-Jacobsen argues that identification and desire are far more closely entangled than usual, and their implication not evident, because Freud and we now lack the (middle) voice which might have best expressed this entanglement.

25. "Strategic location" is Edward Said's term for the "author's position in a text with regard to the Oriental [or other politically charged] material he writes about." *Orientalism* (New York: Vintage Books, 1978), 20.

26. Fredric Jameson, "The Existence of Italy," in *Signatures of the Visible* (New York: Routledge, l990), 168.

27. Five hundred mice is not the perfect political recipe. The call for multiple affinities and mutuality overcomes severe limitations in the traditional united front politics of individual and subgroup subordination to a single, unified agenda. But the centripetal forces that constitute identity politics can also be exclusionary, and the bridging relationships between groups ephemeral and unstable.

The different possibilities are suggestively and perhaps inadvertently conveyed in the closing moments of *Tongues Untied.* Riggs juxtaposes footage from a civil rights march in the 1960s, led by the Reverend Martin Luther King, Jr., with a gay rights parade in the 1980s. The purposefulness and intensity of the marchers is apparent in both, but a significant contrast occurs in the mix of races and sexes who march under the banner of civil rights and the all-black contingent that marches under the banner of black gay pride. The very terms on which black gay identity come to be constructed make the type of solidarity evident in the civil rights march extremely difficult. This is a problem facing identity politics generally, not only black, gay males. A useful starting point for a critical rethinking of identity politics is Judith Butler, *Gender Trouble: Feminism and the Subversion of Identity* (New York: Routledge, 1989).

6. Eisenstein's *Strike* and the Genealogy of Documentary

1. I have structured this discussion of *Strike* as though the film were released today in order to emphasize its similarity to the ways in which boundaries between fiction and nonfiction, narrative and non-narrative, have blurred. *Strike,* from this retrospective angle, is as fully part of the genealogy of documentary filmmaking as those Soviet films that were described as precursors and foundations in earlier historical periods when the very conception of documentary was distinct from what it is today.

I presented an earlier version of this chapter at the Fourth Annual Berkeley Film Conference, November 6, 1993, and at the "Visible Evidence" documentary conference at Duke University, September 8–12, 1993. I am indebted to Nahum Chandler and Terrence Turner for specific suggestions and comments that I have tried to incorporate.

2. Walter Benjamin, "Theses on the Philosophy of History," *Illuminations* (New York: Schocken, 1969), 255. "Writing with lightning" is a phrase used by President Wilson in speaking of D. W. Griffith's epic feature, *Birth of a Nation* (1915).

3. Standish Lawder, "Eisenstein and Constructivism," in P. Adams Sitney, ed., *The Essential Cinema,* I (New York: New York University Press, 1975), 83. Lawder's account has useful information on the social context in which *Strike* took form.

4. Sergei Eisenstein, "Notes on *Capital,*" quoted in Jacques Aumont, *Montage Eisenstein* (Bloomington: Indiana University Press, 1987), 161.

5. Jacques Aumont, *Montage Eisenstein,* 163.

6. S. Tretyakov, V. Shklovsky, E. Shub, and O. Brik, "Symposium on Soviet Documentary," in Lewis Jacobs, ed., *The Documentary Tradition,* 2nd ed. (New York: Norton, 1979), 33–34. Also translated as "*Lef* and Film" (from *New Lef* no. 11–12 [1927]), in *Screen* 12, no. 4 (Winter 1971–72): 74–80.

Shklovsky is referring here to "story" as the overall, coherent account one would render of a particular tale and "plot" as the actual successive arrangement of situations and events as read or seen. Both documentary and fiction would have plots in this sense whereas fiction's plot would resolve into a story and documentary's into a claim or argument about the historical world.

7. Gerald Mast, for example, in an entry typical of film history books, describes Eisenstein in relation to the larger picture of the development of narrative film

even as he also acknowledges that "The Eisenstein films break all the rules of narrative construction. They lack a protagonist and focal characters; they lack a linear plot of the rising or falling fortunes of a single person." *A Short History of the Movies,* 4th ed. (New York: Macmillan, 1986), 159. David Cook, in *A History of Narrative Film* (New York: Norton, 1981), also treats Eisenstein as though he were a part of the evolution of a film language that becomes, virtually by default, narrative film language. Calling *Strike* a "nonnarrative chronicle" (147), Cook nonetheless contextualizes it in relation to other narrative films like *The Gold Rush* (Chaplin, 1924) or *Der Letzte Mann* (F. W. Murnau, 1924) and the rise of the classic period of silent Soviet cinema. Film historians repeatedly acknowledge Eisenstein's elusiveness and then proceed to incorporate his work into what is finally a narrative fiction film tradition.

Standish Lawder makes almost an identical point while placing Eisenstein in relation to constructivism:

> On the one hand, its bold rejection of almost every traditional element of commercial feature film (no stars, no hero, no happy ending, no sub-plot, not even a plot really, but merely a single incident); its profusion of imaginative camera tricks and clever devices (weird dissolves and superimpositions, spinning titles which dissolve into machinery, the shots through glass, through the tiny spy camera, shots reflected in convex mirrors); its intensely charged sense of realism (the documentary-like photography of real setting in factory and elsewhere)—and, on the other, the film is *so* loaded with wild experimentation that it seems today like an exercise in excess. ("Eisenstein and Constructivism," 69)

Lawder's description reads perfectly until we reach his concluding evaluation. What seems to Lawder like "excess" in relation to the positivist tendencies of observational documentary or the realist tendencies of fiction now arrives before us as realism of the sort Brecht had in mind when he rejected dramatic theater and its realism in favor of discovering the underlying mechanisms that such realism obscured.

In a history of documentary comparable to Mast's history of narrative film, Jack Ellis describes how "Vertov's aesthetic position demanded anti-narrative, antifictional forms. His iconoclasm was intended to free film from bourgeois obfuscations of story and the effete pleasures of theatrical performance in order to arrive at the truths of the actual world." *The Documentary Idea* (Englewood Cliffs: Prentice-Hall, 1989), 31. Though an accurate rendition of Vertov's polemics, the account also tacitly supports his exaggerated and reductive view of narrative fiction. The effect of such accounts is to erect an artificial barrier precisely where boundaries blur in remarkable ways.

8. Meyer Shapiro, "Leonardo and Freud: An Art-Historical Study," *Journal of the History of Ideas,* 17, no. 2 (April 1956); Annette Michelson, ed., *Kino-Eye: The Writings of Dziga Vertov* (Berkeley: University of California Press, 1984).

9. Sergei Tretyakov, "Symposium on Soviet Documentary," in Lewis Jacobs, ed., *The Documentary Tradition,* 2nd ed. (New York: Norton, 1979), 29.

10. Sergei Eisenstein, "About Myself and My Films," in *Notes of a Film Director* (New York: Dover, 1970), 13–14. Written in 1945, the essay retrospectively assigns the motivation Eisenstein remembered himself having had back in the 1920s. "Fictitiousness" disturbs him greatly. The emotions spectators feel at a play are real, but they derive from identifying with a fictitious situation. "Thus art . . . enables man through co-experience *fictitiously* to perform heroic actions, *fictitiously* to experience great emotions. . . . Why strive for reality, if for a small sum of money you can satisfy yourself in your imagination without moving from your comfortable theatre

seat?" (13). Constructivism, though, called for an end to this mirroring without reality, and Eisenstein vowed,

> First master art.
> Then destroy it.
> Penetrate into the mysteries of art.
> Unveil them.
> Master art.
> And then snatch off its mask, expose it, destroy it! (14).

We clearly recruit Eisenstein to the history of the growth and development of narrative fiction at considerable peril.

11. The spilled ink clearly doubles as a metaphor for spilled blood. It contrasts tellingly with the rising water that floods the streets of the worker's quarters in *Metropolis*. This water is also dark and blood-like, but its overflow suggests the self-destructive quality of the workers' rebellion. The flood threatens their own children and their homes. Violence worsens their own lot. In *Strike* the spilled ink is clearly not the workers' own doing; it is class violence visited upon them. The most heinous acts are carried out in the name of the existing, hierarchical order; any act that could overthrow it would be preferable to the class violence Eisenstein describes.

These thirty-three shots are not quite as stunning in their composition as the attack by the Cossacks on the workers' tenement buildings that precedes them, where horses and soldiers chase workers on every balcony, every connecting bridge, every level of the buildings, murderously permeating space the workers considered as their own but could not defend. The concluding thirty-three shots bring to a culmination the process of rendering us touched by the production of signs. The shots are:

1. The factory manager pounds his desk.
2. A knife moves down through the frame.
3. On a slope in the countryside, a great tumbling avalanche of bodies rushes forward.
4. Workers flee toward a rise, advancing past the camera.
5. Workers flee through a wooded area, in reverse direction from shot #3, moving toward the right and downward.
6. Workers flee at the same rise as shot #4 again, moving in different directions, bumping into one another, giving the impression of chaotic flight.
7. A knife swoops down, with a hand now more visibly wielding it.
8. A steer's head is struck by the knife.
9. The steer's whole body fills the frame as it buckles and falls.
10. An abstract shot of hands against the sky, reaching out, fingers splayed. The hands begin pointed largely upward and then tilt to the right onto a diagonal line.
11. A worker at the abattoir walks toward the camera alongside a corral carrying a rope and wearing a leather smock.
12. Another abstract image of hands against the sky, contorted, twisted, writhing.
13. Soldiers pour down a slope in the woods, sweeping through, past trees, moving to the right in a line. The foreground remains empty as though the camera views their advance from a place of concealment, out of the line of march.
14. A man slits the steer's throat. The motion of the knife is like a giant unzipping gash that opens up the animal's throat; the steer's eyes remain open.
15. Soldiers fire in the woods, toward the upper right corner of the frame, at unseen targets.

16. The steer butchering continues. The knife moves back to the left after unzipping its throat. A pan is thrust toward the animal's throat to catch the blood but it overflows the pan and spreads across the floor. Two men are partly visible in the frame. Though workers, their situation is entirely different from that of the workers pursued by Cossacks.
17. Another image of slashing the bull's throat, with its head twisted, its throat pointing upward. Workers' hands hold the steer in place.
18. Soldiers fire their rifles in the woods, advancing to the right. A tree in the foreground seems to shelter the camera and the documentary worker who wields it.
19. A line of soldiers fires volleys in the woods. Clouds of smoke drift toward the right producing, in retrospect, the pressure that causes the subsequent action.
20. A fence buckles, quivers, as two men jump over it. They bound away and the fence falls behind them as scores of other workers dash forward.
21. Workers and several of their wives sweep past to the right, streaming down an embankment into the background with a river in the far distance.
22. Workers seen from behind, fleeing. They sweep leftward, these scores and scores of proletarians; a tree stands squarely in the center of the frame.
23. Soldiers fire their rifles to the left after the men fleeing, an officer with a pistol also fires. Smoke wafts upward and the handful of visible soldiers are positioned to fill the frame from left to right and top to bottom.
24. The same shot of workers fleeing as #22, with the tree in center frame.
25. Another shot of soldiers advancing past the same tree as in #22 and 24 but now seen from a reverse angle.
26. Another reverse angle puts the camera back on the same side of the tree as it began. Soldiers stream past the tree while workers, in the background, keep ahead of the advancing soldiers. Both groups move leftward in the frame.
27. Men and women stream down a slope similar to the first one we saw in #3. They move rightward and down as a tumbling mass of bodies.
28. The head of the steer, its throat slit with the arms of the workers attending to it.
29. A medium shot of the legs of the steer as they kick and thrash. The body convulses on the abattoir floor.
30. With its throat slit, the steer's blood continues to flow, slopping beyond the semi-useless pan.
31. A composed image of workers' bodies strewn across the field where they fell. Many are heaped on top of one another like grotesque bales of hay. Women's bodies are prominent in the composition.
32. About a one second dissolve from the image of dead proletarians to that of soldiers seen from the waist down marching back to the right, as though walking on the bodies.
33. The workers' bodies again, but now the camera pans left as though following the marching line of soldiers and the carnage they have left behind. The image is perfectly composed with gaps of field and heaps of bodies similar to the imagery of a harvest. Fade to black.

The four shots that conclude the film follow.

12. Eric Rhode takes exception to this treatment, reading the portrayal of the workers as fully realist but wrong. "His workers are boyish, bloody-minded and never seen to work. . . . At home among the machines, these workers swing from girders like monkeys and seem hardly different from the police informers whom Eisenstein protractedly compares to various beasts of prey." Eric Rhode, *A History of the Cinema* (New York: Hill and Wang, 1976), 95. Regarding it as a combination of newsreel and circus, Rhode finds the film wanting in relation to the contempo-

rary realities it presumably portrays. The present essay takes a different tack in which *Strike* belongs squarely with other innovative documentaries that break with empiricism, realism, and the chronicle to approximate the distinct reality of the Marxist dialectic itself.

13. Frank Lentricchia, in *Criticism and Social Change* (Chicago: University of Chicago Press, 1983), makes this point memorably in his discussion of Kenneth Burke's 1935 address to the American Writers' Congress. "In effect Burke asks Marxists . . . whether or not it is their ambition to become workers. . . . You can't expect, [Burke] says, in effect, to his progressive friends, on the one hand, to keep painting these riveting portraits of workers under capitalism, of degradation and alienation—you can't expect people to accept these portraits as the truth, which is your rhetorical desire, after all, and then, on the other hand, at the same time, expect people to want to identify with workers, or become workers, or even enlist their energies of intellect or feeling on behalf of workers. . . . You must, as Marx would urge, rethink your representation of workers. . . . [You must] make sure that their fate and ours are bound up with each other" (25–26). This is precisely what Eisenstein has done.

14. Eric Rhode's condemnation of Eisenstein's portrayal of the workers sees the transformation but assigns it to the wrong code: he lumps workers and spies together as "species of beast" and misreads an iconography of (unspoken) desire as boyish frolic (*A History of the Cinema,* 95).

Roland Barthes constantly approaches the significance of the homoerotic but just as constantly fails to name it in his essay, "The Third Meaning," in *Image/Music/Text* (New York: Hill and Wang, 1977). Barthes likens the third or obtuse meaning to "pun, buffoonery, useless expenditure . . . it is on the side of the carnival" (55). Barthes also sees a correspondence to disguise but does not connect it to suppression and the homosexual closet: "The characteristic of this third meaning is indeed—at least in [Eisenstein]—to blur the limit separating expression from disguise, but also to allow that oscillation succinct demonstration—an elliptic emphasis, if one can put it like that, a complex and extremely artful disposition . . ." (57). Barthes insists that the third meaning is a "signifier without a signified" because "it does not copy anything" (61). A stranger case of blindness and insight than Barthes's could hardly be imagined.

A singular exception to this myopia is Thomas Waugh's essay on Eisenstein, in which he pointedly identifies the unseen homoerotic elements of Eisenstein's films. Tom Waugh, "A Fag-Spotter's Guide to Eisenstein," *Body Politic,* no. 35 (1977).

15. The most notable discussion of Vertov's use of reversals to address issues of consciousness and historical materialism is Annette Michelson, "From Magician to Epistemologist: Vertov's *The Man with a Movie Camera,*" in P. Adams Sitney, ed., *The Essential Cinema,* I (New York: New York University Press, 1975).

16. Though Eisenstein did not take it as his inspiration, a similar and equally Brechtian conception of how artistic form that separates us from the centered, bourgeois consciousness of individuated, realist representation can give rise to a dialectical form of spectatorial consciousness occurs in Althusser's seminal essay "The 'Piccolo Teatro': Bertolazzi and Brecht," in *Lenin and Philosophy and Other Essays* (New York: Monthly Review Press, 1971). In this essay Althusser describes the necessity for distance and incompleteness, for separation from the illusory consciousness of characters which can only give the impression of dialectics by isolating itself from the real conditions that surround it. "Sheltered from the world, it unleashes all the fantastic form of a breathless conflict which can only ever find peace in the catastrophe of someone else's fall: it takes this hullabaloo for destiny and its breathlessness for the dialectic" (140).

Althusser goes on to argue that the key character in Marxist theater is the spectator and the key goal the production of a new consciousness that is, of necessity, incomplete: "incomplete, like any other consciousness, but moved by the incompletion itself, this distance achieved, this inexhaustible work of criticism in action; the play is really the production of a new spectator, an actor who starts where the performance ends, who only starts so as to complete it, but in life" (151). Althusser's insightful essay gives due recognition to the importance of Bertolazzi and Brecht but regrettably ignores Eisenstein entirely.

17. The only exception is in the representation of women who are consistently presented, when presented at all, in subordinate roles and in poses of suffering or death. Eisenstein does not escape convention in this regard even if his motivations for these images are not the conventional ones.

18. "500 mice" is a reference to a scene in *Born in Flames,* discussed at the conclusion to chapter 5, "Performing Documentary."

19. This argument parallels, but in a more specifically dialectical vein, the argument of Hayden White regarding narrative and time. He asserts that to understand historical acts we must "grasp together" the acts, their motivations, and their consequences which it is the work of plot to do and which, I argue, it is the work of Eisenstein's modernist collage to do dialectically. If, as White reasons, supporting Ricoeur, narrative has as its "'ultimate referent' nothing other than 'temporality' itself," then Eisenstein's dialectical referent finds embodiment in a plot itself constructed dialectically, by the viewer as much as the filmmaker. See Hayden White, "The Question of Narrative in Contemporary Historical Theory," in *The Content of the Form* (Baltimore: Johns Hopkins University Press, 1987), esp. pp. 50–53.

20. Though common sense calls for historical authenticity according to fixed protocols of verification and validation, Eisenstein astutely recognizes the problem this poses for film. Authenticity will be in the eyes of the beholder as much as in the images themselves. (The image cannot authenticate itself.) Validation hinges on the spectator's ability, first, to determine when an image's indexical link to the pro-filmic event (what happened in front of the camera) can be justifiably equated with a historical event (rather than fiction or other types of event that only occur due to the presence of the camera) and then, second, to interpret this event within the spectator's own social arena in an appropriate manner.

Seth Feldman, for example, notes that rural viewers of Vertov's *Kinonedelia (Cinema Weekly)* newsreels could interpret the images of queues at city stores as evidence that the urban population was suffering privations as much as they were while urban audiences could interpret shots of everyday rural life as evidence that rumors of food hoarding in the country were unfounded. Such interpretations, though, require the two-step process described above that Eisenstein rejects in favor of a more existentially situated form of historical consciousness. The form of interpretation preferred by Eisenstein sacrifices specificities of the sort Vertov documented in favor of "the Marxist method itself," rendered no longer as an abstraction but, in keeping with the First Thesis on Feuerbach, as the fullest embodiment of sensuous experience.

As a further distinction, Vertov's conception of consciousness functions more entirely within a reflexive frame. As Annette Michelson put it, admiringly, "[*The Man with a Movie Camera*] renders insistently concrete, as in another dialectical icon, that philosophical phantasm of the reflexive consciousness, the eye seeing, apprehending itself through its constitution of the world's visibility" (Annette Michelson, "From Magician to Epistemologist: Vertov's *The Man with a Movie Camera,*" 98). The trace of tautology here amounts to the absence of a materialist dialectic: the eye apprehends *itself* through its constitution of the world's visibility. This is revolutionary in its own right but radically distinct from the transformative constitution of a subject who has not yet come into being. Althusser clarifies the difference effectively when he argues that *"there is no dialectic of consciousness"* in and of itself, that there is "no dialectic of consciousness which could reach reality itself by virtue of its own contradictions: in short, there can be no 'phenomenology' in the Hegelian sense: for consciousness does not accede to the real through its own internal development, but by the radical discovery of what is *other than itself*" (Louis Althusser, "The 'Piccolo Teatro': Bertolazzi and Brecht," 143). What we discover (or "Remember") in *Strike* is an arrested reality that seems "indifferent and strange," undialectical in its incapacity to imagine anything other than what is. This world is the realm of the factory managers, the lumpen-proletarians, the spies, henchmen, and Cossacks who are radically other than that consciousness we and the slaughtered workers bring into being. The tension of one with the other, the space between, is precisely where the dialectic arises as something in excess of either reflexive or individual consciousness.

Michelson praises Vertov for his destruction of the veil of illusions within this phenomenological frame. Her essay has contributed significantly to our understanding of Vertov as inspiration for a radical aspiration that struggles to persist. Her reading of Vertov is shared by Dai Vaughn, who praises *The Man with a Movie Camera* because it "refuses to allow us to accept the screen as a plane of reference for reality, and instead seeks to dissolve all such planes of reference successively . . . in the hopes that reality will 'emerge' from the process, not as a creature of screen illusion but as a liberated spirit." Dai Vaughn, *"The Man with a Movie Camera,"* in Lewis Jacobs, *The Documentary Tradition,* 2nd ed. (New York: Norton, 1979), 56. But while Michelson extols this process, Vaughn condemns it. For him it is too abstract, too divorced from the "social and hence the human point of view" (57). Though I think Michelson's reading is more persuasive, many do find Vertov too removed and distant. Eisenstein, at least in *Strike,* finds a better balance, a more compelling way in which to make the abstract concrete.

21. The historical importance of the present moment is often lost in historiography and documentary that effaces that moment with the techniques of realism and zero-degree style (style that feigns a near-transparency to that which it represents). Eisenstein and Vertov, like those modernist, and contemporary, filmmakers discussed in chapter 7, "Please, All You Good and Honest People," make use of montage, or collage, to establish a vivid sense of tension between a represented past and an experiential present.

What is at issue is whether or not a film, as performance, constitutes its subject (the one "out there," the topic, to which it refers as well as the one "in here," the viewer, that attends to it) while giving the appearance of finding both subjects already made, in need of little more than discovery and description, or address and (mis)recognition. For both novelistic and historiographic realism "the principal purpose . . . was to substitute surreptitiously a conceptual content (a signified) for a referent that it pretended to describe." Hayden White, *The Content of the Form,* 37.

22. Tom Gunning, "The Cinema of Attractions," in Thomas Elsaesser, ed., *Early Cinema: Space, Frame, Narrative* (London: BFI Publishing, 1990), 58, 59.

23. Standish Lawder, "Eisenstein and Constructivism," 65.

24. The same contrast can be made with the opening of *Peeping Tom,* in which an arrow flies to the center of a bull's eye in one shot and a human eye opens in the next. The assaultative gaze and the dynamics of sadomasochism are here joined together in unmistakable form. Eisenstein shares much more with the camera eye of Dziga Vertov in which the figure of the filmmaker himself is reflected (in *The Man with a Movie Camera*) except that Eisenstein eschews this type of open reflexivity

to allow his camera to reflect on history more obliquely through the style and plot with which he organizes events.

25. Francis Ford Coppola retains the parallel editing but eviscerates its meaning in his *Apocalypse Now* (1979). Coppola merely negates, or represses, the horror, the stench, the dark underbelly of capitalist logic when he crosscuts Willard's execution of Kurtz with the ritual slaughter of a bull. The relations are abstracted outside the realm of class conflict into a realm of ritual practices, individual dementia, and self-purification. Eisenstein has done away with this self and its quest for an authenticity denied by its social conditions at the very same moment as they hold it forth as an ideal.

Coppola neglected what Eisenstein teaches. He has shaped a morality tale by restoring an apparent solidity to the very terrain of individual and melodramatic consciousness that Eisenstein burst asunder. Coppola may well identify with Kurtz, the lone, misunderstood maverick, creator of his own universe of hierarchy, order, and pleasure, who is consequently marked for termination by the hegemonic order. Eisenstein has none of these illusions about his social position or individual ego. His identification is with the masses who become mere decoration in the negative space of Coppola's mise-en-scène. As Stan Brakhage says,

> What did Eisenstein have to start with, to celebrate? Heroics! He was confronted by a mass of people, which for most of the history of the world is a pretty ugly apparition in any form in which it occurs. He made *this* the hero. He strung people out in the most incredible patterns, across vast landscapes and around city streets, in order to create an image of the heroic mass. (*Brakhage Scrapbook: Collected Writings 1964–1980* [New Paltz, NY: Documentext, 1982], 171–72.)

(Brakhage still shares some of the romantic sensibility of a Coppola, seeing in this achievement a mythic representation that would congeal history into formal patterns; Eisenstein's effort also poses an acute contradiction between the individual artist and the collective goals of the nation-state. At least Brakhage recognizes that Eisenstein's achievement lies in giving realization to contradiction, or dialectics, while Coppola simply scavenges techniques.)

26. Walter Benjamin, "Theses on the Philosophy of History," *Illuminations* (New York: Schocken, 1969), 261.

7. Please, All You Good and Honest People

1. Anthony Wilden, *System and Structure: Essays in Communication and Exchange*, 2nd ed. (London: Tavistock, 1972), 65.

2. This essay is strongly indebted to Hayden White's writing on history, particularly to his book *The Content of the Form: Narrative Discourse and Historical Representation* (Baltimore: Johns Hopkins University Press, 1987) and to his Patricia Wise Lecture for the American Film Institute, "The Fact of Modernism: The Fading of the Historical Event" (Los Angeles, 1992).

3. Fredric Jameson, "Marxism and Historicism," *The Ideologies of Theory: Essays 1971–1986, II, The Syntax of History* (Minneapolis: University of Minnesota Press, 1988), 148–77.

4. It would be unproductive to specify all of the source materials composing the Gulf War text as I received it, which was inevitably some fraction of the totality of coverage. It did include portions of NBC, CBS, ABC, and CNN coverage, many of which were taped for further study.

5. I discuss formal and political reflexivity in more detail in *Representing Reality:*

Issues and Concepts in Documentary (Bloomington: Indiana University Press, 1991), 69–75.

6. Hayden White, *The Content of the Form,* 150.

7. Hayden White, "The Fact of Modernism." Fredric Jameson, *Postmodernism, or, The Cultural Logic of Late Capitalism* (Durham: Duke University Press, 1991).

8. These two formulations attempt to stress the similarity between historical consciousness and reading comprehension. The formulations derive, loosely, from Anthony Wilden, *System and Structure,* especially chapter 4, "Montaigne on the Paradoxes of Communication," and from David Bordwell, *Narration in the Fiction Film* (Madison: University of Wisconsin Press, 1985). I substitute *histoire* for story rather than Bordwell's neo-formalist term, *fabula,* to stress the linkage between the reader's imaginative act of textual comprehension and the historian's equally imaginative act of historical representation. Bordwell's relentless formalism, though, limits comprehension to a one-dimensional process that can never attain to dialectical consciousness. His pat formulas describe a very different, restricted type of comprehension, even for classic Hollywood, despite his use of similar terminology. For example, Bordwell writes, "Psychological causality thus permits the classical viewer to integrate the present with the past and to form clear-cut hypotheses about future story events" (David Bordwell, in *The Classical Hollywood Cinema* [New York: Columbia University Press, 1985], 43). This activity remains strictly limited to one level of textual intelligibility. It therefore becomes a dead-end in relation to the questions posed here rather than their foundation.

The notion of "the story so far," of a story held in suspense in precisely the dialectical manner suggested by this chapter's lead epigraph, differs sharply from what Walter Benjamin referred to, with sexist disparagement, as "the whore called 'Once upon a time.'" ("The historical materialist leaves it to others to be drained by the whore called 'Once upon a time,' in historicism's bordello. He remains in control of his powers, man enough to blast open the continuum of history" ("Theses on the Philosophy of History," *Illuminations,* ed. Hannah Arendt [New York: Schocken, 1969], 262.) That congealed sense of a bygone past, full of enchantment and mystery for that very reason, yields to a never-ending story ("the story so far") we ourselves forge more than receive.

9. Wilden, *System and Structure,* 99–100.

10. Realism is inevitably bound up with paradox. It is no accident that Hayden White, on the second page of *Metahistory,* launches a footnote on realism that consumes an entire page of text. In it he describes realism as "*the* problem for modern historiography" (3). The crux of the issue for White is the difficulty of identifying what a historical conception of reality is. The usual declension that associated history with fact, myth with concept, and fiction with both does not strike him as adequate. His own preference is to examine the artistic elements of realist historiography. Mine is to examine the forms taken by quasi- or sur-realist representation that seem to give effective embodiment to historical consciousness. Hayden White, *Metahistory* (Baltimore: Johns Hopkins University Press, 1973).

Among the numerous paradoxes that circulate within the realm of realist representation are: (1) the text as source of knowledge which is also (only) pleasure, (2) the past as something knowable but also as something lost, (3) other cultures as both strange and familiar, (4) the particular (situations, events, individuals) as both unique or specific and typical or general, (5) stylistic emphases as an expression of an individual style or voice and as a form of distortion of fact or manipulation of the viewer, (6) the indexical linkage of image to source as a bond involving both a pro-filmic referent (what occurred before the camera) and a textually produced signified (what occurs to the viewer, often in the guise of a naturalized referent).

The texts of particular interest to me do not seek to unravel such paradoxes, to deconstruct them, so much as make use of them, dialectically, in ways that further the goal of engendering historical consciousness.

11. Fredric Jameson, *Signatures of the Visible* (New York: Routledge, 1990), 158.

12. Fredric Jameson describes some of these qualities in relation to Lacan's interpretation of the veil painted by Parrhasius which prompted Zeuxis to ask what lay behind it (in *Signatures of the Visible,* 139–40). Lacan contrasts this with the grapes Zeuxis painted that deceived birds. The grapes seem real; the veil, in seeming real, is what it is but also suggests something more, behind or beyond itself.

Jameson's choice to refer to Lacan on this point may seem an unnecessary detour, but it is one followed, more vigorously, by others as well. What I am describing here as a dialectic has also been described in relation to the psychoanalytic concept of lack as the desire for a lost plenitude. In this scheme fascination with the "loss" carried by any form of representation in relation to what it represents is a peculiarly male fascination. Preoccupation with a host of losses is reduced to preoccupation with one—the loss of the penis—and the anxiety this produces then gets projected onto women as bearers of the lack, of the mark of castration. Elements of this interpretation of lack clearly figure in texts discussed here, perhaps most vividly, or overtly, in *Dear America: Letters Home from Vietnam.*

Preoccupation with the incompleteness of representation, including the representation of time, though, can also be understood as a precondition of historical consciousness. This radical difference in perspective may be one point at which Freud and Marx have yet to converge. It may also be that the choice of a Marxist or psychoanalytic reading of loss or lack requires different kinds of contextual justification, different analyses of symptomatic display that would support a social or a more properly psychic form of reading. To reduce a preoccupation with the ways in which representation, especially, here, cinematic representation, is "at a loss" in order to show how this preoccupation is a direct function of male subjectivity risks sacrificing its political potential to evoke what might be or ought to be. That it has functioned (in its more phenomenological manifestations such as the early writings of Christian Metz and those of André Bazin) to project loss away from the male subject may well be true. It is, however, a partial truth about the potential function of incompleteness or lack in cinematic representation.

For a thorough reading of lack and male subjectivity specifically from a psychoanalytic perspective, see Kaja Silverman, *The Acoustic Mirror* (Bloomington: Indiana University Press, 1988), especially chapter 1, "Lost Objects and Mistaken Subjects: A Prologue." A more promising merger of psychoanalytic and historical analysis occurs in Mary Ann Doane's *The Desire to Desire* (Bloomington: Indiana University Press, 1987), especially in the first chapter; later chapters tend to limit themselves to a more strictly psychoanalytic reading. Perhaps the most successful use of psychoanalytic readings of lack and male subjectivity within a resolutely historical framework is Carol Clover's *Men, Women and Chainsaws: Gender in the Modern Horror Film* (Princeton: Princeton University Press, 1991). Unlike the other works cited or more recent efforts by the same authors—Silverman's *Male Subjectivity At the Margins* (New York: Routledge, 1992) and Doane's *Femmes Fatales* (New York: Routledge, 1991)—Clover does not make psychoanalysis the most fundamental reference point for her work. Fredric Jameson's work, with which this note began, is remarkably rich in its readings of historical consciousness and the search for a Marxist hermeneutic that can do justice to it, but it is strangely silent on the issues of gender that cut across all considerations of representation.

13. Robert Burgoyne, *Bertolucci's* 1900: *A Narrative and Historical Analysis* (Detroit: Wayne State Press, 1991), 41.

14. Hayden White, "The Fact of Modernism," 7.

15. For an extremely useful portrait of the complex and deliberately blurred boundaries between French surrealism and anthropology, between art and science, see James Clifford, "On Ethnographic Surrealism," *The Predicament of Culture* (Berkeley: University of California Press, 1988), 117–51.

16. Hayden White, "The Fact of Modernism," 9.

17. Mary Ann Doane, *The Desire to Desire.* See chapter 1 in particular.

18. See chapter 5, "Performing Documentary," and John Peradotto, *Man in the Middle Voice: Name and Narration in the* Odyssey (Princeton: Princeton University Press, 1990), for more on the nature of middle voice. These thoughts on mood and voice are indebted to informal conversations with Hayden White.

19. In one "live" report from Kuwait, discussed later in this chapter, CBS anchor Dan Rather invites us to come with him "just over here." As he moves off-camera we cut to a pre-recorded, and clearly edited, sequence as he takes us through an Iraqi bunker full of rocket launchers that could have been used against a landing from the sea. Rather points, apparently toward the offscreen ocean, and intones how we can imagine the consequences of this deadly force on Allied forces upon hitting the beach. Not only conditional mood, it is a remarkably "for the boys" recounting that wishfully erases the very distance that this mise-en-scène displays between Rather and the troops.

20. Jean Baudrillard argues that this is the *primary* effect of the Gulf War text in his monograph *La Guerre Du Golfe n'a pas eu lieu* (Paris: Galilee, 1991). Andrew Ross, following Paul Virilio, makes a similar if somewhat more tempered claim in his "The Ecology of Images," *South Atlantic Quarterly* 91, no. 1 (Winter 1992): 215–38. A brief, incisive commentary on both Baudrillard and Virilio's positions on war is Gary Genosko's review of Baudrillard's monograph "Virtual War," *Border/Lines,* no. 24/25 (1992): 51–52.

21. See chapter 5, "Performing Documentary," and Hayden White, *Metahistory,* 13–21, for further discussion of contextualist historiography.

If we reconsider *Land without Bread* in this light, the larger frame within which both the discovery of poverty among the inhabitants of Las Hurdes and the tone of the commentary belong is that of anthropological forays and amateur travel adventures. Apprehending the implicit, larger context allows us to make sense of the ironic tone and satiric commentary as an attempt to produce a heightened consciousness of Western complicity in the apparently ethnographically authenticated living conditions of others. Commentary like "We had a difficult time trying to photograph the idiots," or "Here is another type of idiot," takes a reflexive turn of considerable force.

22. White addresses the Holocaust as a more profound example of the type of event represented by Kennedy's assassination, and rightly so. A highly suggestive work on this same topic that poses the question of how the Holocaust can be represented in film is Ilan Avisar's *Screening the Holocaust: Cinema's Images of the Unimaginable* (Bloomington: Indiana University Press, 1988). I am indebted to his parallel discussion of modernist techniques (although he does not use that term) and in particular to his discussion of Alfred Radok's *Distant Journey,* aka *The Long Journey* (Czechoslovakia, 1948). Radok's film, like the texts considered here, utilizes but also breaks with realism, forging crucial links between the individual and the collective, the interior psyche and social subjectivity.

23. Richard Hofstadter, "The Paranoid Style in American Politics," *The Paranoid Style in American Politics and Other Essays* (New York: Knopf, 1966). The line of argument I am following runs something like this: "History [for the paranoid style] *is* a conspiracy, set in motion by demonic forces of almost transcendent power, and

what is felt to be needed to defeat it is not the usual methods of political give-and-take, but an all-out crusade" (29). "Feeling that they have no access to political bargaining or the making of decisions, they find their original conception of the world of power as omnipotent, sinister, and malicious fully confirmed" (39). "What distinguishes the paranoid style is not, then, the absence of verifiable facts . . . but rather the curious leap in imagination that is always made at some point in the recital of events" (37). "The plausibility the paranoid style has for those who find it plausible lies, in good measure, in this appearance of the most careful, conscientious, and seemingly coherent application to detail, the laborious accumulation of what can be taken as convincing evidence for the most fantastic conclusions, the careful preparation for the big leap from the undeniable to the unbelievable" (37–38).

A prime example of the "big leap" is when Garrison describes the plot to kill Kennedy and hide the evidence as "fascism," as a coup d'etat to sustain the Cold War. Stone cuts at that point to a close-up of defendant Clay Shaw smiling, recognizing, no doubt, that those who have followed Garrison's tireless march through endless streams of evidence will come to a screeching halt before following him into the melodramatic field of fascist dreams. That Stone chooses to make this cut at such a crucial point in the entire line of reasoning suggests an awareness of the limitations of the very style that also gives *JFK* its exceptional power. (It may also be a grim moment of acknowledgment that "the people" have yet to make the leap from a conspiracy to kill Kennedy to a coup d'etat including the FBI, CIA, Johnson, Warren, and many others at the very heights of power.) For further discussion of Stone's distanciation from Garrison and the provocative resonance of his film in relation to the Gulf War text, see W. J. T. Mitchell, "From CNN to *JFK:* Paranoia, Melodrama, and American Mass Media in 1991," *Afterimage* 19, no. 10 (May 1992): 13–17.

24. Doane, *The Desire to Desire,* 131.

25. Ibid., 133.

26. Wilden, *System and Structure,* 290.

27. I discuss "technologies of knowledge" in relation to Teresa de Lauretis's notion of "technologies of gender" (itself posed in relation to Foucault's "technology of sex") in *Representing Reality,* 51.

28. Barthes offers the term "third meaning" in his discussion of still frames from Eisenstein's films. See "The Third Meaning," in *Image/Music/Text* (New York: Hill and Wang, 1977).

29. A prime example of Stone's use of collage and retrospection is the set of brief scenes depicting stages in the making of a photograph (developing, cropping, enlarging, and so on). These scenes only make sense after the fact, in retrospect, *if* we put the pieces together in a new pattern that then provides an account of, and accounts for, the media representation of Lee Harvey Oswald as lone assassin. What Stone has disassembled and distributed through the film are stages in the production of the *Life* magazine cover of Oswald. By starting this collage in advance of the assassination and far in advance of this issue of *Life*'s actual appearance, Stone uses collage to evoke imaginatively the breadth, techniques, and thoroughness of conspiracy. This use of film technique is not overt; we may even miss it. The indirection or obliqueness is precisely what may also prompt feelings of manipulation rather than insight.

30. Fredric Jameson takes up the theme of paranoia and the cinema in his *The Geopolitical Aesthetic: Cinema and Space in the World System* (Bloomington: Indiana University Press, 1992). He argues that an array of American films from *The Parallax View* to *All the President's Men* explore conspiracy as an allegorical representation of

the prevailing global economy or world system. *JFK* is too recent for inclusion in the discussion, but Jameson does single out the assassination of Kennedy as "the paradigmatic political assassination in (Western) modern times" (47) because of the simultaneous media relay of this event around the world. This relay itself offered a "glimpse into a Utopian public sphere of the future which remained unrealized" (47). (I find this somewhat idealist, and prefer to regard the event as a prime example of those modern horrors that can be visualized but not explained.) A utopian "glimpse" is what *JFK* also provides. The paranoid terms of a conspiracy narrative block a wider-eyed grasp of the world system at work, but they also give vivid, affectively charged expression to the elusive powers of precisely such a system.

31. *Who Killed Vincent Chin?* (Renee Tajima and Chris Choy, 1988) examines the murder of Vincent Chin by Ronald Ebens and his stepson. Ebens was an out-of-work auto worker in Detroit, who, in most of the news media coverage, was said to have mistaken Chin for Japanese, blaming him for his current state of unemployment. The film uses a wide variety of source materials not only to raise questions about the structural conditions that might give rise to the consciousness attributed to Ronald Ebens but also to propose novel alternatives to the prevailing forms of historical representation.

32. Robert Burgoyne, *Bertolucci's* 1900, 11.

33. Raul Ruiz, *Of Great Events and Ordinary People*. This comment is made on the soundtrack in voice-over. It is meant as a critique of the documentary tradition in which an array of images is assembled into a meaningful statement by means of voice-over commentary. Ruiz opts to insist on a heterogeneity that attests to the structural disjunctions in consciousness produced by pseudo-totalizations like the nation-state.

34. Jean Paul Sartre, *Anti-Semite and Jew* (New York: Schocken, 1948), 19–20.

35. See Richard Hofstadter, "The Paranoid Style in American Politics," *The Paranoid Style in American Politics* (New York: Knopf, 1966).

36. This line of reasoning, if we may call it that, also figured heavily into the defense lawyer's arguments in the case of the Rodney King beating. The Los Angeles Police Department officers argued that Mr. King "was in control" of the situation (and that they were not). They only responded to what Mr. King did. Willing backward becomes an exercise in willing oneself into passivity, at best an agent of fate, or, here, police policy and procedures.

37. Leslie Devereaux, "Experience, Re-presentation and Film," in Leslie Devereaux and Roger Hillman, eds., *Alternative Visions* (Berkeley: University of California Press, 1995).

38. Fredric Jameson, "Marxism and Historicism," *The Ideologies of Theory,* 157, and George Simmel, "The Web of Group Affiliations," *Conflict* (Glencoe, Illinois: Free Press, 1955).

39. I discuss *Dear America* in relation to other American and a selection of Vietnamese films dealing with the war in "Dear Vietnam: The Shadows of Forgotten Warriors," *Cinemaya,* nos. 17/18 (Winter 1992–93): 10–14.

40. See my "Sons at the Brink of Manhood: Utopian Moments in Male Subjectivity," *East-West Journal* 4, no. 1 (1989): 27–43, for further discussion of films such as *Running on Empty* and *The Accused* in terms of the idealization of the masculinity of late adolescents, caught in that transitional moment between boyhood and the full-blown manhood that will render them unavailable for idealization.

41. A prime example of the latter is *Frank: A Vietnam Veteran* (Fred Simon and Vince Canzoneri, 1984), in which Frank recounts his experiences in what amounts to little more than an extended close-up. It is a work of remarkable power not unlike Shirley Clarke's much earlier film *Portrait of Jason* (1967).

42. This issue is pursued with considerable insight in Susan Jeffords, *The Remasculinization of America: Gender and the Vietnam War* (Bloomington: Indiana University Press, 1989).

43. Like the rest of the film, the final moments offer therapeutic reconciliation most ostensibly for whites. Of the eighteen faces of soldiers that we see during a photomontage in this final scene only two appear to be black, and two female. The great bulk of the letters appear to be written, and read, by whites despite the disproportionate number of people of color among non-officers. The style of recitation is muted and respectful, laden with overtones of suppressed feeling, but exhibiting none of the colloquial idiosyncracies of either the untrained voice or the minority communities whose absence is so striking.

44. Kaja Silverman, *The Acoustic Mirror: The Female Voice in Psychoanalysis and Cinema* (Bloomington: Indiana University Press, 1988), 74. The quote is from Michel Chion, *La voix au cinéma* (Paris: Editions de l'Etoile, 1982), 57.

45. Silverman pursues these matters yet further in her more recent book, *Male Subjectivity at the Margins* (New York: Routledge, 1992), especially chapter 2, "Historical Trauma and Male Subjectivity."

46. White, "The Fact of Modernism," 4–5.

47. Stephen Heath very succinctly characterizes the work of the beginning in most narratives: "A beginning, therefore, is always a *violence,* the violation or interruption of the homogeneity of [the initial state]." Heath, "Film and System: Terms of Analysis, I," *Screen* 16, no. 1 (Spring 1975): 49.

48. The Gulf War text shares a template for other events which can be iteratively repeated in its mold: the unanimous, uncritical celebration of the U.S. "dream team" of professional basketball players at the 1992 Barcelona Olympics repeated many of the same tropes of team play, moral redemption after the humiliation of defeat (in the previous Olympics), superior professionalism, and unparalleled prowess. (This despite the best efforts of Charles Barkley to take up the Saddam Hussein role of spoilsport, disclosing the more ruthless and mercenary underbelly of athletics: "I don't know anything about Angola [as an opponent] except they're in trouble.")

49. For example, who are "we"; where are "we"? Where do "we" go during this type of advertising pause? What kind of messages are these? Why are they inserted into this text in this way? How do they alter the text and what "we" hear or what "we" say? What relation is there between a "sponsor," a message, and news? If these messages must be kept apart, marked off, how do they differ from the other messages "we" receive? Would a reversal, in which we begin in the domain of advertisements and then promise to return after messages from our news team, make a difference? *JFK*'s retroactive construction of the cover of *Life* magazine begins to suggest how such questions can take on the force of historical re-vision. Similarly, the juxtaposition in *Who Killed Vincent Chin?* of Ronald Ebens's sense of fate and Mrs. Chin's cry for justice compels an awareness of their incommensurate worldviews; and the intense anxieties signaled in the letters home in *Dear America* contrasted with the receptive encouragements of General Westmoreland at least suggest a chasm between the subjective interiority of fear and the official discourse intended to calm it. The Gulf War text makes no such effort at radical disjunction, retrospection, or the envisioning of an alternative future.

50. The reference to the maternal voice that surrounds and bathes the child does not imply that women drag men down into the half-light of the imaginary, or beyond, into the darkness of a primal unity. It is a *fantasy* which exerts its sway precisely because separation and autonomy come at so high a price in our culture. The voice may be maternal, given the hierarchical pattern of our dominant sex-

gender system, but it calls to both men and women. Potentially transformative, the fantasy projects the fear of engulfment onto this maternal voice in proportion to the psychic investment subsequently made in a gender hierarchy of independence and dependence. (It is men who are typically more fully invested and for whom this voice signifies nightmare as much as bliss.)

51. White, "The Fact of Modernism," 6.

52. Brian Henderson, "Toward a Non-Bourgeois Camera Style," *Movies and Methods,* I (Berkeley: University of California Press, 1976), 427.

INDEX

BILL NICHOLS is Professor of Cinema Studies at San Francisco State University. He has edited two widely used anthologies, *Movies and Methods* I and II, and has examined central issues in social representation in his two previous books, *Ideology and the Image* and *Representing Reality*.